Ending the Glorious Race By God's Grace

The Life of Richard Cortez

Copyright © 2012 Richard Cortez

All rights reserved.

No portion of this book may be reproduced, stored in a retrieval system, or transmitted in any form or by any means— electronic, mechanical, photocopy, recording, scanning, or other— except for brief quotations in critical reviews or articles, without the prior written permission of the author.

Cover Art by: Kim Hinnant © 2014
Back Cover Image: "Used with permission from Microsoft."

Unless otherwise stated Scripture quotations are taken from THE ENGLISH STANDARD VERSION (ESV) © 2001 by Crossway Bibles, a division of Good News Publishers.

Scripture quotations marked NKJV are taken from THE NEW KING JAMES VERSION © 1982 by Thomas Nelson, Inc. Used by permission. All Rights Reserved.

Library of Congress Cataloging-in-Publication Data

Cortez, Richard, 1927-
Ending the Glorious Race By God's Grace / Richard Cortez
      Pages cm
Includes bibliographical references
1. Autobiography   2. Christian   3. Reformed
ISBN 13: 978-0-9974392-1-2

Printed in the United States of America

Table of Contents

Introduction VIII

Dedication IX

Fearfully and Wonderfully Made 1

Childhood Years 7

   Ira Ogden Elementary School 7

   Economic Hardships 10

   The Early Thirties 11

   Culture & Environment 14

   Racial Struggles 18

The Early Forties 21

   2716 W. Salinas Street 21

   My Mom – Loving, Caring and Compassionate 27

   My Dad – Industrious, Sensible and Wise 32

Growing Up 39

   House of Neighborly Service - 1941 42

   Newspaper Boy and Other Jobs 46

   Mom and Dad – Heart of the Cortez Family 52

My Introduction to the Music World 53

   Washington Irving Junior High School 54

Plenty of Work For a Young Entrepreneur 58

Tech High School 1943-1946 63

High School Concert and Marching Band 64

The Danny Cortez Orchestra 71

Pearl Harbor Attacked 77

U.S. Navy Calling 77

Anchor's Aweigh 77

Assigned to the USS New Jersey 87

On the Deck of the USS New Jersey 88

Departed the USS New Jersey… Headed for San Francisco 91

Island of Guam - 1947 95

Hispanic "Swabbies 98

The SEABEES have landed 101

Rollover in a Jeep 105

The Enemy Found in the Chow Line 106

Typhoon Threatens Guam 106

Heading for Okinawa 109

Life in Okinawa – Cold & Lonely 112

Surprise Visitors in the Middle of the Night 114

July 10, 1947 – Bound for Hawaii 115

July 12, 1947 – Shanghai, China 115

July 16, 1947 – Arrived in Tsingtao, China 117

July 20, 1947 – Yokosuka, Japan 118

July 30, 1947 – Arrived at Pearl Harbor 119

At Last – Los Angeles 123

December 2, 1947 – Discharged from Navy 125

Home at Last 127

Trip to Mexico City 127

Our Dream Home – 2905 Buena Vista 130

1948 – Civil Service Job at Fort Sam Houston 132

Golden Gloves 134

Duck Hunting 142

Gilbert Joins the Marine Corps – August 1948 144

Our Lady of the Lake College - 1953 151

Milkman 155

Alamo City 20-30 Club 155

The University of Texas - 1954 160

Married Life 171

La Trinidad Methodist Church 171

Met my Beloved 174

Married to Lupita – August 28, 1959 177

St. Mary's University in San Antonio – May 29, 1960 183

New Career As Band Director 189

Band Director – Natalia, Texas – September 1960 189

The Hawaiian Islands 215

September 1966 215

Malihini's Arrive in Pahoa 227

    Christmas in Hawaii 236

Volcanoes National Park 245

    History of the Birth of the Hawaiian Islands 247

Papaikou 255

    Kalanianole Intermediate School – September 1968 258

    Kinoole Baptist Church 264

Palo Alto, California 279

    1972 - 1973 279

    Watsonville – 1973 - 1974 285

Back in San Antonio 291

    Tafolla Middle School – 1974 - 1988 295

    Tafolla Middle School Band 301

Rare Moments at Tafolla 311

    The Mystery of the Broken Toilet Paper Dispenser 316

    Rhodes Driving School – 1981 - 2001 317

    The 80s at 208 W. Ligustrum 320

    Babes & Tots Daycare 325

Camping Trips 327

    Camping with Rick & Eddie 328

    Bastrop State Park 329

    Hiking in Grand Canyon - 1980 330

University Park Baptist Church **339**

Lake of the Pines 341

My Mom, Weak in Health But Sustained in Faith 348

Newly Weds **353**

Marriage of Mayra & Sam Cerda – June 4, 1983 353

Marriage of Rick & Belle – January 8, 1985 @ UPBC 360

Purchased Duplex on Babcock Road – August 1986 362

Moved to 8519 Bristlecone Street – August 24, 1987 368

Mayra & Sam Move to Massachusetts - 1987 369

Lupita and I Visit Sam & Mayra – November 1988 369

Driving Ruby to Massachusetts – December 1989 372

Second Trip to Massachusetts 376

Saying Goodbye to Massachusetts 378

Marriages and Missions **381**

Marriage of Ruby to Tim Conway – January 29, 1994 381

Grandkids 384

Agua Caliente, Chihuahua, Mexico – May 1997 387

Torreon Mexico – July 1998 393

Marriage of Adela to David Butterbaugh – July 31, 1999 394

Grace, Grace, Grace **399**

Free Grace Baptist Church 1991 - 2002 399

Attack on U.S. by Terrorist – September 11, 2001 406

Grace Anne Goes to the Hospital 408

Grace Community Church – October 20, 2002 .... **411**

Thirty Years of Teaching **431**

Substitute Teaching After Retirement 434

Defensive Driving 436

Tennis 437

Moved to 6415 Honey Hill – February 2007 441

Letters & Alzheimers **445**

Letter from January 1, 2009 445

Letter to Dr. Kalter – October 2, 2009 448

Alzheimers Strikes Our Home – December 2009 449

A Letter From Ruby – December 30, 2009 458

Letter From January 24, 2010 460

Lupita – Recommended for Hospice Care 461

Care Giver at Home **463**

Letter from February 22, 2010 463

Letter from April 11, 2010 466

Letter from September 2, 2010 470

Letter from September 16, 2010 472

Letter to Grace Community Church 474

Letter to Rick – October 30, 2010 478

Letter From Ruby – October 31, 2010 481

Letters Between Ruby and Me 483

Letter from January 20, 2011 485

The Saddest Day of My Life – March 11, 2011 488

Invited to Live with the Conways **493**

The Denton Conference – April 21, 2011 495

Trip to Michigan – June 20, 2011 496

Letter From June 19, 2011 497

Vangie Comes to Live with Me – August 2011 498

Hawaii Trip with Vangie 498

More Letters **509**

Letter From December 6, 2011 509

Short Trip to North Carolina – December 8, 2011 510

Letter From December 31, 2011 511

Cataract Operation – Dr. Lisa Marten 524

Denton Conference 2012 526

Mission Trips **527**

Trip to Brazil 527

Trip to Guadalajara, Mexico – June 18, 2012 528

Trip to Puerto Rico "La Isla Del Encanto 529

My Testimony **535**

DEDICATION

I want to dedicate this book to the memory of Lupita, my beloved and faithful wife of fifty-one years. She passed into eternity on March 11, 2011. I also dedicate this book to the memory of my dad and mom, Eloy and Felicitas Cortez, who labored tirelessly to raise four children in a clean, healthy, Christian environment during the difficult depression years of the early twenties. My father instilled in us a life of principled obedience, and my mother's life was characterized by love and compassion. I am deeply indebted to these two precious parents. I owe a debt of gratitude to my good friend and brother in Christ, Edward (Eddie) Karisch, who has provided encouragement and technical advice as well as editing. His help and knowledge far exceeded my expectations. Jacquelyn Johnson, a young attorney and a dear friend, is greatly appreciated for her enormous contribution in her labor of editing. It is my privilege to announce and congratulate my bosom buddy and editor Eddie Karisch, on his marriage to the beautiful Carole Zea on February 2, 2013. Chris Connell, a dear friend and faithful Christian brother, deserves huge recognition for contributing of his time and skills to the completion of this book. His experience as editor of his college newspaper has been extremely valuable. Another person who contributed greatly is Claire Castleberry, a wonderful sister in Christ. Her previous editing experience was instrumental in getting this book edited properly.

INTRODUCTION

It is my desire that this autobiography honor the supreme sovereign God, the Creator of heaven and earth and sustainer of all life. My ultimate goal is to glorify the Lord, and to enjoy Him throughout the rest of my life.

"But as for you, continue in what you have learned and have firmly believed, knowing from whom you learned it and how from childhood you have been acquainted with the sacred writings, which are able to make you wise for salvation through faith in Christ Jesus." (2 Timothy 3:14-15)

"No more precious assurance can I have, than this, that I am under the constant loving guidance of my heavenly Father-- that He appoints the bounds of my habitation, and overrules all events for my good - that my whole life is a plan arranged by Him! Every apparent little contingency, as well as every momentous turn and crisis-hour - forms part of that plan!" John MacDuff "The Thoughts of God".

"O God, you have taught me from my youth; and to this day I declare your wondrous works. Now also when I am old and gray-headed, O God, do not forsake me, until I declare your strength to this generation, your power to everyone who is to come" (Psalm 71:17-18).

"… Let us also lay aside every weight, and sin which clings so closely, and let us run with endurance the race that is set before us."

Hebrews 12:1

CHAPTER 1
FEARFULLY AND WONDERFULLY MADE

I was born in 1927, during the Great Depression. These were turbulent economic times in America. It was the year that Charles Lindbergh made his historic and heroic non-stop solo flight across the spacious Atlantic Ocean. Just as amazing was a young mother giving birth to a new child. The mid-wife who was assisting was aware of the sacred act of childbirth. This was a time when newborn babies were considered "a heritage from the Lord," not objects to be discarded.

"For you formed my inward parts, you knitted me in my mother's womb." (Psalm 139:13).

On December 5, 1927 at 6 p.m., Eloy Cortez waited patiently while his wife Felicitas went through labor. Only moments before they actually laid eyes on me, I was safe and secure in a water wonderland, my every need attended. There is absolutely no way I could have imagined a completely different environment just inches away from the comforting beat of my mother's heart. Yet, in a blink of an eye, I emerged into an unexplored existence. I entered a new world.

"I praise You, for I am fearfully and wonderfully made" (Psalm 139:14).

The miracle of an infant's birth is the glorious work of the same God that created the heavens and the earth. Ricardo Cortez entered this world at 610 Gould Street on a cold winter day in San Antonio, Texas.

Richy at age one

My mother brought forth into this world four children: three boys, Danny, Richard (me), Gilbert, and one girl Vangie. The youngest Evangeline Ruth (Vangie) was born when I was four. Danny was the only one that had the "privilege" of being born in a hospital. The rest of us were "delivered" at home with the help of a mid-wife. Needless to say, Vangie was Daddy's girl from the very beginning.

My most vivid childhood memories are at our home at 2710 Perez Street. It was a relatively quiet neighborhood. I can say my life began here in a very simple and peaceful environment. Chubby Virgina Mae Pedroza, our next-door neighbor was a couple of years older than me. Every morning, like clockwork, her little brother would stand on the back porch and respond to the call of nature, instead of going to the restroom in the house.

My birthplace

Arturo Guerrero, a skinny little kid who lived across the street from us, was to play a part in our future musical life. In fact, he became an accom-

Gilbert, Richard, Danny & Daisy

Vangie, Gilbert, Richard, & Danny

plished bass clarinet player in our junior high and high school bands. Vangie was fortunate to make friends with Anita, a little neighbor that lived four houses from us. Her family owned the little corner grocery store, which was very convenient for our family.

At one point, a couple moved in next door to us. They were quiet and kept to themselves. However, one day they shocked us! The lady came running to our front porch screaming hysterically. She was barefooted and wearing nothing but her slip. Her husband was chasing her in a fit of violent anger. My mother was ironing, and we kids, who were still very small, were playing quietly inside. My mom quickly let her in and locked the door while we all huddled into one room.

While the lady hid in a closet, my mom went to talk to the man who almost knocked the door down. Her warning that she would call the police did not faze him. He went to the back door, broke the glass, opened the door, found his wife and forcefully whisked her out of the house. Right about that time the police arrived and took him in. This man owned a taxicab company, and was usually a good husband as long as he was sober, but when he was drunk, he was very jealous and became violent.

Eloy Cortez Family—1937

God Created me—and you—to live with a single, all-embracing, all-transforming passion—namely, a passion to glorify God by enjoying and displaying his supreme excellence in all the spheres of life.

John Piper *"Don't Waste Your Life" (Page 31)*

CHAPTER 2
CHILDHOOD YEARS

IRA OGDEN ELEMENTARY SCHOOL

Ira Ogden Elementary was the first school I attended after we moved to 2710 Perez Street. Just starting a new adventure in our young lives, even the short walk to school was exciting. The required vaccinations were dreaded by all incoming children. It was a particular problem when it came to sharp "needles" poking my skin. I remember one nightmarish experience where it took the nurse and at least two other people to hold me down for the shot as I wrapped my legs around a round pillar in the nurse's office. After much fuss, I finally got the shot in the wrong arm and off-center.

Miss Murphy, my first grade teacher, was tall, friendly, and a genuinely caring person. My second grade teacher was okay unless anyone had the sniffles in class. She would ask you to blow your nose, and if you didn't have a handkerchief, she would give a prompt command, "There is paper in the trash can; use it!" You would obey and blow your nose right in

My first grade class (me – first row, fourth from the right)

front of the class. Talk about embarrassment at an early age! And if you misbehaved, your punishment was to stand in the corner, inside the trash can. This would probably be considered "cruel and unusual" punishment nowadays! I think I preferred the board on the seat of the pants, which came later in high school.

Meanwhile, at home Gilbert was being a good brother. Not being able to go outside after a rainy night, he decided to give his little sister a ride in her stroller. He was three years older than her, so he felt confident pushing her around the house. In an instant he steered the stroller through the screened back door. They both went flying down several steps into the muddy backyard. The stroller with Vangie landed safely and upright on all four wheels, and she was miraculously unharmed. Gilbert on the other hand, landed face first in the mud. Fortunately the rain had softened the ground. My mom thanked God for His mercy and watchful care over little children in the face of danger.

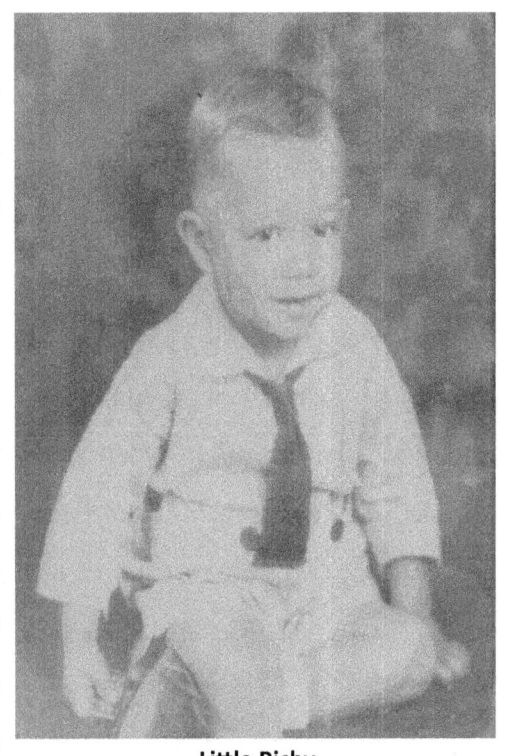

Little Richy

Besides the "extraordinary" challenges in the elementary classroom, the social life and relationships on the playground were to teach me major lessons. I was to receive an award for winning a health contest in my classroom. Because it was a citywide contest, the awards were being presented at San Pedro Park.

That morning as I walked proudly to the teacher's car that was to transport us to the park, we went past the school's sandbox. My "best friend" Martin was there to give me a "send off." With his two little hands full of sand, he deliberately threw it on my crisp white suit. I would have wrestled him to the ground if I hadn't been all dressed up. In the days ahead we continued to be good friends.

Another episode in elementary school involved Gilbert. One day he vanished from school. The principal promptly sent my older brother Danny and me to go search for him. After searching around the school area, we decided to go to Elmendorf Lake Park that was a few blocks from the school. We were concerned because we had heard that several people had drowned in that lake, and feared the worst for Gilbert. Once we got there we found him. He and one of his little school chums were sliding down the grassy slopes along the river. Of course my dad was not one to spare the rod of correction. Needless to say, we had to keep a closer watch on him. Later we found out that truant officers track down kids that play "hooky" from school. But the family was relieved that the Lord had protected those two little rascals from serious harm.

ECONOMIC HARDSHIPS

A few months later, we moved to Leal Street next to the Wong family. Helen and Jimmy, two kids in the family, were about our age, so we quickly made friends. In later years Jimmy became a firefighter with the San Antonio Fire Department. Surprisingly, Danny happened to be in the fire department at the same time.

Other schools I attended were David Crockett Elementary on West

On top of Big Brother's shoulders

Commerce, and Burnet Elementary on the Eastside of town. After about three years we moved again; this time to Saunders Avenue. We lived there for only one year. If I recall correctly, all these moves during my childhood were due to economic reasons.

At one point, we even shared a house on Chestnut Street with my Aunt Mamie. As kids, we just went along and did what kids do. A good example was when Gilbert dunked Vangie's doll in the toilet. I'm grateful that my aunt was patient and tolerated us at this mischievous stage.

At Burnet Elementary, things were going pretty smooth until Gilbert was kept after school. After a short deliberation, Danny and I went to his classroom, and in defiance of his teacher, whisked Gilbert out and took him home. The next morning our classmates observed curiously as the principal beckoned the three of us to her office. She and the teacher lectured us severely and nearly to tears. They said that obeying our father's rule to come home together did not warrant our rude and disrespectful behavior toward the teacher. My father was a strict disciplinarian, but felt we had learned our lesson in the principal's office.

THE EARLY THIRTIES

Radio was fairly new and rare during those early days. This was an innovation that thrilled the whole family. It was an unusual special privilege to have our own radio in the living room. On certain nights we sat around the radio listening to news, music, and narrated and dramatized stories.

We looked forward to hearing popular shows such as Jack Benny, Fibber McGee and Molly, Red Skelton, Inner Sanctum, The Shadow, The Lone Ranger, Bob Steele, and others. My dad was always fascinated with the blow-by-blow descriptions of championship fights, including the world champion Joe Louis, the "Brown Bomber." Radio was a modern luxury, and I'm sure my dad had to make a measure of sacrifice to purchase this new, unusual gift for the family.

I thank God we always had food on our table. "Mom and Pop" neighborhood stores were popular, convenient, and practical, before the big supermarkets showed up. This was before plastic credit cards. Instead of cash, check, or credit card, we just took a small spiral notebook to the store. The cashier (usually the owner) would record the amount of the purchases in his store ledger and in our notebook. The amount owed would be paid at the end of the work week, which was payday for most people. Our favorite store was a Chinese-owned grocery at the corner of Zarzamora and Martin streets. I guess we kids liked it because we always got "pilon" when we paid our balance. "Pilon" was a treat (a small bag filled with candy and/or cookies). Gradually larger stores like Piggly Wiggly and Handy Andy began to pop up everywhere which caused the "Mom and Pop" stores to be concerned. Today HEB and Wal-Mart and other big superstores dominate the market in San Antonio and have virtually eliminated small family-owned grocery stores.

Rainy days were always thrilling because we were permitted to put on our bathing suits and play in the rain. However, one day I slipped on the wet sidewalk and my forehead hit the sharp edge of a solid rock porch step. All I recall is my mother attempting to keep the deep cut on the left side of my forehead closed with her thumb and finger. I would panic at the thought of being sewed up. I do not remember going to the doctor or hospital.

One thing we dreaded when we were sick, was seeing grandma coming up the sidewalk. Her presence usually meant an enema. That was supposed to be some kind of cure all. I don't know which was worse, an enema or castor oil (laxative). Of course, we didn't have a choice in the matter. My mother tried to disguise the castor oil mixed with orange juice. It left a greasy residue on top of the drink. All you could do is hold your nose and try not to vomit. That caused me to hate orange juice for a long time.

Growing up in the thirties in San Antonio was all fun for us, especially when it was time for school. We were enjoying life, innocent and unaware that our city as well as the country was going through economic hardship. There was much social change and labor unrest. In 1930, San Antonio had a population of 231,543.[1] Families could walk safely in their neighborhoods night or day without fear.

Violent crimes were rare. With the friendly small town atmosphere, people had no fear of leaving their homes and cars unlocked. Window bars were a rare sight, except when used for ornamentation. News of even a single murder was shocking to the community.

CULTURE AND ENVIRONMENT

The technological age and the communication mediums of today gradually crept in during my years growing up. Children today have instant exposure to rampant senseless killings, sexual immorality, drunkenness, strife, and domestic violence. Daily doses of these and other heinous crimes can be seen on television or on the internet.

Children are victims of broken homes, abuse, and divorces. In my early years, divorce was uncommon and frowned upon. Today divorce has become a commonplace practice in our society. Homes are fractured and family relationships are thrust into confusion and insecurity. The children are the ones who suffer the most. To a child it is incomprehensible that the two people they love the most are suddenly separating. Grieved, broken hearted, feeling discarded and unloved, youngsters seek refuge elsewhere. However, I have personally known several who matured and experienced extraordinary security through their faith in God. It has been said that the hurt and the pain of divorce is worse than death. It is not shocking anymore to hear that divorces are so easily attainable.

In Texas, a divorce can be obtained with only one spouse filing an application. There seems to be no reverence or acknowledgement to the vows made before God, as well as to the solemn commitment of marriage.

$1.00 a Picture—Expensive Goat!

Cortez Kids (Danny, Richard, Gilbert, Vangie)

Richard preparing for the Rodeo

Busy minds at work (Vangie, Richard, Gilbert, Danny)

The number of broken homes in our country is devastating. In 2011, 877,000 divorces occurred in the United States.[2]

The expression "single parent" was not common while I was growing up. Nowadays over 25% of all households in San Antonio are single-parent homes[3]. The role of the father and of the mother in our society was distinct, recognizable, and generally acceptable. It was understood that the father worked and provided for the family's needs. It was normally accepted that he was the head of the family. The wife for the most part was submissive to her husband. She was usually a devoted hardworking wife and homemaker. She managed the home, raised the children and fed the family.

This was God's plan from the beginning. "She looks well to the ways of her household and does not eat the bread of idleness. Her children rise up and call her blessed, and her husband also, and he praises her" (Proverbs 31: 27-28). "Older women likewise, are to be reverent in behavior, not slanderers, or slaves to much wine. They are to teach what is good, and so train the young women to love their husbands and children, to be self-controlled, pure, working at home, kind, and submissive to their own husbands, that the word of God may not be reviled," (Titus 2:3-5)

I thank God that my wife of fifty-one years was faithful in her role as mother, and stayed at home raising the children. Even when she ran a daycare center for two years, it was in our home. I am convinced that motherhood is the most essential and the most indispensable occupation in the world.

During World War II, many women, single and married, supplemented the work force at home while the men went to war. After the war, many continued in their jobs even though most of the husbands had returned. And of course child daycare centers experienced a boom! Working mothers swamped the job market in numerous positions, including government, business, industry, military and education, just to name a few. This would forever change the fabric of the American home, which would eventually cause devastating consequences. Many homes went through a revolutionary transition in which the role of father, the breadwinner, and mother the homemaker, evolved in an extraordinary manner. In some cases the roles were reversed.

With all this confusion, it's no wonder juvenile delinquency became a major problem. I witnessed this while teaching in the public schools. In the last twenty to thirty years, youth disrespect for authority, including teachers, parents, and law enforcement, has increased. Plus, an aggressive feminist movement in our country brought about many ramifications that affected our society. The country experienced a second-wave of feminism from 1960 -1980, which included women's roles in suffrage, sexuality, family, and workplace. Much of the debate focused on gender equality. Spiritually, women are equal with men in the eyes of God. But He in His sovereign wisdom assigned distinct roles for each.

RACIAL STRUGGLES

Another issue we had little awareness of was racial discrimination. There were incidents that occurred, like the time when a Hispanic San Antonio councilman and his family were refused entrance into a public swimming pool in New Braunfels, Texas. Years later, this gentleman, Henry B. Gonzalez, excelled and distinguished himself as a champion of the people in the U.S. Congress. He was one of the few politicians in my lifetime who had a matchless record of integrity and whose career was free of scandal. On one occasion, this "gentle" congressman with an impeccable record landed a fist to the jaw of a man in a San Antonio restaurant who called him a communist. This did not affect the congressman's record in the least!

Speaking Spanish in elementary school was considered almost as bad as using "profanity." These violations would send us straight to the principal's office, which everyone feared. The African-Americans suffered the worst discrimination even in the peaceful city of San Antonio. The rear seats on city buses were specifically designated for them. Department stores had restrooms and water fountains clearly labeled " Colored" and "White." Theaters also had separate entrances and segregated balcony seats.

Most everyone seemed accustomed to these practices with no serious problems or disputes. In fact, San Antonio later had the distinction of being one of the few cities in the country that integrated the schools without major problems.

During our teen years another incident occurred. Our dance band, comprised mostly of Hispanics, was returning to San Antonio from an out-of-town job. We stopped for a snack at a Seguin restaurant. Well, we sat, and sat, for a long time without being greeted or waited on. We were totally ignored! We finally quietly walked out, but we had an idea why we had been ignored. Later, back home in San Antonio we were informed of the discrimination in that town.

A more pleasant memory during those early years was having the convenience of ice and milk being delivered to our homes very early in the morning. Ice was delivered in different size blocks. A 12-inch octagon card with large numbers placed on the front window of each home would indicate the pounds of ice desired. The upright number would tell the iceman how much ice was needed. He would grab the ice with his tongs and carry it on his back into the house. and place it inside the icebox.

This was literally an "icebox" with a compartment for the block of ice and another one for food. The "ice pick" was a convenient tool used to split the ice block into small pieces for use at the dinner table. We didn't have the luxury of icemakers with the option of ice cubes or crushed ice.

We were content with this until the advent of the modern refrigerator, which truly became an amazing invention that made life more convenient.

Likewise, the milk truck came before sunrise and before the rooster crowed. The milkman's large order book told him what products to deliver at each house and exactly where to place them. All kinds of fresh dairy products were delivered.

Richard, Danny, Gilbert and Vangie

---

[1]   Population of San Antonio in 1930 City of San Antonio, Department of Planning and Development

[2]   CDC/NCHS National Vital Statistics System. http://www.cdc.gov/nchs/nvss/marriage_divorce_tables.htm Retrieved June 12, 2013

[3]   Bureau of Statistics: Statistical Brief. Page 4. http://www.census.gov/prod/1/statbrief/sb94_26.pdf

CHAPTER 3
THE EARLY FORTIES

2716 W. SALINAS STREET

Our family finally settled more permanently at 2716 W. Salinas Street. My two brothers and I shared the back bedroom. This room had about eight windows, but only one bed for the three of us. One door led to the kitchen and another to the backyard. In the privacy of our "own room," we energetic adolescents engaged in periodic mischief. This often got us in trouble. That was our domain and fun place! During one pillow fight, I accidentally broke one of the windows with a shoe. To this day I'm thankful for the loyalty of my brothers who never "tattled" on me. We were young and lively and the days were not long enough, so we played into the night.

On warm summer nights, some of our inseparable neighborhood rascal buddies would come over after a long day. We would just sit around or lie on the grass and look up at the stars. These were quiet, peaceful San Antonio nights. There was no fear at night. We could leave our homes any time of day or night without bothering to lock our doors or windows. Those days are gone!

During my early teen years, the outskirts of San Antonio, to my recollection, was 24th Street on the Westside. Beyond that was mostly undeveloped wooded areas. Downtown San Antonio was the center of all commerce, entertainment, and social life. As kids, we would casually walk downtown.

The State Theater on Main Avenue catered to young kids every Saturday morning. Together with kids from all over town, we looked forward with excitement and anticipation to this Saturday morning event. Entering the lobby of the theater was a beehive of activity. The excitement and the loud yelling of kids and the smell of popcorn would have been overwhelming for any adult attempting to enter. Most just dropped their kids off in front of the theater. Tom Mix, Buck Jones, Dick Tracy, Flash Gordon, The Lone Ranger, Ken Maynard, Roy Rogers, Tarzan, and others were our heroes. There were serials that lasted for several weeks, but each movie would end with a cliff-hanger. That was disappointing, but it kept us coming every Saturday. It was worth the dime that we paid. We didn't even mind that we had to walk three miles from our home.

On the way to the theater we always went past and through the Katy Railroad Depot on West Commerce and Medina. Seeing travelers and noisy trains coming and going was a thrill in itself. The Indian statue on the very top of the depot dome seemed to point the way for us.

Returning home after all the excitement, we would act out the action we had seen. Danny, being the oldest, always ended up playing the hero, whether it was the Lone Ranger, Flash Gordon, or Dick Tracy. The rest of us had to be content playing the role of Indians or the bad guys. The other kids that usually played the secondary parts were Max, Andrew, Camilo, Lee and Freddy. These were some of the friendly little rascals in our neighborhood. We used mom's brooms as make-shift horses, which we rode all over the place.

We were a bunch of kids enjoying life. We were growing up in a clean wholesome environment. The term illegal drugs was unknown to us. All we knew was that drugs were for sick people. "Grass" was something you mowed and "Coke" was something you drank. Violence in our world was limited to Cowboys and Indians in the movies. There was no need for anyone to carry or use knives or guns for protection or aggression. Sure, there were a few sporadic incidents from time to time, but if one person was killed, it was shocking and would create sensational news. For the most part we grew up in respectable, responsible, and disciplined families. Families were united and stuck together. Juvenile delinquency was at a minimum.

One unexpected crisis that crept into our peaceful home which would affect our lives for several years was when my dad had to be admitted to a hospital in Carlsbad, Texas. He was diagnosed with tuberculosis. We kids didn't comprehend the illness, but knew it was serious, because he was in a hospital far away. My mother, who had a limited education, found a job as a maid at the downtown Plaza Hotel. About a year later, she was hired at the Gunter Hotel as a room inspector. Out of necessity, our parents placed us with different relatives in town. I stayed with my Uncle Seferino and Aunt Rebecca. These were the loneliest days of my childhood!

One day my uncle had planned to take me to the movies. He and my aunt argued about a dollar she failed to return to him. She finally went to the bathroom where she soaked the dollar under the water faucet. Reluctantly, she gave it back to him, dripping wet. I felt a little uncomfortable because that dollar was for the movies. Many afternoons I would sit on the front porch staring at the bus stop, about a block away, waiting anxiously for my mom to come visit me.

Eventually my mom was able to hire a lady to stay at our home so we could all be together again. Marillita was a kind little old lady and a terrific cook, but we were too young to appreciate her. We played all kinds of tricks on her and teased her about "her boyfriend" the vegetable man, who came by once a week. A little bow-legged she would hobble to our favorite hangout; The House of Neighborly Service (a popular community center) to call us to dinner.

Since we practically lived there and were always involved in some kind of activity, I'm afraid we didn't respond very quickly. This sweet soul was worthy of a medal of honor or a huge trophy for her patience and endurance beyond the call of duty. Years later, after my dad returned and the family was back to normal, we heard that Marillita, who was back in her home, was sick. She apparently had a nervous or mental breakdown. Years later I couldn't help but think that we had probably contributed to her mental condition.

Times were hard, and money was scarce. So when we were at a very early age my father taught us the importance of work and the value of money. He stressed the importance of saving. He had a unique little bank that would only take dimes and would open up only when it reached five dollars. He believed that "idleness is the devil's workshop."

Gilbert and I started out by volunteering to help the vegetable man. The man gave us the task of going from house to house selling small baskets of veggies, mostly tomatoes. The man would always advise us to place the best tomatoes on top. We were thrilled to receive a designated amount of money for each basket we sold.

Being little rascals, we managed to find excitement and "adventure" (mischievous acts) in our neighborhood with the help and encouragement of Max and Andrew Morales. Gilbert and I, along with the Morales boys would get bored; anxious for excitement we organized the "Night Raiders." First we made mud balls which we used to "freckle" houses at night. They had to be soft and mushy enough to stick.

The houses we selected were mainly people who were unfriendly or even hostile toward children. On one occasion a man rushed out with a shotgun threatening to shoot whoever it was that was throwing rocks on his tin roof. We hid behind a thick hedge hoping he wouldn't come out shooting. Our most ingenious project was the creation of a huge slingshot on top of our favorite tree. A large branch that formed a "V," and inner tubes were all we needed. We would position ourselves atop our favorite tree which stood at a strategic and safe distance from the street. After dark, perched quietly in the tree, we waited for passing cars.

One person was the spotter, another held the "ammunition," and the third was the one who fired the shots. If the timing was right and the aim accurate, we could hit the side of a car with a mud ball, and quietly celebrate on top of the tree. We felt safe in our dark hideout atop the tree. One night a police car approached slowly and stopped in our target area while we sat petrified in the tree. After that we decided to abort this mission.

Another ridiculous idea we had involved a dare. The aim was a nighttime entrance into a nearby church. A couple of us got into the dark building and just started quietly crawling around furniture and pews through the whole assembly area. I guess we were trying to prove we were fearless.

Another intriguing activity I enjoyed as an inquisitive little squirt was throwing a big red ant into a spider web on an outside corner of our house. The ant would wiggle desperately to free itself from this sticky web, not realizing her movements would cause her demise. The wiggly movement of the ant would alert the spider. I would wait patiently for the long-legged villain to show its long black hairy legs. Finally the spider would appear and confidently advance toward its next meal. I'm sure the ant would scream at the top of its voice, if it could! With little struggle, the spider would overcome the helpless ant. When it would proudly prance to its hole with its prey, I would go into action. I would discharge my homemade rubber gun, and put an end to this crafty long-legged bully.

A positive activity that became popular in our neighborhood was movies in the Cortez garage. My brother Danny had the ingenious idea of showing movies using a simple old-time, but very practical movie projector. He started showing cartoon characters in our garage one night a week. Being something new and novel, this attracted the kids in the neighborhood. Before long our garage was full on movie night. Of course, there was a small fee of a penny or a milk bottle cap, the latter of which was used to play games.

MY MOM— LOVING, CARING AND COMPASSIONATE

My mother was warm, loving, patient, and definitely not a disciplinarian. In fact, there were times she had to intervene when my father was laying the belt to one of us. I can remember my mother vividly on washday Monday. She would place a large, round, galvanized washtub on top of short stacks of red bricks. Kindling and a small fire were already started under the tub while she poured water into it with a garden hose. With a knife in hand, she would begin shaving a big bar of "El Chivo" soap.

The shavings from the soap in the hot water would create suds, a broom handle was used for stirring. This process provided the clothes washing detergent. Then she would use the broom handle as a plunger and agita-

Vangie, Gilbert, Mom, Richard & Danny

My Adorable Mom

tor. Some clothes required the use of the scrub board. Another galvanized tub with clean water was placed right next to the first one. It was used for rinsing the laundry. After that she would wring out the clothes with her bare hands. Then came the chore of hanging everything on the clothesline. I have never seen clothes so crisp and sparkling clean as those that were dried in the sun.

It was a great relief for my mom when dad bought her the first washing machine. This was an amazing invention which featured rubber rollers to wring out the clothes. That must have been about the time we bought our first radio. Some folks discovered that with simple amateur crystal sets they were able to receive some radio reception. However, my dad managed to

Felicitas Cortez

My young mom

get us a real radio. We were overwhelmed, not realizing that we were entering into a new age of technology and entertainment.

Fast forward and many years later, Gilbert and his wife Sophie had a grand idea to celebrate mom's 80th birthday. They planned it from their home in Garland, Texas. Mom's family was invited: brothers, sisters, children, grandchildren, great-grandchildren, and a few close friends. The Fellowship Hall at University Park Baptist Church was colorfully decorated with white table cloths, balloons, streamers, and flowers. A long table was loaded with delicious food, desserts and drinks.

Gradually people started trickling in. Gilbert had an excellent idea of photographing each family as they arrived (with his Polaroid camera). Then all the pictures were attached to a huge four-foot tall birthday card. Each of the family members would then write "well wishes" or a short message under their picture. The party was a huge success with many pictures and movies taken to remember the event. My mother's delight of course was her 16 grandchildren, and 18 great-grandchildren. There were

In Loving Memory of Mom and Dad

times when she was overwhelmed with all the hugs and kisses when they came to visit.

My mother went to be with the Lord on Nov. 21, 1990 at the age of 83. Even though this was a difficult time, the Lord granted me comfort and peace. It was a celebration of a glorious blessed life. She had lived a long, happy, and relatively healthy life. She was buried next to my dad at Rose Lawn Cemetery. The inscription on their tombstone is one of my favorite bible verses. These are the words of Christ, "I am the resurrection and the life. He who believes in me, though he may die, he shall live. And whoever lives and believes in Me shall never die. Do you believe this?" (John 11:25-26)

MY DAD– INDUSTRIOUS, SENSIBLE, AND WISE

My Handsome Dad

My dad was born in Laredo, Texas on December 1, 1901. He never talked much about his family; consequently we knew very little about his background. I did know that he and his sister Mamie were both born to Estevan and Jesusita Frausto Cortez. After Grandpa Estevan's death, Grandma Jesusita remarried and had four children: Seferino (Sefe), Arturo, Consuelo, and Ninfa. I do remember our dad discreetly encouraging us kids to call his stepfather "Tio" Juan. As we grew older we heard very little about my dad's father and mother. Since they had died, we never saw them except in pictures. Uncle Sefe (dad's half-brother), as a young lad, lived with us when we lived at 2710 Perez Street. Ninfa also lived with us while she attended elementary school.

In April 1934, at the age of 32, my dad enlisted in the Texas National Guard as a trombone player. This would provide a little extra income while doing something he enjoyed. At the age of seven, I was thrilled and proud to see my daddy in uniform and marching in parades. However, we were saddened when he would leave for his yearly tour of duty. His unit would usually train in Palacios, Texas, near the Gulf Coast.

Vangie, Gilbert, Richard, Dad & Danny

During these early years, my dad's trust in God and his work ethic were a great testimony for us kids. We felt secure and looked up to him. He was industrious and a hard worker. Even during the Great Depression, he was never without a job. In fact, as far as I can remember, he always managed to keep two jobs: one full-time and one part-time. Out of necessity he would create jobs. Once he opened up a small Mexican candy shop downtown, in a small space next to the Empire Theater. He also opened up a shoeshine stand in back of the "Naciónal" Theater, which opened up an opportunity for my brother Danny to work. My Dad had taught himself the trombone and saxophone, now he was passing that knowledge to me and Danny.

Dad in National Guard Camp in Palacios, Texas

In later years we all benefited by playing these same instruments in our own dance band. No matter what we did or where we went, my dad made sure that Sundays were reserved for church. Plus, he was a very strict disciplinarian which we either feared or respected, or both. When he drew the belt from his waist we knew we would get it - no excuses, no explanations, no mercy! "Train up a child in the way he should go, and when he is old he will not depart from it." (Proverbs 22:6). If we were going dancing, he would ask, "How come you didn't get that gig?" One occasion, when we were still young and dumb, the three Cortez "Caballeros" were all dressed up to go to a dance. When my dad asked

The Three Cortez "Caballeros"

Danny, "What time are you all coming home?", he answered, "About…" Before he finished the sentence, my dad interrupted with "ABOUT?!" Go to your room and change those clothes. "He who heeds the word wisely will find good." (Proverbs 16:20)

My dad worked at Alling Blueprint Company which was located on St. Mary's Street, across from St. Mary's Church downtown. His main hobby which eventually became his great love was photography. He read photography magazines from cover to cover and learned much from them. He developed his own pictures and built his own enlarger in our home. However, we caused him much frustration at times. He complained we always got the urge to go to the bathroom (his dark room), right in the middle of developing pictures.

He also learned to hand color pictures before color pictures were introduced. Eventually, he built up a good business taking pictures at weddings and other social functions. In spite of his limited education, he taught himself photography, the trombone and the alto saxophone. He had great imagination and was a man of vision. He had played in the church band at "El Templo Cristiano," and was also in the National Guard Band. His ultimate dream finally became a reality!

The U.S. Postal Service (USPS) accepted him as a mail carrier after he passed the exam. Providentially, it was our local mail carrier who encouraged him and kept him informed about the job situation at the Post Office. This mail carrier also was instrumental in getting us to join his church. La Trinidad Methodist Church, was our home church for many years. My dad was on the board of directors until his death in 1968 at the age of 67.

Neither snow, nor rain, nor heat, nor gloom of night stays these couriers from the swift completion of their appointed rounds.

THE EARLY FORTIES

Dad looking sharp

Mom and Dad

Dad after a parade

" But as for you, continue in what you have learned and have firmly believed, knowing from whom you learned it and how from childhood you have been acquainted with the sacred writings, which are able to make you wise for salvation through faith in Christ Jesus."

2 Timothy 3:14-15

CHAPTER 4
GROWING UP

Brigido Gonzalez Family

My mother came from a large family, five boys and three girls. They were a loud but happy bunch. My mother was the oldest and was, therefore wiser and more mature than her siblings. My grandfather Brigido Gonzalez and grandmother Juanita Flores Gonzalez lived a humble life and were very giving. My grandmother's pot of pinto beans on the stove and a pile of flour tortillas on the dinner table were delightful treats that we always enjoyed. My grandfather was a kind and gentle man. He was pleasingly plump in stature, and he operated a barbershop downtown. On hot summer nights he would sleep outside on the front porch of his house, because there was no air conditioner. The porch was immediately next to and parallel to the driveway where he parked his car. One morning he woke up and discovered that his car was sitting on four blocks. Someone had stolen his four tires while he slept right there on the porch.

We came from a large, close-knit family (on my mother's side). The whole bunch of us would be drawn to grandma's house on most Sunday afternoons. Some of us would go there directly after church. The little house on Pace Street would fill up with so many family members that we had to set up tables in the shade of the driveway. There the families would spend much of the afternoon eating and chatting. We were just kids, running, playing, and having fun; and we felt secure in seeing the unity of our families.

Cortez Family at Grandma's House

There was always much hugging and kissing among the relatives. As my uncles (my mother's brothers), who were a happy hilarious group, reached their young adult years, they became more brazen and bold. They casually began to bring beer, instead of drinking the usual iced tea. In time, they enticed the older men (my dad and an older uncle) to join in the "fun." These young "Stallions" who were in their late teens and early twenties thought this was a refreshing fun thing. Soon the "social drinking" at grandma's house was getting a little rowdy. They encouraged my dad to join them in taking in some "cold ones" on hot Sunday afternoons. One of the younger men would hold his nose while drinking his beer. He was convinced that drinking Pearl Beer was the manly thing to do even though he hated the stuff. Later he became enamored by it and boasted about his drinking. Another uncle didn't really care for it, but drank to please his brothers. Even though the men had now introduced the beer barrel (wood keg), for the most part the situation was toned down. They enjoyed quenching their thirst, pumping the keg, and seeing the booze foam to the top of the cup. These uncles were consumed with fun and folly on grandma's grassy front lawn enjoying their foamy beer mugs.

I never recall any serious problems. If there were, you couldn't tell, because there was always joking and laughter. Gradually, my dad realized this was a bad testimony for his family and children, so he quit drinking. Consequently, there were murmurs of his being "too good" to drink with them. My father was a no nonsense kind of person. But apparently he had let his guard down to satisfy these young brothers-in-law. We slowed down on the Sunday visits to grandma's, and soon my dad avoided all functions where there were alcoholic drinks.

Our Christian standard of living became somewhat of a target for subtle ridicule. Most of these young relatives were professing "Christians," having "inherited" this title from three of their uncles who were preachers. Tio Felix, Tio Lupe, and Tio Estanislado Flores had been devote men of God. Our families remained in touch but there still seemed to be an underlying tension. However, it wasn't as bad as the Hatfields and McCoys' feuds. I am thankful that my dad stood firm in his convictions even though he became unpopular in the family. But this was a good testimony for his immediate family.

HOUSE OF NEIGHBORLY SERVICE -1940

The House of Neighborly Service (HNS) was a project of the Presbyterian Church we attended. It was a community center located at the corner of W. Salinas and Calaveras Street. We lived just a stone's throw away at 2716 W. Salinas Street, right next to the Lawrence family.

Next to them on the corner was the Venzor family, including Lee and Camilo. Freddy and Teresita who were part of the Alfred Zepeda family, lived across the street. Andrew and Max Morales lived around the corner on Calaveras Street. These are the kids we grew up with in the old neighborhood.

Divine Redeemer Presbyterian Church

We had mud fights in the vacant lot across the street from our house. We pretended to be Tarzan swinging from branch to branch on a tall tree. Once a boy fell and had the air knocked out of him. He was one of two boys adopted by Ms. Phelps and Ms. Callaghan, social workers at HNS. When I asked Ms. Phelps if she would punish him, she replied, "He has already been punished."

In June 1940, at the age of 13, I received my certificate of completion from Vacation Bible School at "El Divino Redentor" (Divine Redeemer Presbyterian Church). About this time, my Uncle Sefe and his family moved into a house, immediately behind ours, on Central Alley. Later, my dad's other sister Consuelo and her family moved in next door to them. So we enjoyed close family relationships for a long time.

Mr. Ben Perez, a mild-mannered ex-prize fighter, was the youth director at HNS. He was probably the person who turned our young mischievous lives around. He was quiet spoken but firm in enforcing the rules. He set values and standards as he coached and monitored all the athletic activities, including basketball, ping pong, boxing, baseball, wood shop and track.

Citywide basketball tournaments were held at Wesley House Gym every Saturday morning during the season. These were exciting and thrilling times, even though the cold Saturday mornings brought goose bumps to our skinny legs. The spirit and the enthusiasm of thirteen and fourteen-year old kids filled the cold air. We all looked up to Mr. Perez our coach, who taught us teamwork, as well as many other positive traits. He taught us values that were to remain with us for the rest of our lives. He was a super guy that taught us by example.

Pioneers was another club that taught us hiking and camping skills. After my short time as a Pioneer, I joined the morally upright Boy Scouts of America. At 14, I followed my brother Danny who was already a Scout. Mr. Jimmy Tafolla (an attorney), was the Boy Scout Master. Earning merit badges through skills and projects kept us motivated to learn more in order to progress in rank. Fifteen-mile hiking trips to Medina Lake in Von

Ormy were always exciting. There is nothing like telling scary stories, cracking jokes, hearing strange noises, and finally going to sleep around a crackling campfire at night. I have great regard and respect for Scout Leaders and the Scouting movement because of the moral and honest values they instill in young people. Their philosophy may have changed throughout the years, but at *Scout Troop 52* character building was a major focus. This was another activity of House of Neighborly Service.

One pastor at the Church had his two arms severed at the elbows. He had lost them in a cotton gin accident in years past. His young son, our neighborhood friend, thought it was cruel and unusual punishment that he should get spanked with two hard knobs which his father applied very effectively. One day after school, another boy beat up this young lad right in front of his home. His father never came out, and claimed he preferred his son learn how to protect himself. This boy had to learn the hard way.

Happy Days!

NEWSPAPER BOY AND OTHER JOBS

Motivated by my father, and by the desire to make a little money, my brother Danny and I got jobs as "hop boys" (Milkman helpers). The Milk routes usually started around 4:30 or 5 a.m. That meant we had to walk several miles in the dark to the Dairy on Fredericksburg Road. We were assigned to different milk truck routes. Once arriving at our neighborhood, my assignment was to "hop" off the truck and deliver the dairy products. The milkman already had all the customer information in a large route book. The customers had designated spots where they wanted the products placed - some on the front porch, others around the back, the side door, or inside a screen porch, etc. Some of the dairy products we delivered were: quarts and pints of milk, orange juice, and chocolate milk. Other popular products were butter and cottage cheese. All drinks came in glass bottles; that was before the days of plastic containers. Early one morning, my brother Danny fell when he jumped off the truck. He broke a bottle, and cut his hand. This was part of the hazard of this early morning job.

At a young age I sold newspapers downtown, in front of the Brady Building. This was right across the street from Alterman's Mens Shop where my Uncle Raymond worked. Houston Street was a busy main drag downtown, and a profitable location for selling newspapers. I worked for the Express-News Company. Our competitor, San Antonio Light, was the only other newspaper in town. The newspapers were the principle means of news media in the city and throughout the country. When tragedy, murders, or wars broke out, the newspaper boys could be heard shouting "Extra, Extra" all over the city. This of course, was before television.

As newspaper boys, we became acquainted with the names of gangsters who continually made the headlines. You could hear these boys roaming and shouting throughout the city, *"EXTRA, EXTRA, John Dillinger has robbed another bank."* "**EXTRA**" in large print on the front page was dispatched immediately to announce spectacular or sensational news. Other infamous gangsters who were terrorizing the country at this time were Baby Face Nelson and the Texas gangsters Bonnie and Clyde. Some regarded these gangsters as legendary heroes because they were getting an upper-hand on the law and the establishment. In general, many people were fed up with the establishment, which is the attitude of many today. In regards to the criminal element, San Antonio for the most part remained relatively quiet and peaceful.

I always looked forward to the Christmas Banquet given by The Express-News. Hundreds of boys from all over the city would converge on the Gunter Hotel banquet hall to feast on the annual Turkey Dinner. This included turkey (with stuffing), gravy, mashed potatoes, candid yams, hot rolls, ham, pumpkin pies, and all the trimmings. An unfortunate incident occurred, when I was selling newpapers in front of the Texas Theater. One large bully newspaper boy started pushing me around and even left his nail prints on my arms. He sold the Light, our competitor newspaper.

My dad, who was not a big man, came and tried to talk to this guy. When he did, this bully got in my face and starting blurting out profanities. My dad immediately responded with a fist to his jaw. The boy backed off holding his chin with threats that his father would come and get even. If I recall, the two fathers were able to talk it over in a civilized manner. One thing I do remember is that the boy's father was built like a lumberjack. My dad was always ready to defend us, even though he was small in stature. But, he could ignite pretty quickly!

This reminds me of another time where my dad's short temper flared up. He and my mother had just entered a city transit bus. The driver took off with a jerky motion that shook the passengers on the bus. My mom, still standing and trying to hold on, complained to the driver to be more careful. He responded with, "Are you drunk or something?" That was a big mistake! He never should have said that! My dad promptly jumped on the little platform where the driver sat, grabbed him, and put a headlock on him. Other passengers finally helped calm him down.

I made friends with many of the working people and other kids downtown. One was a tall and handsome usher from the Majestic Theater. I admired him as he would strut by from time to time in that stately uniform. Sometimes he would buy a paper, and other times I would just give him a free copy. I was thrilled the day he promised to treat me to the elegant and expensive Majestic Theater. The day came when this new friend was escorting this little excited newspaper boy to the theater. With his hand on my shoulder we both walked toward the Majestic. He gently and politely walked me to the rear entrance of the theater. This of course was the entrance for "Colored" people only, which didn't faze me. Well, I ended up on an upper tier that was just beneath the theater ceiling. The seats were tiered wooden slats with no backs, and very uncomfortable. I was just happy that I got in for free! As a young kid, I could boast that I had been inside the elegant Majestic.

Using my first bike, I delivered drugs (prescription drugs, that is) for Webster Drug Store, which was at the corner of West Commerce and Zarzamora. Mr. Webster, the pharmacist, owned that whole corner property, as well as the Pig Stand and apartments across the street. He had wealth, and he clung to his "worldly" possessions. Once while I was waiting on a customer, he whispered in my ear, with a strong intense voice, "You're putting too much ice cream on the cones." This was after I had been promoted to "soda jerk" serving fountain drinks. Apparently I was a very generous soda jerk! In those days soda fountains were commonplace in most drug stores.

About the age of fifteen I had a bigger bike, which allowed me to start my own newspaper route. I was slowly climbing the "ladder of success." I was having fun and making money at the same time. The biggest sacrifice was waking up while it was still dark on Sunday mornings. I walked five blocks to the "drop off" location where all the newspaper boys would pick up their bundles of papers. The individual heavy Sunday papers had to be rolled and tied with string. This was done by wetting the end of the string with your tongue, then slinging it around the upper part of the roll (so it would stick to the paper). You would wrap it around snug, two or three times, then slide it down to the middle. If it wasn't tight enough, you would start the process all over again. The papers were covered with special plastic covers on rainy days. If we accidentally or carelessly missed a house delivery, we would get a phone call. That meant another trip (rain or shine) with an extra paper. This might happen if friends came along to help (or clown around).

Cortez boys Christmas Shopping

One morning, when I threw a heavy Sunday paper unto a dark porch, I heard a loud "Oummmp." How was I to know there was a man sleeping there? For the most part, we brothers always teamed up to help each other. My dad was always very encouraging, and supportive of any jobs we had. He always made sure we were treated fair. Plus, he also encouraged us in the habit of sharing a small percentage of each paycheck with mom.

Extended Gonzalez Family on Easter Sunday

Christmas Eve

ENDING THE GLORIOUS RACE: BY GOD'S GRACE

MOM AND DAD
HEART OF THE CORTEZ FAMILY

CHAPTER 5
MY INTRODUCTION TO THE MUSIC WORLD

The alto saxophone became my new love when my dad began to give me lessons. I was as excited as some kid getting his first baseball glove. I would clean it inside out and make it shine. I would practice sitting down and standing up and in front of a mirror. I pictured myself playing with a big band. I was motivated because Danny was already playing the trombone. Of course, seeing my dad march with the National Guard Band was a thrill we kids all enjoyed. Music would eventually become the passion of my life. In later years I would experience the thrill of marching bands! It started with my high school band (Tech High), The University of Texas Longhorn  Band, the St. Mary's University ROTC Band, and my own Natalia High

School Band. Later, I was privileged to play with the Hawaii County Band. Stirring march music, like John Philip Sousa's "Stars and Stripes Forever", still gives me goose bumps. I thank God for giving me a dad who cared and encouraged me. He was my inspiration.

WASHINGTON IRVING JUNIOR HIGH SCHOOL

Me and my saxophone

After elementary school, junior high was naturally an exciting new adventure. It was a huge step climbing from childhood to adolescence (that state of endearment and confusion). However, it didn't take me long to get used to this new environment. I made new friends and hung out with other kids from our neighborhood. The school was only three blocks away from home. My father had been teaching me the alto sax when I entered Washington Irving Junior High School. I was anxious and really looking forward to playing with the school orchestra. Well, Mrs. Majesky, the orchestra teacher burst my bubble. She did not accept me, "The orchestra does not use saxophones," she said. My dad was not satisfied, so once again he came to my rescue. Mrs. Majesky was correct about saxophones not being used in orchestras, except on specific musical arrangements. Ultimately, I was accepted and was really excited! Here,

I made friends with David Garcia, a cornet player, and his sister, Esther, a piano player. We started experimenting with popular dance music at David's house after school.

His father, a clarinet player, was very helpful and encouraging. We made our debut with a small group playing for free at a birthday party. We felt proud when we were hired to play at another party at the International Institute on Medina and Martin. Wow! We were one happy budding musical ensemble ready to take on any job.

Louis Garcia, who played in the school orchestra and high school band, was another good friend and an excellent trumpet player. He was a Christian and visibly moral even from his youth. He was very successful in his adult years, but still proved to be a humble and faithful friend. In time, I bonded with three other very close friends, Andrew Morales, Alfonso Hernandez, and Ernest Trejo.

There, in the school library one day, Andy and I took vows to be friends forever. We even pricked our fingers and sealed our vows with blood. Unfortunately, as an adult, he met a tragic death while working in his back yard. He apparently had a heart attack. His brother Max, who was now a doctor, tried to revive him by a tracheostomy, but was unsuccessful. Many years later, Max who had a successful medical practice in Dallas, also died. He was brought to San Antonio for burial. It was sad to acknowledge the loss of these two brothers whom we had grown up

Junior High Grads (Richard, Alfonso, Ernest, Andy)

with.

Besides playing in the orchestra, I had the opportunity of participating in several school plays. It all started with Mr. Sprout, my homeroom teacher, who was also the metal shop instructor. One year, as Abraham Lincoln's birthday approached, he assigned the class to research and give an oral report on Lincoln. The day came, and my turn came up. I presented a very simple story. It went like this: Lincoln was riding his horse with several officials on the way to Washington. It was a wet and muddy morning after a storm the night before. Noticing that a little bird had fallen out of its nest, Lincoln stopped, got off his horse, and walked to where the helpless bird lay. He picked it up gently, climbed the tree, not hindered by the tall boots, and wet raincoat he was wearing. He gently placed the little bird back in its nest and climbed down the tree. Mr. Lincoln quietly climbed on his horse and continued down the muddy road with his companions.

At the end of the class, Mr. Sprout approached me and asked if I would

MY INTRODUCTION TO THE MUSIC WORLD

be willing to share that story at the school's Lincoln Day assembly. Not realizing the magnitude of this request, I responded with "Okay." The bell rang and I could hear the chatter of hordes of humanity filing into the school auditorium. Someone ushered me to the front row, next to the principal. Wow, the whole school was there: the students, the teachers, administrators, janitors and cafeteria help. I tried to look above the "thousands" of eyes that were staring at me as I stood behind that "skinny" microphone. Somehow I managed to get through it all, and got Abraham Lincoln to Washington! The applause was "deafening"! That was my first public speaking experience.

The Speech Arts teacher, Ms. Cockrell, apparently admired my "courage" and encouraged me to take her course in Speech Arts. The next semester, I took the course. I studied the art of public speaking. Self-confidence, enunciating and communicating with a clear voice, were most important. This led to several small parts in school plays.

Washington Irving Junior school's first dramatics production of the year, "Rags," Friday had this group in roles. Seated (L.-R.) Mary Anne Peterson, Angelia and Bina Mae Pittman. Center: Eddie Sacre and Mar Acquart. Rear: Ernest Trejo, Alice Rios, Geraldin and Richard Cortez.

I starred in our first production of the year "Rags"

I played the role of a pig, a baker, and a "starring" role of a flag waving Uncle Sam in a patriotic program. It was fun, but music was my main interest!

January 1943, I walked on the stage in a hand-me-down suit from my older brother, and graduated from Washington Irving Junior High. I was leaving behind many friends and wonderful memories.

PLENTY WORK FOR A YOUNG ENTREPENAUR

In 1943, at the age of sixteen, I polished silver and assisted in the mail department at Shaw's Jewelry Store at the corner of West Houston and St. Mary's. This was right across the street from where I had sold newspapers. My brother, Danny, who worked there had recommended me for the job. At the height of the Christmas season, the store was like a bee hive, and I suddenly became an expert at wrapping gifts at a record pace.

The following year, I worked as a pin boy at a USO Bowling Alley, across from the Main Fire Station, behind the Alamo. The automatic electric machines were not popular yet, so the pins had to be set on the rack by the pin boys. If you didn't jump up to your safety spot fast enough you might catch a bowling ball right on your shins.

During our high school years, the Danny Cortez Orchestra played several dances for service men at that same USO. Another job I had as a young lad was as a bus boy at the downtown Kress Cafeteria on Houston Street. They must have been desperate for help to hire this "little squirt." I wonder if Kress was aware of "child labor laws".

In 1944, I was employed as a bag boy at HEB on West Commerce near Zarzamora. It was probably one of the first HEB's to open in San Antonio. The most vivid memory I have of that job was the tyrant boss whom I considered a slave driver. After a long hard day on our feet, the "real" work began! This man would make us sweep and mop the whole store. If he was not satisfied we would have to sweep and mop again.

While in high school, I had a part-time job as the tailor's helper at Penner's Men's Store on West Commerce Street. This store, which is very near City Hall, is one of the few old businesses that is still in operation. I did small jobs, including sewing and ironing the cuffs on peg leg pants for "Zoot Suiters."

That was the popular style at the time, during the mid-forties. Carlos Castro, my high school buddy, recommended me to Max and Sam Penner for the job (now-a-days the sons run the store). Saturday nights after work, Carlos and I had to dodge the winos and other loitering reprobates on the street. Their intent was to acquire money to sustain their drinking habit. One night, three of them chased Carlos all the way to his bus stop. He made it just in time to jump on the bus before being caught.

San Antonio Drug Company, located at the corner of Market and St. Mary's, was another one of my employers during my teen years. I did odd jobs, including messenger trips to the different floors. The Drug Company was located immediately across the street from the fire station, which was later converted to a public library. Most of the jobs I had as a youngster were downtown on Houston Street. This was San Antonio! This was before the introduction of malls. Downtown, the city extended from Dolorosa Street (at Milam Park) to Alamo Street, and from Market Street to Martin Street.

All the major department stores, hotels, restaurants and businesses were downtown. It was a friendly small town atmosphere, where friends, neighbors, and relatives often met. One of the first big malls that opened up in San Antonio was the Wonderland Mall on Fredericksburg Road and IH 410. Later, the name was changed to Crossroads Mall. At present, it is known as Wonderland of the Americas.

The major hotels were the Menger, Gunter, Crockett and the St. Anthony. The major retail stores were Joske's, Wolf & Marx, and Solo Serve. Kress and Woolworth were the most popular five and ten cent stores.

The theaters were all downtown. The most popular and elegant were the Majestic and the Aztec. Plush carpeting, drapes, elegant statutes, unique furniture and paintings, would provide a quiet, tranquil, and relaxing atmosphere. It was a subtle and captivating mood - one of entering another peaceful world, taking you away from the hustle and bustle of the city outside.

Other popular theaters were the Texas, the Empire, the Palace, the Prince and the State. There were two Spanish-speaking theaters - the "Nacional" and the "Zaragosa" located in the same block on West Commerce. They were very popular with the Hispanic population in San Antonio. Later, a more elegant Spanish speaking theater was opened on west Houston Street - the "Alameda." The Joy Theater on West Houston Street was the only burlesque show in town and only stayed for a few years.

The Municipal Auditorium was the center of all cultural activities including: concerts, formal dances, dramatic plays, boxing, Easter sunrise services, and high school & college graduations. It was also the home for the San Antonio Symphony Orchestra.

The San Antonio River was just an insignificant little "Arroyo" (creek) meandering through the city. "Casa Rio" was the first restaurant established on the river walk, right below West Commerce Street at Alamo.

With its Mexican food and atmosphere, it was conveniently located for the people who worked downtown. The "Original" was another one of the oldest Mexican restaurants in San Antonio. Sometimes after a dance job, we would end up at Mi Tierra Cafe, located on Produce Row. It was just a "hole in the wall," but had a variety of delicious "pan dulce"(sweet bread). Today, Mi Tierra Restaurant and Bakery, is a prominent colorful tourist attraction.

Ready for a New Year's gig.

After playing a dance job for three or four hours, we were hungry. The "Golden Star" restaurant on West Commerce was another favorite. It was another place for musicians to hang out. The Chinese owner, a permanent fixture behind the cash register, always had a rigid face; but his delectable hot fish plates attracted people all night long.

That's were I picked up the habit of spreading catsup and picante sauce on fresh soft white bread to create an amazing hot fish sandwich with wedge fries on the side. A cop, sitting inconspicuously at the end of the counter, was also another permanent fixture throughout the night. His presence offered a measure of security in this rough part of town.

CHAPTER 6
TECH HIGH SCHOOL
1943-1946

When I was in high school and Christmas was approaching, I had the opportunity for a part-time job at the main post office (at Houston and Alamo). My brother Danny, being older and wiser, often introduced me to job situations that he knew about. Everyone feared "Macho," the supervisor on the floor at the post office! He looked like Boris Karloff, and was constantly hovering over the employees.

Danny, in his wisdom, gave me some good advice, which I never forgot. "Always carry something in your hands, letters or whatever," he would tell me. "Never be caught empty-handed," he said. In fact, it became a habit with me even after I left the post office. Instinctively, I always carried something, especially if I was on a job. For thirty years, as a band director, I always carried a brief case, sometimes full of music and sometimes empty.

HIGH SCHOOL CONCERT AND MARCHING BAND

Tech Buffalo Band in Battle of Flowers Parade

My two brothers and I played in the Tech High Marching Band. Band practice was during Zero Hour (before school). And we were always out of breath by the time we reached the third-floor band room. We were always loaded down with books and instruments.

Mr. Dossche, a nervous balding band director, turned beet red with disgust when the band didn't respond to his commands. We were the Red and White Tech Buffalo Band, and were proud as can be! We enjoyed many fun activities including: concerts, parades and contests. Football games every Friday night were the high point of every week. The band had to rehearse for the half-time shows on a baseball field about a quarter of a mile away

San Antonio Technical & Vocational High School

from school. Being a technical and vocational school, practice fields did not take top priority. But that didn't deter the school spirit displayed by the students.

During my high school years, drive-in restaurants were a good place to hang out and shoot the breeze. (No, that's not where we did our homework.) Roger's Drive-In on Main Avenue was close to our school and was accessible to those who drove cars.

Another popular weekend hangout for young crowds were the drive-in theaters. You drove into a huge parking lot where all the cars would face a giant screen. You would park right next to a meter-type box that held the speaker. This you would hang inside your car door. You could dress casual and be comfortable. People could walk to the nearby concession stand and stock up on burgers, hot dogs, drinks, and other goodies. You could enjoy all this in the comfort of your car. It was perfect for families with children. Occasionally, some daring youngsters would be caught sneaking in by hiding inside a car's trunk. And of course, the drive-in was a convenient place for young couples to get better acquainted.

One dull rainy day, a couple of my high school buddies and I found it hard to study, so we skipped school and went to the O'Brien (the small dinky "flea bitten" theater) on West Houston Street. Much to my surprise, someone had also found refuge from the rain that should have been in school - my brother, Danny! There he was, sitting in his ROTC uniform, with some of his friends. We all found it very hard to concentrate on our studies on dismal rainy days, so we would take a "little break" from school.

If Mr. Cunningham, the school counselor, or some truant officer would have come, I'm sure all these hooky players would be scrambling to the nearest exit. The Palace Theater on Alamo Street was another popular place to visit on rainy days. That one was too risky though, in cases where we had to hightail it back to school, it was just too far.

After school, many highschoolers would stroll through town, and sometimes just loiter in front of Kress or other stores, even though there was an ordinance against loitering. One afternoon, a whole bunch of young guys (including the three Cortez boys) were picked up by the police paddy wagon in front of Kress. At police headquarters, a rotund police captain sitting behind a desk gave us a long lecture on civil obedience and city ordinances.

For the most part, high school was filled with happy days. Admittedly, tempers would flair up from time to time. If two boys were determined to brawl, the coach would escort them to the gym and provide them with boxing gloves.

Tech, being a technical and vocational school, offered an extraordinary variety of opportunities for students. Some of the subjects offered were: Distributive Education, Retail Selling, Welding Shop, Sheet Metal, Piping Trades, Print Shop, Garment Manufacturing, Machine Shop, Engineering Drafting, Electric Shop, Wood Making, Auto Repair, Dressmaking, Radio Repair, Commercial Art, Cabinet Mill, Architectural Drafting, Home Making, Plastics, Cosmetology, ROTC, Tech Service Reserve (TSR) for girls, Sports, Red Jackets (Pep Squad) and Band.

In high school I had many friends, both boys and girls. However, there was one girl that I was infatuated with. Susie didn't know I existed, but I couldn't help but admire her when I caught sight of her. I would make an extra effort to spot her as she walked down the crowded hallway. I was even annoyed by this wacky clown who was always hovering about her. I couldn't understand what she saw in this guy. Well, I guess he was funny and entertaining! My dream was to date her some day. Amazingly enough the day came, a miracle happened! A Junior-Senior Prom was coming up and I found out she didn't have a date. "Wow, now is my chance," I thought! After some reflection, I said "No way!" Then I finally worked up enough boldness. I was a little nervous as to how I would approach her and pop the question. We had just talked a few times in the hallway. I finally worked up incredible courage to ask her. After some hesitation and stammering, the words finally came out. Her response was, "Of course, Richard!" I nearly passed out when she said that! I was on cloud nine for the next couple of days.

This was so special for me that I chose a beautiful white Gardenia for her corsage. I personally wrapped it up with expensive wrapping paper and a big beautiful bow. I pictured her opening it up in front of her mom, while the other couple waited in the car. Well, it didn't happen that way! Instead, she met me at the front gate, and her mom didn't even appear. I politely opened the back door of the car for her. As we drove off in the dark of the night, I was aghast as she tore open that beautiful gift box that I had labored to put together. Well, at least the strong scent of the Gardenia was rewarding! I still remember that date every time I smell a

Gardenia! It was a magical evening that I would never forget. We had a marvelous time at the prom. That was the first and the last time we dated, but we remained good friends. Many, many years later, at our 50th high school reunion, I met her and her husband. And much to my surprise, she still remembered that date, and even the Gardenia corsage. I was astounded!

Riding the crowded city transit bus to school every morning, loaded with books and at least one saxophone, and/or clarinet for years, got tiresome. But my attitude changed one day when I spotted this stunningly good-looking girl boarding the bus on Martin Street. I would stretch my neck just to get a glimpse of her. She was there by herself at the same time every morning. I didn't know what came over me, but I was consumed with the desire to meet her! I didn't know how or when.

Bertha, Richard & Adela

By the time the bus reached her stop, it was packed with people standing from front to back. One morning it happened! Unexpectedly and surprisingly, I was able to grab a seat next to her. I was petrified! No words would come out of me. I was not a fast talking Casanova like some guys were. But when the bus hit a bump on the road, our elbows accidentally touched. Whoa, I felt a tingling up and down my arm, and goose bumps at the back of my neck. Shortly after that, Bertha and I became close friends, and eventually went "steady."

I was convinced she was the most beautiful girl in school." A few other guys apparently thought the same thing until they found out she was "mine." Walking after school one day, she "innocently" explained how she had accepted this friendship ring from a certain boy. When she showed it to me, I discovered I had a streak of jealousy. I strongly advised her to return it immediately, which she did! We were "in love", we were enamored, and we enjoyed every moment spent together walking to the bus stop after school.

Even though our bus stop was just a couple of blocks from school, it wasn't uncommon for us to walk from school on Main Avenue to Houston Street, and clear across town to Alamo, past Joske's, on E. Commerce, and several blocks beyond Market Street to catch the bus. The heavy load of books, both hers and mine, were not a hindrance. Those moments were warm and wonderful with my high school sweetheart. Unfortunately, in later years, "I let her slip through my fingers", I neglected and lost her when I joined the Navy and became too self-absorbed, prideful, and foolish.

THE DANNY CORTEZ ORCHESTRA

While in high school, Danny decided to form a dance band. Danny was our trombone player. I played alto sax, Gilbert played drums, and with about eight other young musicians, we were off on our "musical careers." We started playing at school assemblies, birthday parties, and were becoming well known. The popular Tech 200 dance (every Monday after school) cost ten cents. The kids loved it because it was in Room 200, a relatively small area in the basement of the school. The crowded condition made it convenient for partners to dance cheek to cheek, or at least in close proximity.

The Danny Cortez Orchestra volunteered to play for the 200 dances. It was decided that the dances would be moved to the school library to accommodate the orchestra and the larger crowds. The kids all loved the music of Tommy and Jimmy Dorsey, Benny Goodman, Artie Shaw, Harry James, Glenn Miller, and other popular big band names. Danny appropriately chose Glen Miller's beautiful "Moon Light Serenade" as the theme song for the band. From then on, we were called to play for weddings, social functions, high school proms, and college dances around town. Then we began to get calls from out-of-town.

Practice sessions for the band started at our house, at 2716 West Salinas. Later, we got permission to practice at House of Neighborly Service, the Community Center close to our house, where we grew up. Neighborhood "fans" of all ages would crowd around the windows to hear us practice. At first we enjoyed playing just for the fun of it! Getting the guys together, getting organized, discussing new ideas, then "diving" into those terrific big band arrangements was a real thrill. Here were a bunch of high school kids on a new "high," playing to our hearts content. We were in our own little world, doing what we loved best. On top of all that fun, we were amazed that we were now getting paid. All those hours of practice were beginning to bring rewards.

High School Barn Dance—October 27, 1944

As the band gained popularity, our high school as well other schools in town were booking us, and keeping us busy. Lanier, our school rivals, even hired us to play at their events. One of many unusual incidents that stand out in my mind happened in November 1944 at our school barn dance. The band must have been playing real "hot!" Some pranksters poured a big bucket of water on us from the outside through the basement windows. It did cool us off on a hot Saturday night, but we kept on playing without missing a beat.

Something funny that could have turned serious took place at a birthday party held in a private home. During one intermission, Heron B. Smith, a quiet but talented lead trumpet player, had a confrontation with some guy in the crowd. When Heron returned after the break he was displaying a kitchen knife that he stuck in his belt. It looked rather awkward (to say the least) when he got up to play a solo. We tried to avoid rowdy crowds and nightclubs. But there are many interesting and hilarious stories to be told.

One awkward situation occurred at Columbus Hall on Martin Street, where we were playing for a wedding. As was the custom, after the bridal party marched in, the bride and groom would do the first dance. As soon as we started playing, a short chubby man stood in the middle of the floor, and shouted at the band "Páren la música, páren la música" (stop the music, stop the music). He requested another number, which we played to satisfy him. Danny expressed his indignation at the insult and embarrassment caused by this individual. We were prepared to pack up and leave the party, but the bride and groom quickly apologized. They asked the little man, the "tipsy" father of the bride to apologize before the whole crowd. I guess he wanted his favorite song since he was paying for everything, without realizing that the bride had already chosen a certain piece. After this slight discord and apology, everything went smoothly.

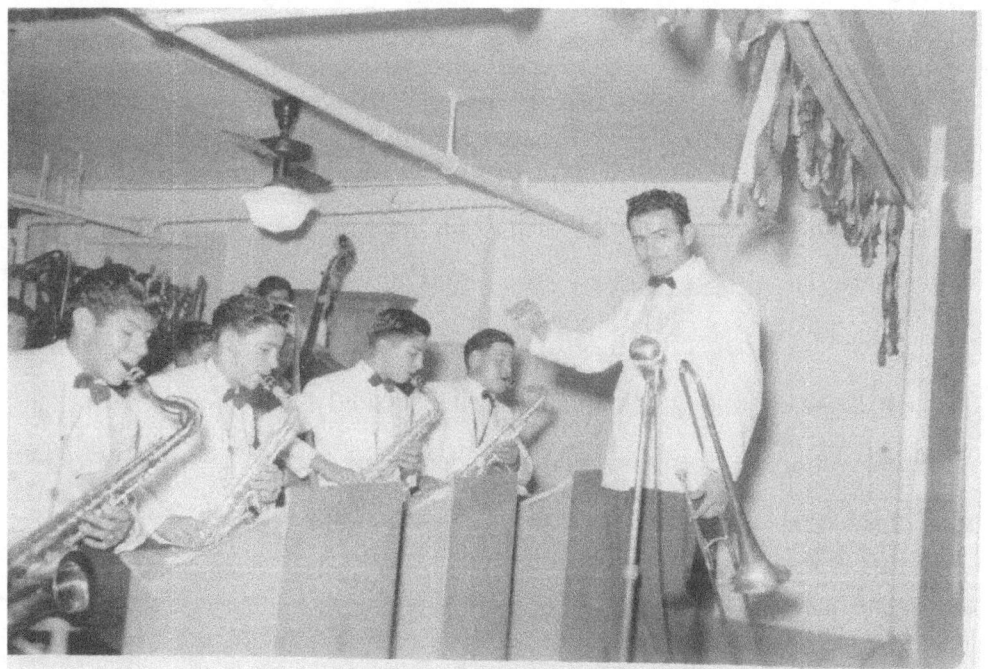

"Moonlight Serenade" - New Year's Eve Dance

Danny Cortez Orchestra

One hot summer night, as we played in a Gazebo in an Austin park, a fight broke out right in front of the bandstand. As we played, two women started shouting and screaming obscenities at each other. Soon they started pushing, slapping, scratching, punching and pulling each other's hair as they fell to the ground. This uncivil and unfeminine altercation happened without the band missing a single beat. I believe a man was the

"Mambo" at Patio Andaluz—Danny Cortez Orchestra

object of this shameful fracas.

A gym in Beeville, Texas, a former Naval base, was another "battle ground." The band was playing for a wedding on a five-foot high stage in a big gymnasium. The bridal party table was right below the stage, facing the dance hall. Everyone was having a wonderful time, dancing, loud conversations, and drinking. About halfway through the night the elegance was shattered by loud angry voices coming from the floral decked bridal table. Suddenly, tuxedo clad "gentlemen" engaged in pushing, shoving, and shouting. The women, in their formal apparel, starting screaming as an all-out-brawl ensued and bottles starting flying. The scuffling erupted into flying fists as the band "provided" lively background music. That is, until one of the groomsmen came up and shouted, "STOP THAT MUSIC!"

For obvious reasons, we tried to avoid jobs at nightclubs and honky-tonks, where liquor flows and trouble can flair unexpectedly.

Patio Andaluz on West Commerce was another dance hall where we played regularly, in a more peaceful atmosphere. They had a big ballroom upstairs, and a picturesque patio outside for summer night dances. Social clubs usually had big formal dances at the Municipal Auditorium.

**Starlight Club
Danny Cortez Orchestra**

La Villita was another beautiful open-air patio in the historic district downtown where we played often. Of course, New Year's Eve dances were the ones we looked forward to. These were the most profitable for all bands. From time to time, we were hired to play in several of the surrounding small towns around San Antonio, including: Austin, Seguin, Brady, Hondo, Uvalde, Lackland Air Base and Fort Sam Houston.

CHAPTER 7
PEARL HARBOR ATTACK-
US NAVY CALLING

I was in high school, when the Japanese attacked Pearl Harbor on December 7, 1941. President Delano Roosevelt said these profound words, "This date will live in infamy," a day to be remembered! Admiral Isoroku Yamamoto, the Commander-in-Chief of the combined Japanese fleet in charge of the Pearl Harbor attack, made this sober statement, "I'm afraid we have awoken a sleeping Giant." The attack on Pearl Harbor came with destruction, devastation, and deception.

ANCHORS AWEIGH

The war cry "Remember Pearl Harbor" was to ring throughout our nation for a long time. The spirit of patriotism in the United States was overwhelming! Students who were seventeen or older were anxiously joining the Army, Navy, Marines, and Coast Guard. My enthusiasm to join the military faced gracious opposition. Since I was so close to graduation, my parents advised me to wait. In January 1946, I had enough credits to graduate, so I rushed to the Navy recruiter and signed up. A small problem appeared – I discovered for the first time that the name on my birth certificate was Estéban Cortez. I rushed to the courthouse, and for fifty cents I had my name officially changed on the birth certificate to Ricardo Cortez. Apparently I was named Estéban after my grandfather, but grew up with the name Richard (or Ricardo).

Young men were still being drafted in 1946, even though the war had ended. In fact, I got my draft notice after I had been in the Navy for several months. My high school diploma was mailed to my home while I was on a ship. The war was over, but many young men still felt it was their patriotic duty to serve their country. While signing up with the Navy recruiter, I was asked for my middle name. I honestly replied that I did not have one. Then the recruiter asked for my mother's maiden name. When I said "Gonzalez," he promptly designated "G" as my middle initial. And that's what it is to this day, "Ricardo G. Cortez."

I was excited, to say the least! After passing all the preliminary tests, I was given a date to report back. Being in peacetime, we were offered the option of enlisting for only two years. I was thoroughly pleased that I had qualified.

It was a cool morning on January 28, 1946. Me and about twelve other adventurous boys from San Antonio and the surrounding area boarded the Southern Pacific Railroad train on E. Commerce. We said our goodbyes to our families. And I said farewell to Bertha, my highschool sweetheart.

It was an exciting time as we rolled out of the station, and heard the rumbling wheels of the train as we settled down in our seats. I struck up conversations with the other young passengers. Here were a bunch of "kids" headed for San Diego, California. Some had never been outside of Texas. It was a long slow ride, as the train made many stops along the way.

It was a dark, cold, early morning when we arrived in San Diego. The only people that were visible on the streets on that cool misty morning were Sailors and Marines. A Sailor in a white station wagon with the U.S. Navy logo on the side greeted us and drove us to the U.S. Naval Training Center. As we entered the immaculate base with the perfectly manicured lawns, I couldn't help but be impressed, and made a remark about the cleanliness of the place. The "old salt" driver was quick to remark, "Tomorrow you will find out who keeps it that way."

What followed upon arriving was an immediate and complete surrendering of everything you possessed from civilian life, including your independence. Now we were property of the government, the United States Navy. The first day we found ourselves in lines - lines for physical exams, lines for shots, lines for uniforms, lines for hair cuts, lines for paperwork, lines for chow, and lines for the head (restrooms).

While waiting in one of those long lines and still in our civilian clothes, one "salty" Sailor who was in charge shouted out, "Is there any one here who is a college graduate?" At least two people eagerly raised their hands. They were promptly handed mops and assigned to clean nearby restrooms. Our first lesson learned, never volunteer! When the bugle blew reveille about 6 a.m. every morning, we would all scurry about and fall in, half asleep. We would then march to the chow hall in the dark cool California morning.

Mess hall duty was something everyone dreaded. This involved getting up in the "middle of the night", and hopefully finding your way to the mess hall. Cleaning and setting up tables, washing dishes, mopping floors, peeling potatoes, and serving food; just some of the chores we had to endure for those long days. One morning, me and three other buddies were assigned to sit around a big shiny metal vat and prepare scrambled eggs for breakfast for hundreds of men.

Our assignment was to crack eggs and deposit them into that basin, being cautioned not to accidentally drop the shells in with the eggs. It was customary to rush at all of our duties. In our haste, a nail from one of the egg crates accidentally fell in the pot. Wow! We panicked, and in desperation called one fat, permanent duty cook that was close by. Very calmly, he stuck his big, fat hairy arm, and fishing around for a while, he held up the nail. There were raw eggs dripping all the way down his arm. With his free hand, he wrung out his hairy arm into the vat. We were stunned! I gave up eating scrambled eggs for a long time after that.

The daily routine in Boot Camp was rush, rush, rush; to classes, military drills, airplane recognition, ship recognition, seamanship, introduction to the M1 Rifle, swimming (jumping into the water from a high tower), flag signals, first aid and safety. We were pressured to accomplish much in a short period of time. And, of course, it was "march, march, march," or "double time, double time," everywhere we went! One of the last classes given included recognition and prevention of venereal diseases. The last day of class the instructor warned, "The best prevention is to keep those thirteen buttons buttoned." (Referring to the thirteen buttons that keep the fly flap shut on the Navy bell-bottom trousers)

Loud commands by various leaders, and would-be leaders would ring in my ears - rush, rush, rush, double time, double time! We marched everywhere we went, with the taller guys up front setting the pace. The shorter people, like myself, were forced to strain and take longer steps, which was painful on the calves. One afternoon, after classes, marching, and all assignments completed, we quickly marched back to the barracks. Our squad leader shouted out, "Muster (fall in) in fifteen minutes." This meant we had to shower, change clothes, and fall in for chow. After much scrambling and tripping over each other, we were now on our way.

After marching for a little while, I felt a little draft below my tummy. Glancing down, I noticed all the thirteen buttons to my fly were unbuttoned, and the flap was down. In the rush to get out of the barracks, I buttoned only the top two, and overlooked the bottom eleven. Very discreetly, I was able to close that "window" before reaching the mess hall. Customarily we wore what was known as the "undress blues" for evening chow.

Every morning we did calisthenics on a huge asphalt marching ground. I couldn't help but admire the beautiful mountains all around us, unlike the flat plains of Texas. Wooden rifles were used for marching and exercising to the rhythm of the live Navy band. I enjoyed the band and embraced the thought of being part of it. Our "free time" was spent studying, writing letters, and washing clothes. There were "convenient" long wooden troughs with water spigots outside our company barracks for washing and scrubbing our clothes. Like mom, we used our hands and scrub brushes.

And, I believe we were provided with Octagon Soap, to avoid "dish washer hands." Instead of clothespins, we used little "clothes stops" (short pieces of string with metal ends), to tie our clothes on the clothesline. We didn't have the luxury of washers, dryers, or laundromats. At least we didn't have to iron our clothes. The Navy way was to roll all our clothes inside out with our printed name facing up. We laid them out on our bunks for inspection, so they had the appearance of being ironed. Frequent inspections would insure that all was rolled tight, and according to regulation. Boot camp was exhausting and challenging and seemed to have no end. It was a constant desperate rush to complete what seemed impossible at that time. No one wanted to fail and have to repeat the course. One night was designated as Talent Night for all interested. That's where I ran into a friend from back home. Johnny Rodriguez was a trumpet player and fellow musician from San Antonio. Graduation day finally arrived and we were able to wear our dress blues for the first time. We looked sharp as we marched in review, past the base commander and other high-ranking officers. I was now a seaman first class and looked forward to some exciting sea duty. First, we were given leave to go home.

It was awesome rolling into the railroad station on E. Commerce in San Antonio, and seeing all the family, friends, and my high school sweetheart, Bertha. It was great being home with my family. We ate and partied, and my dad always had his camera at the ready. I was a proud and happy "swabbie", with a disgustingly shaved head where you could spin my white hat around.

Later, Danny joined the Marines. The Danny Cortez Orchestra continued in San Antonio, with my younger brother Gilbert as the leader. Mike Hettler was the featured vocalist. The band continued in popularity and did so well that they were hired to play on an amateur radio show. Radio station KCOR presented this show in a big auditorium at San Fernando Gym in downtown San Antonio. The show and the band, backed up by plenty publicity, created much interest in the community. Huge crowds would fill up the place every Sunday afternoon.

Boot Camp picture

Danny Cortez, US Marine Corps

Welcome Home Party

Gilbert Cortez Orchestra

Home on Leave

"Whatever you do, work heartily, as for the Lord and not for men, knowing that from the Lord you will receive the inheritance as your reward. You are serving the Lord Christ."

Colossians 3:23-24

CHAPTER 8
ASSIGNED TO USS NEW JERSEY

I returned back to Long Beach, California for assignment on the U.S.S. New Jersey. I didn't know it at the time, but that was one of the largest battleships in the world, together with its sister ships, USS Iowa, USS Missouri, and the USS Wisconsin. As I boarded this magnificent gray battlewagon, I was astounded at how huge it was! It appeared to be as long as a city block. My adrenalin accelerated as I climbed the gangplank to board "my ship", it was immense, and had the appearance of being freshly painted. And later I found out who kept it clean and spotless. Now I knew the true meaning of the popular term, "ship shape", I was a seaman gunner's mate. Part of our assignment was to keep the deck outside our compartment scrubbed clean. The ship was anchored about three miles out from the city of Long Beach. In my spare time I would go exploring through out this massive metal structure. I was overwhelmed - it was like a "small city", there was a ship's store, laundry, tailor shop, post office, library, barbershop, band room, and a brig (with Marine guards), just to mention a few. What was really impressive were the nine huge 16" guns that were capable of firing accurately at targets twenty miles away.

There were also twenty 5" guns, as well as 40MM aircraft guns throughout the ship. I roamed through compartments high and low, through gun turrets, up to the bridge, forward and aft, exploring, but never covering it all. Some nights I would climb up to the bridge to look through the huge telescopes. I could get a beautiful view of the night-lights in Long Beach and the Pike.

One morning as I looked out to see Long Beach and the shoreline, I was surprised that there was nothing there but water and the horizon. Much to my amazement, this huge ship, which was anchored had turned completely around during the night. I could have pictured a small toy boat turning around in a stream, but not this massive metal structure turning around. I didn't dare reveal my ignorance to anyone.

ON DECK THE USS NEW JERSEY

The Pike was a Long Beach amusement park with a boardwalk along side the ocean. When we went on liberty, it was the favorite hang out for

On Deck of USS New Jersey

many Sailors and Marines. Since I didn't drink, I would team up with a couple of my "dry" buddies and we would head for the dime-a-dance hall. You could pick from about a dozen or more girls (who stood along the wall, like wall flowers), who just waited for you to ask them to dance as long as you had your dime ticket. They could not refuse you, because that was their job. The idea was to keep the service men happy for the price of a little dime. If you hurried when the music started, you might pick one of the prettier ones.

Some weekends. we would take the train from Long Beach to Los Angeles. I would take two or three of my buddies to visit my Uncle Arturo Alvarez in Compton. Conchita, His wife, and their two little girls, Sylvia and Jeanie, always got excited when we came. The kids would shout "Here come the "hailers". They made us feel right at home with plenty food, rides to famous places like Hollywood Grumman's Chinese Theater, and restaurants. And, no matter what time we came in at night, our beds were always ready. Aunt Meme, Eluterio and Ninfa, were equally hospitable when we visited them in Wilmington.

Sometimes we would bunk out at the YMCA. On a couple of occasions, we just slept in theaters that were open all night, just to keep from going back to the ship. Our folded up pea coats served as pillows for a small measure of comfort. It was strange waking up during the night to the sounds of galloping horses and shooting. We wanted to take full benefit of our liberty.

However, most mornings we would hurry back to the ship on time for a super breakfast that far excelled any on shore. Half asleep we would drag ourselves into the small dinghy boat that would transport us to our ship. The ship was anchored about three miles out in the harbor.

The time came for the ship to get under way and all liberties were cancelled. However, there were some exceptions and I was one of them! Because I had passed a surprise locker inspection weeks before, I was given liberty privilege for four hours. This gave me the opportunity to call home from the marina. Back on ship, we finally got underway after all the boatswain's mate pipe calls, bells, bugle calls and loud announcements on the P.A. System. It was exhilarating to see the ship cutting through the Pacific waters and the wind blowing the huge waves over the bow. We were traveling along the California coast heading toward Washington State. Some of us did not know that the New Jersey was to be placed in dry dock for maintenance and repairs in Bremerton, Washington. So we enjoyed a few short liberty trips to Seattle. My memory of that state was much fog, drizzle and overcast, day and night. One night while on liberty in Seattle, I was forced to sleep on a pool table at a YMCA. All the cots and sofas were taken! The scuttlebutt (rumor) was that a small skeleton crew would stay on the ship and the rest of the crew was to take a troop train back to San Francisco.

DEPARTED THE USS NEW JERSEY... HEADED FOR SAN FRANCISCO

I had enjoyed my few months of duty on this ship, but now the captain was bidding us farewell and good luck on the P.A. System. We packed our seabags and were transported to the train station. A troop train took us through the breath-taking green forests and mountain passes with meandering rivers far below. The train hugged the coastline all the way from Washington down through Oregon, winding and ending in Northern California.

The scenery was awesome; but the cold sandwiches, Spam, and sauerkraut on the train were something we had to tolerate. We arrived at Yerba Buena Island (YBI) in the bay of San Francisco. Arriving there, very tired and sleepy, it seemed like a weird dream as we were shuffled from one lo-

USS New Jersey underway

cation to another, not knowing where we were going. Finally, we arrived at our destination: the USS Hermitage, a transport ship that was docked and ready to take on passengers. As we went up the gangplank, I couldn't help but notice that this ship was an eyesore compared to the USS New Jersey. This old veteran ship had carried many troops overseas during the war. Now it would be transporting five thousand Sailors and Marines to the Island of Guam in the middle of the Pacific Ocean. From there, all these men were to be transferred to other ships. Yes, we were crammed like sardines in a can. We slept on canvas bunks, which were closely stacked, one on top the other, from the deck to the ceiling. There was no fresh water to bathe or brush our teeth. There was salt water, which was useless. Conditions were so hot, most of the men just laid on the deck during the daytime. In fact, many of them sat on blankets playing cards while waiting in line for chow. I found a way to avoid these long lines.

A Navy Lieutenant announced that a band was being formed and would

Weekly Division Inspection

have auditions. I tried out and was accepted as a tenor sax player. So, a stage band was organized to entertain the five-thousand swabs and jarheads in the evenings.

Besides practicing and entertaining the troops in the evenings with the band, I now had a special pass that would get me to the head of the chow line. Needless to say, some guys in the long lines would occasionally voice their complaints. Another privilege I had was discount coupons for the ship store and the Geedunk (Concession) Stand.

However, something awkward happened at the first band rehearsal. I was playing away on my sax right next to a porthole with the ship rocking and the waves swaying. My stomach felt queasy and I had to rush to the head (restroom). You guessed it - I was seasick! I was miserable! I couldn't stand the sight of food, so I had to "dry heave". Soon after that, things went pretty smooth. It was a long, hot, boring trip, and the evening band concerts provided some form of entertainment. Some men were so frustrated with the heat and the ship's poor conditions; they cut holes on the air vents above their bunks to get more air. Thoroughly disgusted, some slashed holes in their canvas bunk beds when we were approaching our destination.

CHAPTER 9
ISLAND OF GUAM
1947

We finally spotted the beautiful swaying palm trees along the beaches on the Island of Guam. The year was 1947. There were fluffy clouds blowing in the Pacific breeze as the sun was setting. A gentle tropical rain started coming down as we reached the shore. With seabags on our shoulders and wide-eyed anticipation, we made our way to waiting 6-by Trucks (Chevrolet 1 and 1/2 ton, G506). It was now dark as we were led to our sleeping quarters. Wouldn't you know it, with 5000 Sailors and Marines ashore, accommodations were limited. So, some of us (yours truly included), were escorted to the nearby brig (jail) where we spent the night.

We were exhausted from that long, hot voyage on that rusty transport ship. Anything would do, we just wanted to sack out as soon as possible! From Guam, we were supposed to be transferred to other ships. After a few days, ships started to arrive and large groups went to their new assignments. The rest of us remained behind and just waited patiently.

Days turned into weeks and weeks into months, but still there was no sign of ships. Eventually, we were informed that our records had gone back on the USS Hermitage. We got the impression they were lost! Here we were, stranded on an island in the middle of the Pacific Ocean with no assignments and uncertain about our future.

Thinking of home

In the meantime, we were to fall in for muster (roll call) each morning. To our surprise, each day we would be assigned menial jobs, such as cleaning out the heads (restrooms), and other *priority tasks*. The Navy was going to keep us busy to prevent us from being bored and getting "rock happy" on this *island paradise*. In our frustration and discontent, some of us learned the art of escaping from work parties. We would manage to sneak out after roll call. After a couple of months of rain and just hanging around with no definite assignments in sight, everything was getting tedious. The only consolation was payday! That's when the action began with opportunities to release tensions. The men indulged in gambling, beer drinking, and fights that broke out sporadically. "Toddy" (a canned chocolate drink) was the only other drink that was available besides beer.

One good friend of mine shared part of his life story while he was "tipsy." He was anxious to leave home from Indiana to join the Navy to get away from a miserable broken home life. He drank to drown his bad memories and that's when he would sorrowfully talk about his misery. His dad was cruel and had worked him hard in a lumber mill. One late night, I noticed he had not returned to his bunk. After looking around, I walked to the head, a square wooden screened structure located several yards from our quonset hut. There I found him, sound asleep, completely naked and sprawled on the potty seat, (One of many holes on a wooden plank). I half-carried and half-dragged him back to his bunk.

Among the many unusual characters, there was one scraggly individual who came from the mountains of Tennessee. It was visibly obvious that he wore new clothes all the time - week after week, and month after month until they were dirty and hard; then he would throw them away and buy new ones. Plus, he never showered! One day, the members in his hut ganged up on him, removed his clothes and literally carried him to the outdoor showers. There they introduced him to soap and water, then "gingerly" applied the scrub brush to his smelly body. He was just one of many who had a hard time adjusting to Navy life.

The guy that had it the easiest on base was my good friend, Ralph Adame, from San Antonio. He was the barber, and voluntarily gave instruction in dancing and boxing to his friends in the barbershop after hours. He had many friends, including officers. They were all at his mercy in the barber chair. Occasionally, he would borrow a jeep from his friend, Frenchy, and take us for a Sunday afternoon ride around the island. Besides Ralph, my other close buddies from San Antonio were Lupe Rodriguez, Albert Gonzales, Mauro Veliz, Rudy Martinez, Eddie Ruiz, Gilbert Martinez and Rudy Hernandez, and Cadenita.

Gary Chistianson was one of my close buddies from Long Beach, California. He knew I liked writing letters, so he asked me to write to his sister. To be "nice" I obliged. After a couple of letters, she sent me a beautiful picture, in her bathing suit. Now I was more anxious to get to California! But I found out that a couple of other homesick Sailors were also writing her. Gary said that the guy that made it to California first would be the lucky one to date his sister. Guess who got there first? I'll reveal that when you get to Chapter 11.

HISPANIC "SWABBIES"

At one time, we had a whole quonset hut full of Hispanic Sailors. They were from California, Texas, Arizona, and New Mexico. We had a lot in common. At least we could chat and complain in Spanish. We had a lot of free time to talk and take pictures on the beautiful beaches. At times, some of us would take little hikes to Agana Village just to enjoy a glimpse of the local girls.

Most of them looked Hispanic or Filipino. Of course we thought we had the advantage! We did manage to persuade a couple of the girls from the local tailor shop to take pictures with us. Wow, what a thrill that was! Later, we found out that some Guamanians spoke Spanish, mainly the older folks. Spanish explorers and settlers in the historical past had left their influence here.

After several months on Guam, I heard of a dance band being formed by a Navy lieutenant. I thought, "Wow, what an opportunity!" I rushed to audition and was really excited to be accepted. After several rehearsals, our leader got us a job playing at the Palm Beach Officer's Club every Saturday night. This club was nestled among the palm trees along the shore. We could hear the waves pounding the rocks down below us as we played under the moonlight. It was fun, plus we earned ten bucks. I was ecstatic, being part of a dance band again. Our leader, Lieutenant Nicholas, who played the piano, was able to acquire the instruments for us. I got

Seaman Cortez Lower Right

an alto saxophone, which I was able to take back to my base where I could practice. This made me feel right at home! As the band's popularity grew, we were invited to play other gigs, including an Agana Village birthday party.

I enjoyed writing home and, of course, got letters in return. Some of my buddies who didn't write much would get excited just seeing me get letters. They were curious about things back home in the states. They would even ask me to read my letters out loud. I didn't mind because we were a close-knit bunch. I would even share some of the things I received from home, like cookies and goodies at Christmas time. Usually the cookies would arrive all crumbled up. Canned foods, like beans or tamales, really

Natives or Sailors?

Palm Beach Officer's Club (Richard third from left)

hit the spot. I would warm them by placing them in a bucket full of hot water over a small fire. One of my hut buddies told me he didn't like to write and asked if I would write a letter to his wife. I told him it was not a good idea. He was just a little to too lazy to do it himself.

THE SEABEES HAVE LANDED

One day Construction Battalion Detachment (CBD) 1107 (Seabees- the guys with green baseball caps) arrived from a nearby island. Their label was Material Salvage Unit #3 (MSU #3). So, since we were not attached and with no definite assignment in sight, you guessed it - we were immediately inducted into the Seabees. This was supposed to be "temporary"

Agana Village Party (Richard Kneeling)

until our records returned, from who knows where! It turned out this outfit was made up of a rough bunch of rambunctious characters. We were assigned to working parties (or gangs) of thirty per quonset hut. The CBD had the job of clean up operations on the Island of Guam. Our job was to load useable materials, supplies, food, ammunition, and heavy equipment unto trailer trucks; then transport them to waiting merchant ships in the harbor. A lot of heavy loaders, cranes, cherry pickers, forklifts and flatbed trucks were required to do the job. Some men would work the dock, others on the ship's deck, and others would work in the cargo hole. The hole was the worst, because it was hot with little ventilation. Essentially, we were stevedores (dockworkers).

We would receive pallets full of products, which came in on an 18-wheeler (tractor-trailer truck). The ship's crane would lift the pallets off the truck and swing them across the deck and into the cargo hole. The men in the hole had to swing the pallet into position on the floor. Stacking things up in order was important to utilize all the space available. On occasion, if canned food products, such as canned peaches, or mixed fruit cans, came down, it would be a delightful treat for the hungry men in the hole.

Some of the larger objects we loaded were jeeps, forklifts and trucks. Once I saw a cable break and left a 6-by truck dangling on the railing of the ship. On another occasion, one Guamanian helper was accidentally crushed as he stood between giant heavy planks and the side of the ship.

During the one-hour lunch break, a 6-by truck would transport us to our base for lunch. Most guys would nap after lunch. I found time to remove my dirty, sweaty clothes and shower. Some called me "powder baby" on the way back to work. I didn't mind those remarks because I felt clean and fresh. Stevedore work is hard, dirty, and dangerous.

At times salt tablets were given to the men working in the hole who would come out all sweaty. There were two sly swabs in my outfit who didn't mind volunteering to work in those disgusting sweltering holes. Instead of filling their canteens with water they would fill them with potato saki (an Asian alcoholic beverage). They would come out flushed, swooning, and cheery at the end of the day.

Sometimes, we would get help from local worker gangs. I came across an older gentleman who spoke Spanish. When my commander found this out, he assigned me to communicate in Spanish with this man. From then on I served as translator. This Guamanian leader would in turn communicate to his gang members, who completed their tasks much faster. This helped to speed up things especially since we had deadlines to meet. Some Sailors on the merchant ships that we loaded were curious as to how long I had been on the island. They thought I had learned the native language, not realizing it was simple Spanish.

One of the men in my gang was always in and out of the brig. One evening, he and his good buddy stole the commander's jeep and decided to go joyriding. They went on a drinking and shooting rampage through one of the villages and creating havoc. Fortunately, no one was hurt. They would do daring and foolish things like this and would end up in the brig. Yes, these were the two who liked potato saki.

ROLLOVER IN A JEEP

We were enjoying a day off from work because we had finished loading a ship. Our boatswain mate (gang leader) asked some of us if we wanted to go for a jeep ride around the island. Some of the guys had been relaxing with a few beers, including our driver. He was the type that was serious and always looked sober even while drinking. Since he had checked out the jeep, he would be our driver. Seven of us jumped on, three in the front, and four crunched up in the back. I was in the left rear seat. We were enjoying the ride and the scenery as we cruised along the shoreline and through winding palm groves and wooded areas. The driver was accelerating even as we cut some sharp corners on the road. I mentioned to my friend next to me, "We're going to turn over, if this guy doesn't slow down on these sharp curves." I can remember his reassuring response as if it were yesterday. "No way, there is too much weight for us to turn over." Just as I was repeating this in my mind, I was flying through the air as the driver failed to recover from another sharp curve. The jeep rolled over on its side onto the narrow asphalt road and part of the shoulder. I was one of the fortunate ones with just a bruised left elbow. Two guys were pinned under with scratches and bruises on their bodies, but no broken bones or serious injuries. We turned the jeep over and drove back to our base. This was one of those popular World War II Jeeps, before roll bars were introduced.

THE ENEMY FOUND IN OUR CHOW LINE

The lines at the chow hall at our base on Guam were always exceptionally long. There was no dress code, so some of us wore blue dungarees with white hats. Most wore Seabee's informal clothes with green hats. This made it convenient for a few Japanese soldiers to come down from their mountain hideaways and get in the chow line. They had remained in hiding among the thick wooded mountain areas and caves since the end of World War II. They were not readily discovered because they would blend in with Filipinos and other Asian men that were stationed there. One of many war stories tells of one secluded Japanese soldier who refused to believe that the war was over. He had managed to survive in the Guam jungle several years after the war had ended.

TYPHOON THREATENS GUAM

The Guam skies were usually filled with beautiful fleecy clouds, which often brought down tropical rains. One day, we were informed that a typhoon was approaching the island. Early that night, the wind started howling, bending the palm trees and blowing objects around. We bedded down wearing full foul weather gear, from head to toe. As we lay quietly in our quonset hut, loud speakers could be heard above the wind announcing warnings and instructions. We were to hang on to only a few valuable belongings, in case we were ordered to abandon our huts.

As I lay in my bunk with the wind and rain whirling loudly and wildly outside, I was wondering how long the support cables for our huts would hold out. I just lay there and prayed! There was dead silence among the men. Suddenly, I heard a piece of roof's sheet metal from the other end of the hut get blown away. Then I heard a loud rattle and two more came loose and were swept into the night wind. "When will they announce for us to leave this place that's slowly falling apart"? I asked myself. After a few more pieces flew away, the announcement was made to file out in an orderly manner.

Our base (with many quonset huts) was located on a fairly high ledge. About twenty feet below our base was a much stronger Red Cross building. We hurried down to take shelter in this building. The typhoon raged through out the night while we huddled in this haven of mercy. We remained there for two nights eating hot dogs and sauerkraut. Our quonset homes were no match for the violent storm. Everything was flattened to the ground. Our base was devastated with debris and corrugated metal sheets strewn all over the area.

"God is our Refuge and strength, a very present help in trouble. Therefore we will not fear, even though the earth be removed..." (Psalm 46:1-2) Of course, being a Construction Battalion Detachment, guess who would rebuild the base. Well, we did a large part of it! When the job was complete, I think the base looked better than before.

During the war, the Navy Seabees were the men who specialized in building vital airplane runways in rapid fashion throughout the Pacific Islands. These runways provided extremely important strategic landing fields. From there our planes could strike at the Japanese and give much needed support to the U.S. troops. Many times the Seabees did their jobs in the open and at risk of enemy fire, especially snipers. Yes, at high risk, theirs was a huge contribution to the battles in the Pacific.

Scuttlebutt was that we were to leave Guam. Sure enough, the time came and we were officially notified that the whole unit would be going to Okinawa. Lieutenant Nicholas, my bandleader, offered me an opportunity to stay on Guam if I wanted to. I was persuaded to go with my outfit, because of loyalty to my unit and close buddies. Later I realized that I might have been better off staying on Guam. You will understand what I mean when you read the next chapter.

CHAPTER 10
HEADING FOR OKINAWA
FEBRUARY 4, 1947

Gary and me relaxing on the open sea

We were ushered into an LST (Landing Ship, Tank). This is a relatively small landing craft that was used during the war to carry fighting equipment such as jeeps, tanks and troops. A huge ramp on the bow (front) of the ship would open up and all kinds of motorized vehicles would roll out onto the beachheads. These small ships were appropriately called "floating match boxes", because they had the shape of large match box - flat on the bottom and flat on the bow and stern. In the open sea they would toss back and forth because there was nothing on the bottom to cut through the water. If we thought that rusty USS Hermitage that had brought us to Guam was "uncomfortable", we had a new rare experience ahead of us. I cannot remember how long it took us to sail to Okinawa, but it seemed like forever! This LST was rolling and bouncing up and down and from side to side. At times I was sure it was going to roll over on one side. You had to hold on to something all the time and put your sea legs to work.

"Eternal Father strong to save
Whose arm does bind the restless wave
Who bidd'st the mighty ocean deep
Its own appointed limits keep
O hear us when we cry to the thee
For those in peril on the sea"

                Eternal Father Strong to Save (Navy Hymn)
                William Whiting, 1860

From my journal, Feb. 6, 1947 - "It's starting to get cold, and the water gets rougher all the time. The ship rocks so much that it's hard to write." Feb. 7 - "Everyday we eat topside where tables were set up. It was cooler and less crowded than below. It was crazy trying to keep my balance walking with a tray of food while the wind blew the soup in my face. Today we ate fish, as usual." We eat standing up holding onto our tray, to keep it from flying away. After awhile we even lost our taste for food. Most of it we would vomit over the side of the ship - many times the wind would blow it back in our face. If we had enough time, we could rush to the stern (rear) where the wind would not blow in our face. You were literally rocked to sleep if you didn't mind rolling from side-to-side on your bunk. Who can sleep like that? There was constant wind and spray on the deck. (I can imagine the hundreds of landlubber Soldiers and Marines getting sick to their stomach right before hitting the beaches.) Right about this time I was regretting not having stayed on the beautiful island of Guam.

As I think back, how could I complain when thousands of men during the war rode this LST and sacrificed their lives as they landed on enemy beaches. As we approached the harbor in Okinawa on Feb. 9, 1947, it was dusk. Something unexpected happened! A Sailor, who was usually pretty quiet, jumped in the water and swam to the shore. I never knew what became of that guy who couldn't wait for the ship to reach port. Someone made the comment, "He must have had a girlfriend in Okinawa." He was a truck driver for our outfit; nice guy, kind of a loner, originally from Louisiana. This incident would be stretching the popular slogan that states "A Sailor has a girl in every port."

From my journal, February 11, 1947: "For two days we have been working till late at night unloading beer, toddy, and other equipment from the LST. It was very cold and rain was coming down hard."

February 12 - "Today, our gang (#3), Seller's gang disembarked and went to our new camp on a 6-By truck. We were the last gang to enter the new camp that seemed to be buried in mud. The first thing we did was to fix the potbelly stove that sat right in the middle of the Quonset hut. That old stove doesn't even give enough heat to keep my big toe warm. That was going to be our central heating for the long cold winter."

February 16 - "Every night and day it gets colder and colder. I can't do anything to keep my feet warm at night. I've even tried real thick soccer player's socks. The stove is doing it's very best (and that's not much). Sleeping with all my clothes on, a foul weather jacket, and two blankets seem to help some."

LIFE IN OKINAWA - COLD AND LONELY

We continued our task as a Material Salvage Unit; hauling things to the docks and loading the merchant ships. The cold weather on Okinawa was quite a contrast from the warm tropical Island of Guam. Of course the environment and the Asian culture here is much different. This is a land where you would see females working in the fields and carrying big loads on their heads. Young native boys would hang around our camp during the day and offer their services, including cleaning our huts, shining

shoes, washing clothes, or even offering their sisters for "special" service. All this was done for nominal fees, mostly cigarettes. These locals were obsessed with cigarettes, even the very young kids. Evenings were cold and lonesome.

However, the soft sentimental songs of Jo Stafford on the radio captivated us. Her songs were background music to "Dear John" letters, which were read on the radio. These were actual letters that service men had received from girlfriends or wives that had deserted them. On those nights, absolute silence through out the Quonset hut was demanded, and you could hear a pin drop. I didn't realize it then, as I lay quietly on my upper bunk, but later, I myself would receive a "Dear John". I turned out to be one of those "victims" of love. I had foolishly neglected my sweetheart back home by not writing or calling her when I had opportunities. I was simply a proud Sailor who probably had too much salt air in my big head. One day I got the notice that she was getting married to the close friend who was supposed to be "taking care" of her while I was gone. Served me right!

SURPRISE VISITORS IN THE MIDDLE OF THE NIGHT!

In this MSU outfit, you could always expect the unexpected. One very cold Okinawan night, when everyone was tucked in trying to keep warm, I heard some soft and unusual noises at the other end of our Quonset hut. When I reluctantly pulled my head out from under the blankets to make sure I wasn't dreaming, I was able to hear the unimaginable - female giggles! The only dim light was coming from the potbelly stove in the middle of the hut. The giggles were coming from two or more young native girls that had been smuggled into the camp by a couple of daring desperate Sailors. The giggles and soft voices were now obvious as they moved slowly around the hut. In the dark, one guy from a near-by bunk came up shaking me and asking, "Hey Cortez, do you have any cigarettes?" Everyone knew I didn't smoke but I usually kept a few for the local kids who did our chores. I had to burst this guy's bubble; I was completely out. These enterprising gals were making the rounds taking care of business and loading up with cigarettes. The reckless desperado homesick Sailors that brought them in were able to take them off base without being detected. That cold blistery night, our Quonset hut, our home away from home, had been used for ignoble purposes.

March through April 1947: "It started getting a little warmer with occasional rains. We have been loading Merchant ships night and day, rain or no rain. If we don't meet certain deadlines, we will have to work overtime. But the latest scuttlebutt (rumors) is that we are scheduled to leave for Hawaii."

JULY 10, 1947 - BOUND FOR HAWAII

July 10, 1947 was a momentous day for a bunch of exuberant sailors. We boarded the USS General Anderson, which was headed for Hawaii. Fortunate for us, this ship was going by way of Shanghai and Tsingtao, China, then to Japan. Hey, that was an unexpected surprise! Our overseas job and obligations were almost complete and we were on our way to the good old U.S.A.

JULY 12, 1947 - SHANGHAI, CHINA

Wow-wee man, and anchors aweigh, we are bound for the Orient - China, Japan, and who knows where! Older Sailors told stories of "sweet liberty" on these shores. On July 12, 1947, we entered the dirty and unsightly Yangtze River, headed toward Shanghai. What a letdown that was. We saw many small Sam Pan boats where families live from day to day. Life on this river looks very unhealthy. We finally arrived and docked in Shanghai. The adrenalin started pumping as we anticipated going on liberty (on shore). We were all in our crisp white uniforms with polished shoes and snow-white hats squared away. When our section was called we hurriedly made our way to the place where we would stand inspection. I noticed that the officer on duty, who would grant us liberty had a clipboard. That turned out to be bad symbol for some of us! That clipboard had a record of names and current immunizations. Some of us were totally shocked when we were denied liberty because we didn't have the required shots! We were thoroughly disappointed and disgusted to say the least. We went back to our quarters moping and whining, but did not change out of our uniforms. I guess we were hoping for a miracle. In fact, later in the afternoon there was a different officer on deck. We took a chance and went forward. Much to our surprise, this officer just motioned us to go on ahead. We rushed ahead and didn't look back. As we stepped off the gangplank and to the dock, a huge crowd, mostly young kids, surrounded us. Most seemed to speak good English and either were peddling things or would pick your pocket. As we walked to the near by curb, a "limo," a black, four door, early 40's, model sedan was waiting for us. The chauffeur in a black suit, white shirt and tie, opened the doors for us. He was a familiar tour guide whom some Sailors knew from previous R&R trips. He offered to show us around.

As we drove slowly through the crowded narrow streets of Shanghai, large groups of people started gathering around our car. They seemed to slow down the driver as they shouted remarks at him. At least a couple of times he stopped, got out and shouted back at the small mob that had gathered. My limited Mandarin told me there was strife or conflict brewing. About the third time that this happened, one tall red headed Sailor got out of the car, surprised the crowd, shouting obscenities and waving a big bottle of gin. A few of the leaders backed off bowing their heads with the well-known "Okay Joe, Okay Joe." One little short fellow got our permission to squat and ride on the back floor of the car for a couple of blocks. The only thing we could figure out is that the crowds, mostly peasants, were probably jealous of this successful "tour guide". When that brash Sailor got out of the car, that mob could have easily overpowered us. Most were very short in stature, but they were many, and very rowdy.

The rest of the day went smooth as the guide drove us through different parts of town. He knew where the best shops and stores were and he took us there. I bought a beautiful large suitcase with dragons painted on the sides, silk smoking jackets, silk scarves, colorfully decorated photo albums. Later in the afternoon, we decided to ride rickshaws back to the ship. We went through one dark alley and came out with another coolie pushing the rickshaw from behind. These little guys find all kinds of ways of making money! And many of the little kids are professional pickpockets. One of my shipmates lost his wristwatch in the push and shove crowd that greeted us on the dock when we first arrived. Shortly after our little adventure in Shanghai, our ship got underway headed toward Tsingtao, China. That was one great moment in time. It took me back to the history books, and Terry and the Pirates comic book series. The expression "digging your way to China" became a reality, except for the fact that we "sailed" there.

JULY 16, 1947 - ARRIVED IN TSINGTAO, CHINA

The stop in Tsingtao was short, and liberty did not allow us to see very much. We were allowed some sightseeing, but didn't have time to wander too far. From there we would continue our trip to Japan.

JULY 20, 1947 – YOKOSUKA, JAPAN

Our ship arrived in Yokosuka, Japan. At this point, I was reflecting and being thankful for the opportunity of visiting these beautiful exotic places at the U.S. Government's expense. We had worked long and hard and now were enjoying the "fruit of our labor". At that point in time, I still considered the Navy "an adventure, not just a job". I welcomed every challenge, and tried to maintain a good attitude in spite of some adverse conditions from time to time. The tasks and the "rough necks" I worked closely with were things that I had to tolerate while doing my job to the best of my ability. The enticements, temptations, and other negative influences could easily impact the mind of a young man far from his home environment.

"No temptation has overtaken you that is not common to man. God is faithful and He will not let you be tempted beyond your ability, but with the temptation He will also provide the way of escape, that you may be able to endure it."
(1 Corinthians 10:13)

One of the men on ship had bought a special tailor-made gabardine dress blues uniform. It was made either in Hawaii or China. It had real colorful dragons on the inside cuffs as well as on the inside collar. These designs were naturally hidden, as they were non-regulation. This uniform could only be worn while on liberty. It even had a small pocket hidden on the inside back of the jumper. He claimed that was for a small black jack he used to carry for defense. Anyway, he needed money so he sold it to me for twenty-five dollars. It fit perfectly and I had myself a real "salty" and flashy uniform. Now I was ready for liberty in Hawaii and San Francisco.

JULY 30, 1947 - ARRIVED AT PEARL HARBOR

I was really excited... we were "closer" to home. But we still had work to do in Pearl Harbor. In all the excitement about being in Hawaii, one small thing stands in my mind... fresh milk! We were in the chow hall and cold refreshing pitchers of farm fresh milk were placed in front of us. I was craving for that creamy, white stuff as the cool condensation ran down the outside of the pitcher. The metal pitchers were emptied almost as soon as they were placed on the tables. Powdered milk was the

"Land Ho" – Hawaii at last

only milk we drank overseas. But liberty in Honolulu was the best thing we had experienced in a long time.

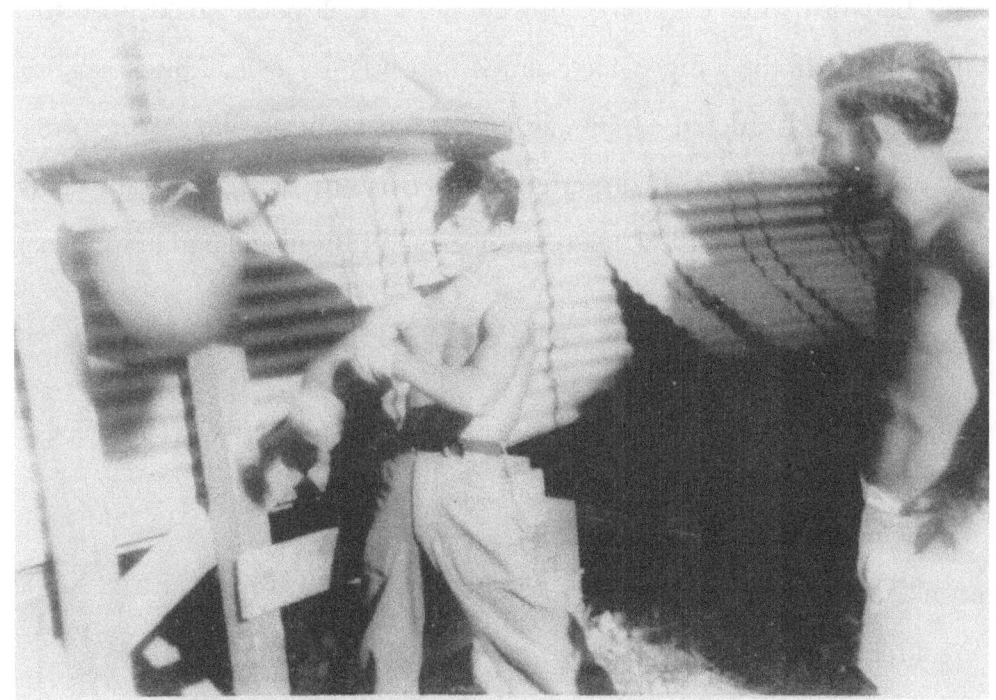
Punching Out Frustration on Guam

Hotel Street seemed to be the most popular place for many of the Sailors and Marines. Besides a USO, there were nightclubs and brothels. Sailors and Marines always ended up fighting, especially after a few drinks. There were also plenty of Shore Patrol (SP) with their nightsticks to break up these brawls. SPs are the Navy equivalent to the Army's Military Police (MP). Going out on liberty with four or five buddies did not work well. Every one wanted to go in different directions. After that, I would just team up with one close buddy who thought pretty much the way I did. I was anxious about calling a pen-pal I had been writing to years before I

Two Swabs and a Jarhead in Honolulu

joined the Navy. I held my breath as her phone rang. Wow, she was still there, Ooh LaLa! But Whoa there, Sailor. You're just a few years late! This young lady was already married and had children. Her voice was nice on the phone, but she bid me a sweet aloha and goodbye, sailor boy! I was disappointed, because I had nothing to brag about to my buddies!

At Pearl Harbor, we continued work for about five months. Finally, we sailed back to the good old USA, the land of the free and the home of the brave. While there, I enjoyed visiting with my uncles and aunts who had been so hospitable to my friends and me before we went overseas. Uncle Arturo and his family lived in La Palma, and Aunt Mamie lived in Wilmington.

All hands on deck

CHAPTER 11
AT LAST– LOS ANGELES, USA

I finally found enough courage to visit Beverly Christianson, Gary's sister, who lived in Van Nuys, California. I was naturally anxious to see if she was as pretty as the pictures she had sent me. I was quite nervous as I stepped on her front porch and rang the doorbell. I was not disappointed! She was a beautiful sandy blond. She was cordial and very friendly. I met her parents and family who made me feel right at home. We had much to talk about, especially about their son. Gary was one of my best buddies overseas. Beverly and I walked around the block, involved in long, casual conversation. We were both anxious to know more about each other. On my second visit, her parents surprised me when they said they were going out and would leave me and Beverly alone to get better acquainted. It was evening and we walked around the neighborhood hand-in-hand on a beautiful moonlit night. I was on top of the world!

A couple of days later I borrowed my uncle's car and took her to a drive-in theater. I noticed she had come to the car from the back of her house when I picked her up. Later, she explained that a "friend" had come to visit at a very untimely moment. Coming home after the movie, she asked me to stop just a short distance from her house. There was a light mist outside as we sat in the car, just chatting and saying good night. Just then we heard a knock on her window. She recognized the person and opened her door. Through the dark night, I saw an image that resembled a line backer for the L.A. Rams football team.

He (an acquaintance) took her hand and asked her to come out. She refused and told him to leave. "I'm with Richard." He attempted to draw her out of the car by grabbing her hand. I held firmly to her other hand! Some words managed to come out of my mouth like - "If you don't mind, she is with me, and I'm taking her home!" He was hoping she would step out of the car, but she scolded him. "You're being rude and ugly." She finally persuaded him that I was taking her home. After a few tense moments, he walked away mumbling "I'll see you at your house!" She tried to convince me that he was "just a friend" and nothing else. That was the last time I saw her even though we kept in touch by phone and by mail.

DECEMBER 2, 1947 – DISCHARGED FROM NAVY

It was a dark, cold night, as I traveled from L.A. to San Francisco in a Greyhound bus. I curled up on the very back seats with only my Navy peacoat to keep me warm. A strange lonely feeling came over me as the big bus rolled into the dark night. I was truly being "separated" from the Navy, from all my buddies, and memories, as I headed toward my final base. I have to admit I had mixed feelings, even though I would be discharged and on my way home. The Navy had been my home for two years, and now I was headed to my other home. From my boot camp days to my final return trip to San Francisco from Honolulu, it was an exciting adventure. As a seaman on a formidable Battleship, to a "Stevedore" with the SeaBees on Guam, Okinawa, and Hawaii, I accepted each challenge with enthusiasm. The "clean up operations" on these islands after the war was the hardest work I have ever experienced.

When I considered the huge number of Americans that sacrificed their lives on those islands, I felt blessed! My meager labor was a picnic. But it made me grow in maturity and responsibility. Plus, in only two years I visited parts of the world that I never imagined, including China and Japan. Even though I appreciate home and value my country, I never remember getting homesick. However, whenever I saw the U.S. Flag flying or heard the Star-Spangled Banner, I could feel proud goosebumps up and down my spine. One cannot help but feel privileged to be a part of this wonderful country when you are in a foreign land. And I honor and glorify the God that made it all.

December 2, 1947, I was given an honorable discharge at the Naval Air Station in Alameda, California. As a consolation, I received the World War II Victory Medal. Then I was sent home with my separation papers, and a final payment of $455.24. Travel or mileage allowed, included in total payment, was $90.60. Well, that was the end of my short Navy career. Upon separation, I had the opportunity to apply for the U.S. Navy School of Music, if I was willing to re-enlist for four more years. Like everyone else, I was so anxious to come home that I didn't give the offer a second thought. I missed a great opportunity, and I regretted it later.

CHAPTER 12
HOME AT LAST

As the train rolled into the Southern Pacific Railway station in San Antonio, I gave a sigh of relief. I was free from Uncle Sam's ties. I needed rest and would do some soul searching to see what the future had for me. I was getting reacquainted with good old San Antonio. I eventually went back to my saxophone and the dance band. I also felt the need to catch up with some academic studies if I was to get a job. I enrolled at Draughons Business College on Martin Street. It was a one-year course covering Bookkeeping and Typing. I was guaranteed a job upon receiving my diploma.

TRIP TO MEXICO CITY

That year, my dad planned a family trip to Mexico City. This was a once in a lifetime opportunity, so I took leave from business school for two weeks. The trip through Mexico was long, beautiful, and exciting. It took us through narrow treacherous mountain passes. It was scary at times, but we trusted the driver- my dad. After driving through many small towns and remote mountain villages, we finally entered Mexico City.

We were astounded upon entering this huge heavily populated metropolis. The downtown streets were lined up with fascinating water fountains, tall palm trees, and many ornate statutes of historic heroes. We decided on a modest hotel called Vireyes. We got lost the first day in this huge city that was a maze of confusion. The traffic was horrific with cars buzzing around at high speeds and constantly blowing their horns. My dad finally decided to hire a "volunteer" driver to be our guide. We met this gentleman in the hotel lobby who recognized our dilemma. He was conveniently located to spot confused tourists like us. "El Zocalo" (the main street) was buzzing with traffic at all hours of the day. It was chaotic to us, but the locals managed to escape crashing into each other using the skills of a bullfighter maneuvering and avoiding the horns of the bull.

We did get to experience the drama of bullfights in the huge Plaza de Toros arena. This "sport" was as popular as football in the United States. Traditionally, the matador dramatically brings the show to a climatic end by plunging the sword into the bull and destroying it. However, by this time, the bull had already been weakened and was bleeding profusely. Sharp "banderillas" stuck and dangling from his shoulders by "courageous" horsemen are designed to weaken the bull. This makes it safer and easier for the Matador to make his "glorious" kill. That is the tradition! Something positive comes from all this – the bull's meat is given to the poor.

We were fortunate to see one of Mexico's most famous movie comedians. Cantinflas (Mario Moreno), who was exiting the arena at the same place we were. People naturally crowded around him to see and to take pictures as he boarded his car. Our guide said he would give us a treat and take us to his home. Much to our surprise, we arrived in front of his home at the same time he did. We were also surprised that he was very cordial and willing to pose for pictures with us, since we were the only ones there. There were five in our group: Mom, Dad, Gilbert, Vangie, the guide and me. That was an exciting day!

One evening we ate at a restaurant where the famous orchestra of Louis Alcaraz was playing. Wow, what a thrill that was! I even had the privilege of dancing with my sister, Vangie. We were very surprised to find out that most popular restaurants, cafes, and nightclubs do not open until 10 p.m.

The next day, we drove away from the city and visited and climbed some famous pyramids. At Xochimilco (floating floral gardens), we enjoyed a relaxing ride in the famous gondolas, which were colorfully decorated with a variety of flowers. Mariachis came along side our boat to serenade us. Wow, what a colorful treat that was! I thank my dad for that trip of a lifetime.

OUR DREAM HOME AT 2905 BUENA VISTA

The house on Buena Vista was somewhat of a dream home. My dad had to do a lot of bargaining with Mr. Rodriguez, the realtor, but finally got it. The house was in a modest neighborhood, and seemed to fit our family like a glove. The back patio was adorned with a small fishpond attached to the house, together with a rose covered trellis, and a weeping willow in the middle of a green lawn that seemed to be saying "Welcome." Louis Ward and his mom had kept the property clean and well groomed. (A year later I happened to get a job at Ft. Sam Houston in the same office with Louis).

One day our peace at home was interrupted when we heard loud screeching brakes of a car that had rushed into our driveway. In the car was Peter Centeno, who had another car right on his tail. Peter ran into the house through the driveway door. The other irate driver chased right behind him shouting obscenities. Danny reacted immediately and met the man at the door with the barrel of a 22 rifle. He shouted a warning to the outraged fellow to "GET OUT OF HERE RIGHT NOW! YOU'RE ON PRIVATE PROPERTY!" The man backed off without a single word. His road rage had quickly cooled off as he drove away.

Our Family

After a few years our family started to disperse. The inevitable happens when children grow up… they get married!

It's common for parents to reach a point in life when they can afford a larger more suitable home, after many years of hope and hard work. This was the case with my parents, at that time we, their children, started leaving the nest. Danny and Gilbert went first. That just left Vangie and me in that big house. Eventually she got married, and that just left me, the lone bachelor. I didn't mind- I had a vision! I was determined to finish college and maybe get married later.

Our new home was also adorned with enticing Chinese plum trees next to our driveway. One afternoon three young boys took the liberty to help themselves to some of those beautiful yellow plums. My dad, who happened to be home that evening, chased them as they ran across our backyard. Two of them jumped the fence and disappeared into the alley. My dad managed to grab the third one and brought him inside the house. While my dad was on the phone calling the police, my mom was sewing the boy's pants, which he had torn while trying to jump the fence. This is an example of the compassionate person my mom was. My dad knew the boy's theft was a minor offense, but he also thought this could be the beginning of other crimes if left unattended.

1948 - CIVIL SERVICE JOB AT FT. SAM HOUSTON

When we returned from the Mexico trip, the business college allowed me to do make-up work for the lost time. I finally finished the course and received my diploma. They even got me a job with an insurance company. I was very pleased as I drove to my new job.

I was received cordially and was given my first assignment. I was to work down in the basement where all the printing took place. I was literally starting "from the bottom", but I was not complaining. I had a job! However, I had a bigger surprise when I got home that day. I had an important letter from the U.S. Civil Service Commission. They were reminding me that I had qualified as a typist on a test that I had taken at the college several months before. Plus, they were offering me a job as a clerk typist at the 4th Army Head Quarters at Fort Sam Houston. I realized the Lord was with me and that this was providential. He would be faithful to guide me and bless me at all times. Without hesitation I called the insurance company and explained. The boss there was understanding and told me not to worry about a thing.

Vangie, Richard and Gilbert going for a joyride in my 33' Plymouth

I was assigned to G-4 section (Supply), in the Quadrangle on Grayson Street at Fort Sam Houston. It didn't take me long to get accustomed to this new environment. There I was, in white shirt and tie, behind my own desk, with top ranking officers and non-coms buzzing in and out in a beehive of activity.

The Quadrangle was a historical old fort at one time. History tells us that the famous Indian Chief, Geronimo, was held prisoner there in years past.

Now it was the home and offices for the U.S. 4th Army Headquarters. The grounds were more like a scenic park. There was a duck pond, beautiful peacocks with their weird screaming sounds, fairly domesticated deer, squirrels, a variety of birds, manicured lawns, and huge shady oak trees. We could eat our lunches in that beautiful setting, or if we preferred we could eat at one of the dinky cafes on "Snake Hill" on Grayson and New Braunfels streets.

GOLDEN GLOVES

I was getting a little soft working in an office eight hours a day. I decided to join the downtown Y.M.C.A. on Martin Street. Among other things, I started working out on the heavy punching bag. Then I got interested in the speed bag and jump rope. After a good sweaty workout and a shower, I would leave the place rejuvenated. One day I met the boxing coach and he got me interested in joining the boxing team. He encouraged me, "If you take a few lessons, and prepare properly, maybe you could enter the yearly Golden Gloves Tournament." I accepted the challenge and started training with en-

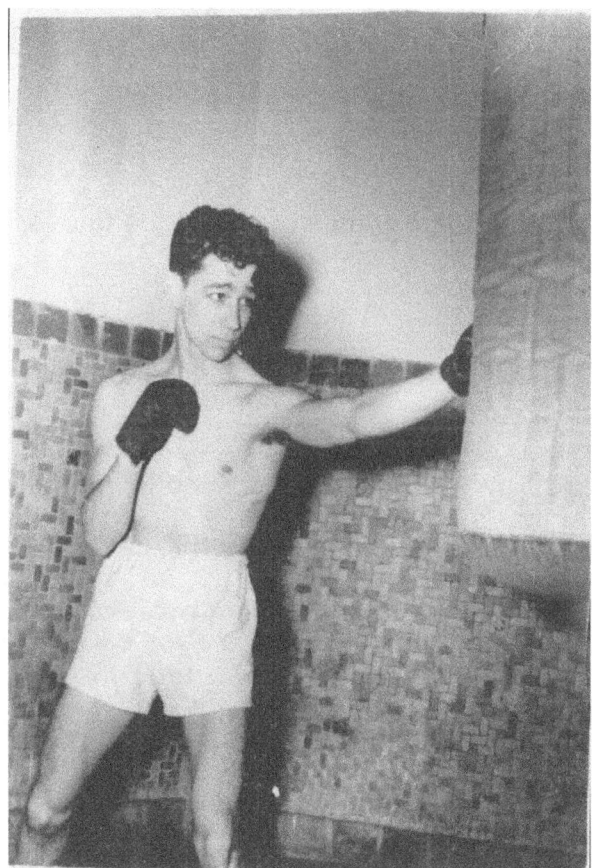

thusiasm. He taught me some good fundamentals, including self-defense, and quick responses with the left and right hands. Then he started matching me with other guys who were of the same weight.

But, he felt we needed to be prepared to fight guys who were heavier, taller, with longer arms and legs. About three weeks before the Golden Gloves Tournament, I got a hard blow to my right ear during training. My ear felt stopped up, and I had trouble hearing. My doctor checked it and said I probably had a broken eardrum. He said, "Check your pillow in the morning for some puss-like fluid." That will confirm that you busted your eardrum. I wasn't about to

wait until morning. All night I kept touching my pillow and ear.

Finally, in the early morning I felt the fluid on my pillow. Well, it was a great disappointment! My body was in good physical condition and I felt confident, but I was unable to fight in the Golden Gloves that year.

I continued working out at the Y just to stay in good shape. Sometimes, I would be in the gym all by myself, except for a big guy that would come and shadow box by himself. He was a heavy-weight who worked as a full-time bartender. In fact, he fought professionally and was known as the "Fighting Bartender". From time to time he would ask if I would get in the ring and spar with him. One day I said to him, "Sure!" He just wanted to go through the motions of moving, bobbing, and defending himself. All I had to do was throw him with everything I had, and not hold back. So, I threw punches with my left, my right, hooks, jabs, and upper cuts, but never touched him.

As the year went by, I decided to enter the upcoming Golden Gloves Tournament again. I was fascinated with the idea even though I had experienced a "knock out" blow the year before. I trained extra hard with the help and encouragement of our coach. He reminded us that in this Tournament there are all types of fighters. There are brawlers (street fighters), who will attack you viciously to hurt you any way they can. Then, there are the ones that box by the "book". They focus on the art of self-defense (weaving, bobbing, counter punching, calculating, and not wasting punches or energy). After much training and good coaching, I was confident that I was closer to being a boxer, and not just a brawler. Prior to weighing in, some of us had to enter into a big steam box (with only our head sticking out). Just a slight weight over might put us in the wrong division. I qualified for the bantamweight division.

The time finally came. I'll never forget! It was a cold January night as our team of ten walked the two blocks from the YMCA to the Municipal Auditorium. I had boxed and spared with most of the team members who were of different weights. My body was fine-tuned! I felt confident, strong, and fearless. The waiting is always the worse part! We sat at ringside; the odor of sweat was pungent. We watched other fights amidst a loud rowdy crowd. The fans want three rounds of action from every bout, or else they respond with loud "Booos". As we got closer to our turn, the coach took us to a nearby dressing room for last minute instructions. "You're well prepared; give it your best."

My adrenalin started pumping as I murmured a quick prayer. We were then led back to ringside. At last the coach says, "You're on!" I climbed up into the ring and someone points me to my corner. There were two "Seconds" (guys that I didn't know) in my corner who assisted and tried to keep me "alive" at the end of each round. I briefly sized up my opponent in the other corner. He was a little shorter than me, but more muscular. He looked like a nice clean-cut kid and he was representing the Boy's Club. The referee calls us to the middle of the ring to explain the rules to follow. The crowd is relatively quiet, anxiously waiting whether to jeer or cheer, or shout out some insulting remarks.

As soon as we returned to our corners, the bell rang. We have three rounds to go and the three judges will determine the winner by points (the most punches landed). The idea is to "feel" each other out cautiously during the first round. At first you try to demonstrate some degree of aggression to put him on the defense.

Ben Perez, ex-prize fighter, used to tell us, "Go in with a commanding smile, this will throw the other guy off!" The first round, we barely worked up a sweat. We mostly did foot work - moving around, weaving, bobbing, and throwing punches, but nothing solid. The bell rings to end round one. As I settled down on my stool, the Seconds immediately went to work on me. "Stretch your legs, take deep breaths, your doing fine, just keep your guard up."

The bell rang for round two and I literally bounced out of my stool. I was sponged down and the water was cool. We both knew that it was time to mix it up! And we did! I put in a few good punches. I knew I had a longer reach, so I applied my jab and landed some to his face. He counter punched well, and also landed some good ones. I never felt hurt or stunned. I still felt strong and confident. We were really battling it out near the end of the round, when the referee came between us. He looked at my face and sent me to my corner. I didn't feel anything, but I had blood running down my face from my forehead. I thought it was just sweat! The ref talked to the guys in my corner and it was determined that I had a bad cut over my left eye.

In amateur bouts like the Golden Gloves, at the first sign of blood the referee has to stop the fight. I still felt in tiptop shape and was very disappointed. I was taken to the dressing room where a doctor, my dad, and Uncle Joe were waiting. The doctor cleaned and carefully examined the area above my left eye. He decided at least three stitches were necessary for a cut on the bone right above the left eye. I was so pumped up with accelerated adrenalin that I didn't feel a thing during the procedure. The doctor explained that the bone above the eye protects the eye but is very vulnerable to blows and scrapes. My opponent had butted his head against mine in the fracas near the end of the second round. Well, that was the end of my brief pugilistic career. But I had the satisfaction of having fought in the Golden Gloves.

Meanwhile, back at the office, at Fort Sam Houston, things started to happen! After working in the G-4 section at Fort Sam for a year, I was called to the personnel office. I was offered a job in the communications section as a Teletype operator. It was a promotion but the hours would be from 3 to 11 p.m. I prayed seriously about this and finally agreed. It would be convenient since I was staying at home with my parents and had my own car. The nights were quiet except for the clicking of the Teletype machines, while I was being trained. With a small skeleton crew, I took on the task of learning to type and read the tapes that came through. There was always small talk and coffee available. One night, some clerk broke the boredom by cleverly luring one of the "young does" into the office. The tile floors were not very conducive for a deer's hooves. It wasn't even funny to see that poor animal slipping and sliding all over the slippery floors. It reminded me of Bambi on the slippery ice pond.

One day a new man was hired. Frank was an older, very friendly gentleman. After a few days we became better acquainted, and in casual conversation he informed me that I had "bumped" him. In other words I had taken his job away from him. I naturally responded by saying that I had been offered the job and had accepted it. I presumed this action happened because I was a veteran. But I knew nothing of this man's situation. Anyway, I was glad he had been re-hired and we became good friends.

I had a good job, making good money, single, and driving a beautiful two-toned hardtop Oldsmobile. I was even enjoying the comfort and convenience of living with my parents. The older men at work challenged me to go to college. They said I was foolish not to do so, especially since I had the benefits of the G.I. Bill. I hated to leave this cushy "comfort zone." However, after two years and much prayer and discussion with my

father, I decided to quit my job and attend college. Now I had to decide which college to attend.

DUCK HUNTING

In the meantime, I took a break to go hunting with a co-worker. I had never been duck hunting in my life, but this opportunity opened up. The subject came up during the slow hours of the night shift in the Signal Section. An invitation by this fellow co-worker sounded exciting. Early the next morning, we met, loaded up and headed toward Mitchell Lake. I was anxious to try out the shotgun that I had borrowed. It was an exceptionally quiet morning as we paddled a small rented boat to the middle of the lake. Since no shooting was allowed until 6 a.m., we were enjoying the tranquility of a serene, calm lake on a cool morning.

Suddenly shots rang out and broke the morning silence! I had a feeling we were the targets, as bullets were whizzing by our boat. My buddy unexpectedly surprised me by firing his shotgun right next to my ear. The duck-hunting season had begun, and it was like a war! After a couple of hours we decided to stalk the ducks along the shore. I walked quietly in the water, hiding my head in the reeds along the shoreline. Lo and behold, I came face to face with about six ducks just sitting in the water about three feet in front of me. I didn't know whether to grab one by the neck, or strike them with the butt of my rifle.

Being a first time hunter, I reacted clumsily. I pulled the trigger on the shotgun and blasted away. There were feathers and pieces of duck scattered all along the area. Well, at the end of the hunt, after much teasing and laughter, we had our legal quota, not counting the scattered pieces of duck left along the bank.

Gilbert, Lee, Richard and Camilo

In our teen years, our favorite thing had been to hunt rabbits near Floresville and Poth. Being ignorant or just foolish, we would shoot the rabbits on the road with our car lights shining on them. They would just freeze and stare at the light. On one such trip, I had a harrowing experience. I spotted a huge jackrabbit in the brush some distance away. He was incredibly still for a jackrabbit! I had him in the crosshairs of my .22, which would not fail me. I nailed him, and he just toppled over. I rushed to pick up my prize. Boy, was I sadly disappointed when I opened the rabbit up. It was a pregnant mother with a litter. I was deeply sorry for doing such a cruel and unkind thing. I regretted that very much and hesitated shooting anything after that.

GILBERT JOINS THE MARINE CORPS

In August 1948, my brother Gilbert, together with his best neighborhood buddy from childhood days, Lee Venzor, joined the Marines. Their boot camp was in San Diego, California, very near the Naval Training Center where I got my start in the Navy. Their training was of course more rigorous than the Navy. These guys probably didn't realize how soon they would put into practice the skills that were pounded into them in boot camp. Gilbert signed up for four years. After returning to the states from a tour of duty on Guam, he had plans to visit home in San Antonio.

While he was still in California, a notice came out that his outfit would be shipping out to South Korea. He was attached to George (G) Company, 3rd Battalion, 5th Regiment, 1st Marine Division. This was the beginning of the Korean War, which would last from 1950-1953. In June 1950, the North Korea Army surprised South Korea by their unprovoked attack across Korea's demilitarized 38th parallel.

In Gilbert's book "A Ground War", he states that the Marine Corps' two functions are "train to fight, and to fight." And this they did in Korea, by pushing back the invading masses of the North Korea and Chinese armies and taking back South Korea. The Marines accomplished their mission, though being outnumbered and fighting in a variety of adverse conditions, including extremely hot, to ice-cold weather day and night.

PFC Gilbert Cortez, US Marine Corps

At home, we had not heard from Gilbert for several months until we read a surprising article in the Express-News. The Marines had landed on Inchon, and progressed to the capital city of Seoul. The news article named three Marines who had draped the U.S. Flag over the dome of the capitol. This was the symbol of victory after the defeat of Seoul. Gilbert Cortez was one of those Marines. We were relieved knowing where he was, but concerned because he was still in a combat zone.

Here are some comments from Gilbert's book: "There were two

MSG Gilbert Cortez (Ret), US Marine Corps

Marines in the ditch with me, one on each side. Every once in a while, they would stick their heads up from the ditch. I wondered why they would do such a dangerous and not-so-smart thing when enemy bullets were flying all over the place. Suddenly, one of them was hit in the neck, and I believe you could hear his screaming and cussing for miles around. The other "jarhead" also kept popping his head up over the cliff, when suddenly he too got shot in the neck. Fortunately they survived." These men, who were at high risk, were Official Forward Observers who would seek out enemy positions, then radio the information to the tankers.

"The enemy sustained their pressure day and night with crushing frontal attacks, as well as trying to infiltrate around our perimeter to attack from the rear, thus forming an encirclement of our forces. Their combat tactics were not always successful, although they kept up their stranglehold and consequently lost hundreds of men in each of their attempts."

"That particular night seemed colder than usual. I didn't know till later that the temperature drops to about 30 degrees below zero at night at the Chosin Reservoir. My nose was freezing and running, and I didn't know if I still had ears because I couldn't feel them. My fingers and feet were numbed, and I was quickly losing any feeling in them. The water in my canteen was frozen, my C-Rations were frozen and there was little relief in a frozen foxhole. The cold weather was an enemy as much as the Chinese that were relentless in attack after attack."

"We were all showing sheer exhaustion from the days of continuous fighting. The cold continued to take its toll and weapons malfunctioned due to the freezing weather. The will to fight and even to live required a supreme test of fortitude and willingness to persevere."

"The bitterly cold sub-zero winds of the Chosin Reservoir never stopped its deep and chilling penetration throughout my clothing."

Many gave their lives there and scores came home maimed and with missing limbs and permanent scars. By God's mercy, Gilbert came back alive, but returned to the states with frostbitten hands and feet. But, in the battle-worn minds and memories of these distinguished warriors, the scars are indelible. Many veterans, as was the case with my brother, returned home with PTSD (Post Traumatic Stress Disorder). Nightmare episodes occur that severely affect some members of his family, primarily his wife, Sophie. He still has occasional flash backs, primarily related to his fighting off North Korean soldiers who had jumped into his foxhole.

Gilbert eventually ended up in a California hospital with frostbitten feet. I have great admiration, deep respect, and love for a brother that put his life on the line for me, and for our country. He is my hero!

Wars, which have been around since the beginning of time, do not make sense. Charles Leiter says: "Sin is the ultimate and only problem of humanity. It is absolutely universal in the human race."[1] Man is characterized by malice, envy, hate, and greed, to name a few. That's why we have wars!

The U.S. has fought many wars overseas in foreign lands. As the Marine's hymn states, "From the halls of Montezuma to the shores of Tripoli." Some justify that it's better to fight and defend freedom from tyranny in other countries before it comes to our country. And we have done this through many years.

However, when Pearl Harbor, Hawaii was surprisingly and brutally attacked, our country reacted and responded immediately. It could be compared to a thief breaking into your home in the middle of the night, and killing your whole family. The Japanese Fleet commander that orchestrated the attack made this comment, "I'm afraid we have awakened a sleeping giant." From that point on, the whole country was willing to sacrifice and use every resource available to retaliate. The war cry was "Remember Pearl Harbor."

During the war, Dwight Eisenhower, Commander of Allied Troops, delivered this message to troops before they embarked on the Normandy invasion (D-Day) on June 6, 1944:

> "Soldiers, Sailors and Airmen of the Allied Expeditionary
> Force! You are about to embark upon a great crusade, toward which we have striven these many months. The eyes of the world are upon you. The hopes and prayers of liberty loving people everywhere march with you."

The main point that's been in the back of my mind, since I started writing about my brother Gilbert, is the complete disregard by our present generation for the thousands of painful and unspeakable sacrifices made by veterans during the many wars fought. May God have mercy on us, as wicked and evil men continue with greed and hatred and their plans to acquire more by the most effective methods of destruction.

---

[1] Leiter, Charles. <u>Justification & Regeneration.</u> Granted Ministries..

CHAPTER 13
OUR LADY OF THE LAKE COLLEGE
1953

In 1953 I was still an active musician with music education on my mind. I enrolled at Our Lady of the Lake College (OLL). They had a good music department, plus it was very close to my house. OLL was accepting veterans under the G.I. Bill. I was one of about six male students (Veterans) who were admitted into a traditionally all-girl Catholic College. I have to admit the atmosphere was pleasant! There were many girls from Latin America and other parts of the world that came to this prestigious college. Needless to say, they enjoyed seeing the few men roaming around the campus, even though the nuns were usually hovering close by. The instrumental teachers were outstanding musicians from the San Antonio Symphony Orchestra. We were required to perform recitals from time to time. I even sang a couple of solos as a requirement for my voice lessons. I spent many long hours in the small practice rooms. One girl from Central America, after practicing her piano for long hours would leisurely stroll over to my practice room and just sit there, staring at me while I practiced my clarinet. I believe she liked my embouchure; or maybe she was fascinated with the unusual phenomenon of a man on campus, which was a "rare commodity".

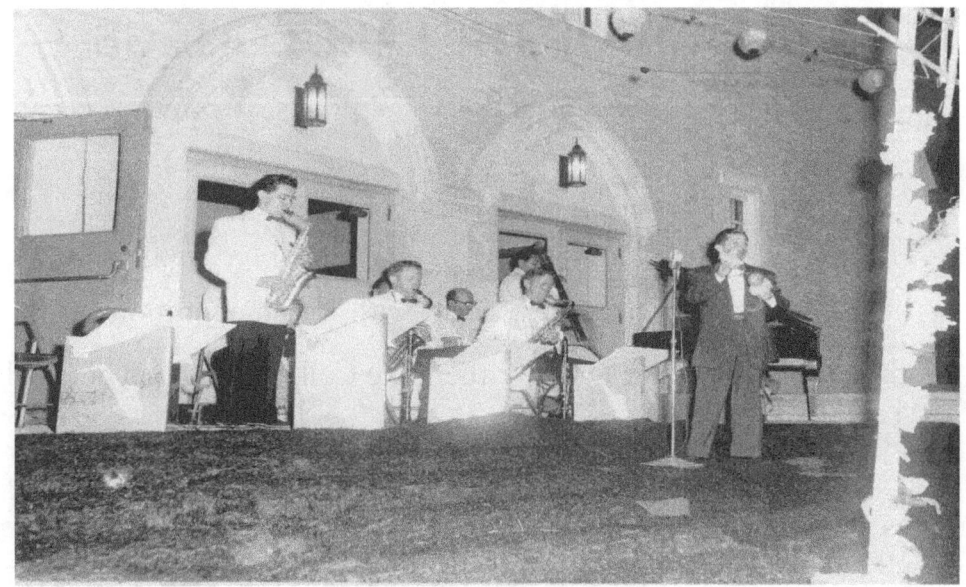

Richard Cortez Orchestra at OLL

I was privileged to have my dance band hired to play for several dances at OLL. One evening, while unloading the band instruments from our car for one of the dances, I could hear voices calling from the girl's second-story dorm windows - "Richar! Richar!" The "Richar" Orchestra was gaining popularity at OLL. Foreign students from south of the border had a little trouble pronouncing the word "Richard."

Some of our teachers were nuns. They were very knowledgeable and dedicated educators. One in particular would quietly "corner" me in the hallway and try to persuade me to Roman Catholicism. I did make friends with another very sweet, thoughtful, and encouraging nun, who was my music theory teacher. She even wrote to me after I had left the college.

(Front Row) Leo, Richard, Carlos (Second Row) David, Arthur, Frank, Isabel & Dad

I had gained favor with some of the nuns and students when they found out I had an orchestra. I had the pleasure of playing at several of their elegant and sophisticated dances. No dates for the girls and no outsiders were allowed! The sisters were very protective and preferred "well-mannered gentlemen" for their young ladies. So, busloads of cadets from the Officer Candidate School at Lackland

Air Force Base were brought in for the dances. Mother Superior would welcome and briefly interview each cadet. Each girl had a little booklet that listed her dance partners for that night. Eventually, the cadet volunteers who were coming to the dances began to dwindle! I wonder why???

I had a lay teacher that taught the men (mostly military or veterans) the piano. Piano was required mainly for the purpose of composing and arranging. This teacher, who was tall and stout, had the attitude of a first sergeant in the Army. Delicate hand positions and motions on the keyboard had to be exact, as those of a concert pianist. She was a spinster and a perfectionist! Once, while I was taking my lesson on that immaculate grand piano, Johnny Rodriguez, who was still in the Air Force, came in for his lesson. As he entered, he made this sly comment, " Well, I'm ready to take my medicine." Suddenly she became enraged! She straightened up, pulled her shoulders back, and motioned me to "GET UP!" Both Johnny and I (two grown men) were ordered to sit on a small bench against the wall. And with a stern voice and sharp finger pointing at us, she gave us a piece of her mind - "You men need to be more serious about this! I don't appreciate that kind of attitude. Don't EVER come in here with those kind of remarks!" In the past I had seen some of her high school students crying as they came out of there. The head of the music department understood our dilemma, and assigned some of us to another piano teacher.

I left the school after one year. There was no doubt that OLL had a fine music department, but there was little emphasis on band director training.

MILKMAN

During summers or vacation times I would seek temporary employment, and the Lord was always faithful to supply my needs. One such job was working for Meztgers Dairy as a milkman, substituting for regular men that were on vacation. I found this very fascinating, especially since I had worked for the same company as a "hop boy" in my younger years.

ALAMO CITY 20-30 CLUB

Richard Teniente was my classmate at Crockett Elementary School. Many years later, I ran into this old friend. As a pharmacist, he was operating two pharmacies in San Antonio. He invited me to an interesting club made up of young business and professional men who were between the ages of 20 and 30. Even though I was still struggling to finish my education, I joined the group. Meetings were at a restaurant on Friday evenings. The atmosphere was friendly and casual with both married and single guys. I was still single and curious to know what the goals of this club were. We would chat over dinner and discuss projects to help the community.

The Alamo City 20-30 Club was an international organization with clubs in the United States, Mexico, Central America and South America. I had occasion to attend at least a couple of conventions in Nuevo Laredo and Monterrey. In between sessions, some of us found time to shop and enjoy the bullfights. At one weekly meeting in San Antonio, someone came up with the idea of a dance and beauty contest. This would bring in a good crowd and raise a big contribution for a local charity. Each member was to scout around for beautiful girls that would be interested. I believe I only drafted two. This turned out to be a very successful project, with flair and a lot of publicity. In fact, one year we placed a float in the Battle of Flowers Parade where four of the girls portrayed cannibal savages. These were fun times.

But it wasn't fun when deputies raided our Cock Fighting Project out on a secluded farm. I was assigned to escort two of the beauty queens home. Just as I was driving out on this dusty road, I saw the deputies' cars rushing in. No, there were no cell phones so I could call and warn my friends. Fortunately, we had several lawyers in the club that were able to settle the matter. As time progressed, Richard Teniente got involved in politics and became president of the SAISD school board. Later, he served as a city councilman. On August 3, 2012 he died and left his position as Justice of the Peace

(Precinct 1), where he had served for eighteen years.

I was always eager and in constant pursuit of part-time jobs while in college. My faithful roommate, Pilo Lozano and I found what we thought would be an enjoyable moneymaker in a pleasant environment – selling ladies' shoes. We started out at Chandlers Ladies' Shoe Store, across from the Majestic Theater on Houston Street. I learned a lot from the cool headed manager, Mr. Cackin. He was calm, intelligent, and very helpful. These traits made him a very perceptive manager that could relate to all people. The atmosphere here was pleasant, and so was Nancy, the cute little cashier. Pilo and I challenged each other to see who would date her first. Pilo lost.

The older full-time salesmen pretended to help us. They were "generous" and allowed us to wait on young ladies that casually walked in during their lunch hour. Of course, these men were already familiar with these "window shoppers" who would just browse around and walk out. However, the thing that really annoyed them was when rich families from Mexico came to buy huge quantities of shoes. These folks would naturally ask for someone who could speak Spanish. Pilo and I were the only ones who were bilingual, so we would make these big sales. These older seasoned salesmen just stood by in disbelief. A man can learn a lot by selling lady's shoes. Some women are vain and insist on wearing small shoe sizes even though they might have huge feet. At times, I was tempted to suggest the shoebox as a more comfortable fit! Most of the time I was gracious and polite, and always brought out at least two or three pair of shoes at a time. Many women enjoy being treated with courtesy and flattery. Occasionally, I had to force a smile and a courtesy "thank you" to a lady who would walk out empty-handed, after trying out six or seven pairs of shoes.

During breaks from college, I also worked part-time at the Grayson Street Post Office Sub Station. This was immediately across from the Fort Sam Houston Quadrangle. I worked the window as a clerk and occasionally went out on short mail routes when business was slow inside. The "judge" (as he was called), was a tall kindly, aging superintendent who would encourage me. He would say, "Enjoy this beautiful day, the birds and the scenery while delivering your mail." Of course, he never mentioned the constant threat of dogs. Once, as I opened a gate to walk to the mailbox on the porch, a dog lunged at me from behind a hedge. My sun helmet dropped over my eyes, the mailbag slipped from my shoulder and fell on my foot. About that time, a little old lady came out making that well known remark - "Oh, he won't bite, he just barks!" It was somewhat voluntary for me to accept this chore, but the judge had "enticed" me. He had a very kindly manner, and he WAS the boss, after all!

In the next block from this Post Office substation was a long wooden building with a lot of offices. This was probably one of the early USAA offices in San Antonio, located at 1400 E. Grayson Street.

THE UNIVERSITY OF TEXAS -1954

I was still determined to get a degree in music and pursue a career as a high school band director. That being my goal, I enrolled at the University of Texas in Austin in 1954. Under the G.I Bill, a Veteran could attend any state university tuition free. So I headed for U.T. in Austin. Now here was a huge university with a sprawling campus. I was fortunate enough to locate a rooming house on Whitis Street, half a block from the Music Building. At that time, the Music Building was right next to the Little Field Fountain. I shared a small room with my close friend Pilo. He was an architecture major and we had close ties as members of the same church in San Antonio. Some weekends we survived on peanut butter and crackers. Occasionally, we would splurge at the nearby Night Hawk Restaurant that was conveniently located around the corner on the main drag. Since it was open twenty-four hours a day, we would end up there at all hours of the night.

On Sundays we could survive with sandwiches, snacks, and drinks after church service at a Spanish Methodist church. On weekdays, I enjoyed nice warm meals at a boarding house across the street from our house. Our own landlady was a sweet little elderly person who never bothered us. However, one day she came rushing over, knocking desperately at our door. With her weak voice trembling, she hurriedly explained that her little puppy was poisoned and very sick. We jumped in her car and drove them to the nearest veterinary hospital. We hurried and made it just in time! She was extremely grateful that the precious little pup's life was saved.

One early Sunday morning, about a week later, she knocked on our door again. This time she surprised Pilo and me with a delightful breakfast of bacon, eggs, sausage, buttered toast, and coffee. However, there were some weekends that I spent "alone". The campus and the whole surrounding area would be like a ghost town with most students going to their homes. That's when I would really get homesick.

The U.T. campus was huge and I did not have a car. So, I was thankful that I could just walk a half a block to most of my music classes. Most evenings, I spent in the practice rooms with my clarinet, violin, or what ever instrument I was learning at that time. As an instrumental major, I was required to get familiar with all of the musical instruments, including all the woodwinds, brass, percussion and some strings. I even had lessons on the harp. Most importantly, we had to learn how to put an instrument together, learn the embouchure (lip formation), the fingering, and play two or three simple tunes, and scales.

All instrumental majors were required to perform with the U.T. Symphonic Band. This was made up of students and teachers. The repertoire for this band was mostly classical, semi-classic, popular show tunes, and "pop songs." It was an exhilarating experience playing and performing with these mature and experienced musicians.

In fact, I feel a rare "high" when performing in a band. I guess that's why I loved music from a very early age. Now, at the university level, I was in the midst of rapturous, captivating and enchanted musical compositions made classical by the Masters. It's an immeasurable sensation that resonates through your mind and body when you are immersed in a sea of melodies, harmonies, and rhythms performed by skilled musicians interpreting captivating musical arrangements.

It didn't take me long to join up with the famous University of Texas Longhorn Band. It was strictly a volunteer organization and was not associated with the music department at that time. If anything, it was more closely connected to the athletic department. It was made up of any qualifying student musicians, even non-music majors who had the zeal and school spirit. Rehearsals were every Monday evening. The director was Moton Crockett, and the band hall was a big wooden structure located across the street from the stadium. It was a well organized fired up organization that "bled burnt orange". Marching routines were "fine tuned" in a nearby field the morning before each game. Out of town games were exciting because we usually had a police escort leading the buses. Sometimes, they would radio ahead to reserve space at a restaurant for three busloads of bandsmen. One of the most memorable trips was the Cotton Bowl football game in Dallas. This is where we played our archrivals, the Oklahoma Sooners. It was always thrilling, exciting, and very competitive.

Marching in the San Antonio Flambeau Parade during Fiesta Week was always like a homecoming for me. The thundering sound of "Big Bertha", the riveting drum cadence, and the one hundred fifty piece Long Horn Band opening up with "The Eyes of Texas" or "March Grandioso" was exhilarating. Being the first band that leads the night parade, the crowds go wild with screaming, yelling, whistle blowing, and streamers in the air. The "Show Band of the Southwest" was making its grandiose entrance into Broadway Street.

The pep rallies in Austin before football games were loud and wild. The band, followed by the cheerleaders and pep squad, would march down the drag (Guadalupe Street) to Gregory Gym. That's where an explosion of noise would begin. The reverberation inside the gym was tremendous, especially when the students got all "fired up". They would get all stirred up and start clapping the rhythm as the band marched in playing "Texas Taps". Then, the cheerleaders jumping and yelling cheers, would cause an uproar in the bleachers. Next, the football players would be introduced. Then with the crowd roaring, the coach would come up front to make an impassioned speech and inspire his gladiators with words of wisdom.

At one particular pep rally we marched down the "drag" in unusually heavy rain. We marched onward with loyalty and school spirit with complete disregard to the expensive musical instruments getting wet. Well, instead of marching to Gregory Gym, we were led to the football player's dorm. There, outside the player's windows, we played, yelled, and showed our school spirit. The scene was a very wet, neurotic crowd of spirit-filled fans. The players, who were dry, content, and warmly nestled in their cozy dorms, waved to their loyal fans through closed windows. The Longhorn Band was a fun experience, but the time spent in all those extra-curricular activities began to affect my grades. I was placed on probation for one semester. Ouch!

I also had the opportunity to play the baritone sax with a dance band made up of university students. We played mostly for fraternities and sororities. Many of these parties were extravagant and wild, but they paid well.

The performance of "Messiah" by Fredrick Handel with the 200 voice University Singers was an inspiring and memorable event. It was truly an electrifying experience! This was a concert performed at the Austin Municipal Auditorium with the University Orchestra accompanying this "grandiose" choir. Music majors were required to sing with this group. This is where my OLL voice lessons really "kicked in."

At U.T. the boys outnumbered the girls, so my social life was very limited. I was fortunate enough to meet a San Antonio girl, which I dated. Once, we attended an Austin Symphony concert and I noticed she was dozing off; I guess she was bored. I have to realize, not everyone likes classical music! A person can get pretty lonely in a huge university like U.T. So it was natural to seek out companionship. And, who better to make friends with than your neighbor. I happened to run across a girl from the boarding house next door. We went out and enjoyed a quiet evening. And wouldn't you know, the time flew by so fast we didn't realize she had gone past her curfew hour. When I brought her home, she quietly and casually opened a front porch window and crawled in unnoticed, by a big full moon. I had been fortunate to borrow a car from a friend who monitored the practice rooms in the music building.

Sometimes I would chat with other students during short breaks. One evening, near closing time I got into a casual conversation with an organ major and a trumpet player. The conversation evolved into a sort of religious debate between a Protestant (me), a Jewish girl, and a Catholic boy. The discussion ended friendly because the three of us agreed on going to the near by Catholic Church to pray. At least we agreed that prayer was essential. The church door was open even though it was about 10:30 p.m. I was a professing Christian at that time, but still had not discovered biblical truth.

From time to time, I would come home on weekends and lead my own dance band. My dad would usually book jobs for me, including weddings, parties, and school dances. He made most of the arrangements ahead of time. I really appreciate my father starting me off in music, and still helping me in promoting the band.

Another reason I was always anxious to return to San Antonio was to see my girlfriend, Teresa. She was real special! She had beautiful soft green eyes. She was petite and her walk was like that of a Persian cat moving gracefully across a soft fluffy carpet. Her voice was soft and gentle, never loud! She lived in a very modest home with her grandmother, two sisters, and two brothers. She was shy and had a sweet quiet nature. She was truly a rare young lady with a kind heart. I loved her very much! But as usual, I was awkward and careless in showing affection. My weakness was that I was too proud and self-centered. I was a bandleader and going to a well-known state university. She was a member of "Las Hijas de Maria", an or-

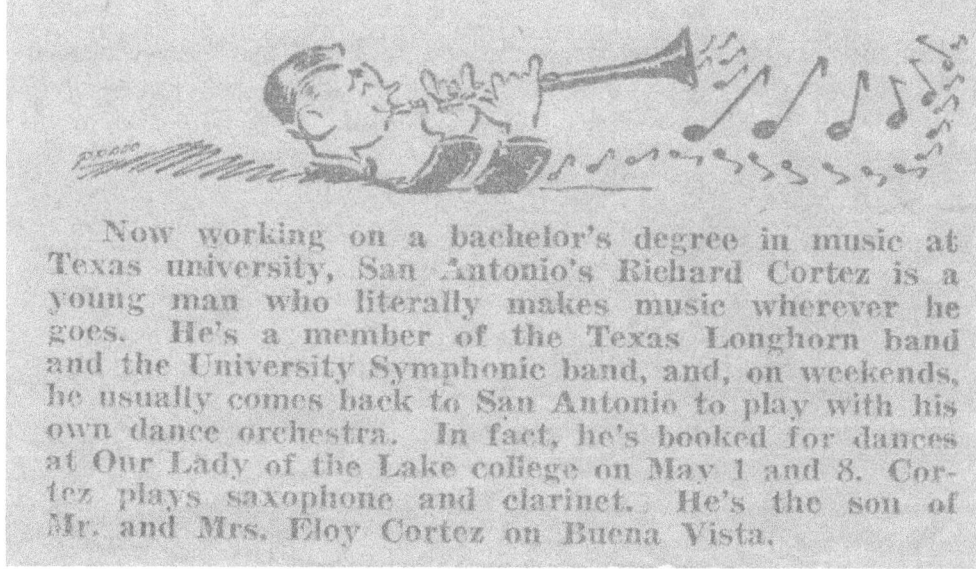

Now working on a bachelor's degree in music at Texas university, San Antonio's Richard Cortez is a young man who literally makes music wherever he goes. He's a member of the Texas Longhorn band and the University Symphonic band, and, on weekends, he usually comes back to San Antonio to play with his own dance orchestra. In fact, he's booked for dances at Our Lady of the Lake college on May 1 and 8. Cortez plays saxophone and clarinet. He's the son of Mr. and Mrs. Eloy Cortez on Buena Vista.

ganization at San Fernando Cathedral. She knew I was Methodist and I knew she was a devout Catholic. But that didn't seem to hinder our growing love for each other. We were in a serene and peaceful world when we were together. I finally had enough sense to give her an engagement ring. We were exceedingly happy and patient as we waited for my graduation.

Years passed as I pursued my education and our relationship continued to flourish. But something unusual started to happen. There were times when I would pick her up from afternoon services at a Catholic church on Ruiz Street. Once, I took a peek inside the church and noticed a certain young man sitting next to her. I gave it no thought at first. But it did bother me after I saw him sitting next to her more often. Needless to say, I confronted her about this. She innocently explained that he was just a "friend". And she was honest! One thing lead to another and in time I began to fear that she would not accept my faith if we were to get married. Gradually, we began to drift apart and we broke our engagement. Several years passed and she married "that friend". But it was obvious that she married mainly for security. Soon after graduating from St. Mary's University, I too got married and moved to an out-of-town job.

After many years had passed, we happened to run into each other in a department store. Even though we were both married and had teenage children, there was still a small lingering flame. After a brief but emotional encounter, we had to admit that our love for each other was not dead. It was like a dim lit candle that never went out. She confessed her serious intention of leaving her church and following me if we had pursued our plans for marriage when we were young. This was regrettable, and we had illusions of what might have been. Inwardly, I toyed with the idea of committing myself to a renewed relationship with her. Wow, this was like a scene in a movie or a soap opera. But this was real life! I cannot believe that I even momentarily entertained the thought of leaving my wife and family for my "old flame". My conscience pricked me and flashbacks of a loyal faithful wife of many years bombarded my mind. I quickly dismissed the foolish thought of abandoning my family. We parted with mixed feelings.

**Gala at Municipal Auditorium
With the Richard Cortez Orchestra**

Patio Andaluz— Richard Cortez Orchestra

CHAPTER 14
MARRIED LIFE

LA TRINIDAD METHODIST CHURCH

The pastor of the Hispanic La Trinidad Methodist Church was a pious intellectual, who preached with power and authority. He was astute and preached in impeccable Spanish. His intellect and knowledge of almost every subject imaginable was very appealing. However, his focus on sin, repentance, and salvation was very limited. I was content because we had a strong confident spiritual leader who stood above everyone. As faithful followers, we all looked up to him with great respect. I didn't realize, until much later, that I was being deprived of biblical truths that proclaim the Gospel of Christ. For the most part, there was unity and harmony among the brethren. Much attention was on godly living, good works, and helping build up the church. Our reward was acceptance and recognition. I blended in well in this environment, since I considered myself moral, responsible, respectable, and socially acceptable. On Sundays, the pews were filled to capacity during both morning and evening services. I made many friends there throughout the years that we attended. We enjoyed worshiping in an organized, well-structured Methodist environment. We dressed well and drove nice cars. Inside, some of us may have been a "little" proud and arrogant.

As a young college student, I learned much from a warm and very caring Sunday school teacher. Miss Annie Reil had remained single, but she had a genuine devotion for young people's lives. I was involved in many youth activities, including trips to Mount Wesley, a Methodist camp in Kerrville, Texas. This was something all the young people looked forward to.

Much of my youth was spent at La Trinidad. Since I was a music major, I was appointed Director of the Youth Choir. It was at this church that I had the pleasure of meeting a beautiful young lady who was to become a major part of my future life.

I sang in the adult choir before being chosen as Director of the Youth Choir. It was indeed a joy working with youth that had a good cooperative attitude. There was one event with the adult choir that I considered real special. We were invited to sing with a combined All-City Methodist Adult Choir. Being in the middle of one hundred singers blending with beautiful and uplifting hymns was one exhilarating experience. The backdrop for this musical extravaganza was the Theater Stage at Brackenridge Japanese Sunken Garden. Willie Rodriguez did a great job of leading that large choir. Just an interesting side note, the beautiful Japanese Sunken Garden was called Chinese Sunken Garden during our war with Japan. After the war it regained its original name.

Leading the Youth Choir

MET MY BELOVED

It was at La Trinidad that I met a beautiful young lady who was fairly new to the church. There were many attractive girls at church, who were bright and came from respectable Christian families. However, in this vivacious young lady, who was originally from Sabinas Hidalgo, Mexico, I saw something very special. She was gorgeous and had a winning personality. She first started coming to church with her sister, Gollita, and Rodolfo, her brother-in-law. Soon, I started giving her rides home after church. She lived downtown in a two-story apartment building on Dwyer Street. Our friendship started to flourish and I would invite her to lunch at

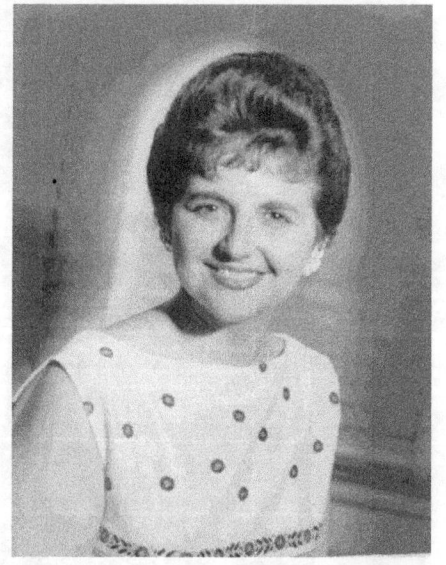

every opportunity. Sometimes I would pick her up at Sophie's Boutique Shop where she worked. There was this beautiful yellow dress she used to wear that I was crazy about! Her big brown eyes were equally beautiful and stunning. We would often double date with George and Irma Romero, who were good friends from church.

My Beautiful Bride

ENDING THE GLORIOUS RACE: BY GOD'S GRACE

Cortez - 50th

Richard and Lupita Cortez celebrated their 50th wedding anniversary on August 28, 2009. This couple is convinced that their long adventure in marriage has reached this point, only by the abundant grace of a good and merciful God. It has been blessed by the presence of Jesus Christ as the middle person in their relationship. There reward is, three children: Rick Cortez, Mrs. Ruby Conway, Mrs. Mayra Cerda, Mrs. Ruby Conway, twelve grand children, and two great grand children. "Unless the Lord builds the house, those who build it labor in vain." (Psalm 127:1) "For every house is built by someone, but He who built all things is God" (Heb. 3:4).

August 28 1959

MARRIED TO LUPITA

I had vowed not to marry until I finished college. But I didn't want to lose "my Lupita". In the beginning, I would drive her home after church. Soon, we were seriously dating. She was sweet and I was beginning to fall head over heels in love with her. We enjoyed just being together and I knew she was the one. Finally, one night, I parked my car at a small park in the King Williams area and proposed to her in a little gazebo. She accepted the engagement ring with excitement and a choke hug around my neck. My parents and family all loved her; her mother liked me and was happy with our engagement. We discussed our situation and Lupita was content and willing to work while I finished my last year at St. Mary's University. We both agreed to live with my parents for one year. We were both happy and agreeable with that arrangement. On August 28, 1959, we took that nervous walk down the aisle and spoke ours vows before God that would

bind us together till death do us part. I was 32 and Lupita was 25. La Trinidad Methodist Church was filled with family and friends.

Pastor Jose Espino officiated over the wedding. Because of the labor and all the meticulous planning, we didn't anticipate human error. However, unexpected little things did occur. A step at the altar, where Lupita and I were to kneel, had an unusual number of ants crawling around. Some alert person spotted them and wiped them out. Much to our disappointment, one groomsmen, Gilbert Vidaurri and his wife were late because they were involved in an auto accident. The soloist who was to sing our favorite song was an hour late. Other than that, all went very well! The wedding party consisted of: My brother, Danny (Best Man), his wife, Adela (Maid-of-Honor), my younger brother, Gilbert (Groomsman) and his wife, Sophie (Bridesmaid), as well as my college roommate, Pilo Lozano and his wife Lily. Others were: Louis Gonzales and Blanquita (Lupita's brother and niece), Idalia (Lupita's sister) Maid-of-Honor, Lynda Diane Cortez as the flower girl, and Rodolfo Rodriguez Jr., as ring bearer.

Vangie did not take part because she was pregnant with Adela. The reception, with all the usual trimmings, food, punch, and cakes, was at the Gunter Hotel Mezzanine. Everyone enjoyed the Ramiro Cervera Orchestra, with singer Emma Hernandez. My dad made sure all this was recorded on film. He took many still pictures as well as movies. Tired, but very happy after a long day, Lupita and I loaded some of our wedding gifts and headed for my parent's house at 2905 Buena Vista.

After opening a few gifts we got back in my merry Oldsmobile and headed for our honeymoon in Corpus Christi, Texas. Driving along, my new bride made a strange request. She had discovered one of her earrings was missing and had a hunch it could still be at the church. She hinted we should go back to the church and look for her earring. I thought to myself, "This is crazy," but I yielded with "Yes dear!" So there we go, headed back toward the church sometime after midnight. I assumed it was of real value to my beloved! And believe it or not, we found it! With the aid of my trusty flashlight we found her little pearl earring lying in the little grassy spot outside the church. This was the place where hundreds of people had kissed and hugged her after the ceremony. We were both amazed as we drove off rejoicing and chatting on our way to a new life.

After that, we were on cloud nine as we "sailed" to our honeymoon destination on the shimmering Gulf of Mexico. We checked in at the Princess Louise Hotel. It wasn't very extravagant, but was reasonable and clean, and close to the sea, on North Shoreline Boulevard. The morning after, we greeted the elevator girl with a cheery smile and "good morning". She looked at us with a strange smirk on her face. In the hotel lobby, a big clock told us it was three o'clock in the AFTERNOON! Oh well, who keeps track of time on their honeymoon. One of our favorite breakfast places was the small and modest Sand and Sea Hotel, also on North Shoreline Boulevard. We were drawn there when we strolled by and noticed crisp white tablecloths on breakfast tables in the dining room. We took leisurely walks along the seawall that was close to our hotel. Lupita was just as happy and bubbly as a little girl. The fishing boats along the "T-Heads" would be preparing to go out for the day. Other fishermen displayed their big troughs and ice chests full of smelly fish, and sold to curious visitors.

During the mornings, we strolled along the sea wall, breathing the fresh air from the Gulf and enjoying the hundreds of seagulls hovering above us. Sometimes I couldn't resist jogging along that long stretch of sea wall with the salt air hitting my face. Relaxing on the beaches under the August sun was sheer delight. We explored the city from one end to the other, at the same time scouting for places to eat. One of our favorites was Chat and Chew on Leopardo Street. Corpus was small, quiet, and very tranquil. Several times we ended up on the grassy park areas along side the seashore. Certain evenings we enjoyed free open-air band concerts and felt sea breezes from the Gulf. We were content to just munch on snacks. Sometimes we ended up eating peanut butter sandwiches. At a time like this who gets hungry! I guess that's where I picked up the habit of always carrying snacks in my car. What was really exciting was the fishing boats that would take us out on the bay for five dollars. All fishing equipment was supplied. The only thing I remember catching were ribbonfish, which are worthless. But the salt air hitting our faces as we left the pier and the "T-Heads" was truly refreshing. The roar of the engines as the boat cut smoothly through the rolling waves still lingers on my mind. The sight-seeing pleasure boats that sailed out in the bay were almost as much fun as the fishing boats. Sailing out in the evening when the sun was sinking was quite romantic.

My beloved and I were in a dream world! We were really enjoying the solitude of this unique bay city. I was exceedingly happy and enamored with my new and adorable bride who I had chosen to be my lifelong partner. Words are not adequate to describe the deep profound admiration that I had for my Lupita. We were two people in love, yet we were one, living in our own little sphere. It was delightful bliss of unparalleled proportions.

"Let your fountain be blessed, and rejoice in the wife of your youth." (Proverbs 5:18)

We found time to visit Bobby Galvan at the Galvan Music Store. Bobby was an old friend, who was an exceptionally hot tenor sax player. We had attended St. Mary's University and played many dance jobs together in San Antonio. After a couple of weeks on the coast, we headed home, tired but happy.

We returned to my parent's home at 2905 Buena Vista. The first week, Lupita and I spent our time painting and sprucing up my old room, which was in the back part of the house. It was cozy and private and we were just as happy as two lovebirds in a cage.

I was the last one in my family to get married. I can't say I was spoiled, but my dearly beloved mother was not one to hold back her usual love and affection. This was her God-given nature. I was the object of much attention, including mother's home-cooked meals, warm embraces and kisses. This was to become an "issue" in our marriage later on. I was going to school as we had planned. As far as I could see, my young bride appeared happy. Concealed emotions and discontent did not emerge until much later. The mutual arrangement we had decided on seemed practical to me at the time. I had much to learn!

I realize now I had been too self-confident and a bit ignorant. One day, "for no apparent reason", my new bride left and went back to her mother's house. This is when my lamp lit up... something was troubling her. I went to her mother's to bring her back. What made the situation more complicated was that she would not explain or give the reason for her actions. Lupita's mother, who had had a difficult marriage herself, convinced her that she needed to go back to her husband. "This is not your home anymore!" she said. I picked her up, physically, and took her out of her mother's small apartment. She was docile and did not resist. This was the beginning of a happy, but sometimes rocky marriage. There would be incredible highs while we both were getting adjusted to this new life. But unfortunately, the Adversary always seems to disrupt a harmonious relationship. We attended church regularly, but still had not tasted the amazing truth and grace of a loving God.

ST. MARY'S UNIVERSITY IN SAN ANTONIO

MAY 29, 1960

My declining financial position had convinced me to leave U.T. and head back home to San Antonio. After scouting around, I was fortunate to get a part-time job with the Post Office. After two years and a little money in the bank, I was more determined and motivated to finish college, and get a music degree. Still single at that time and depending on part-time jobs, I enrolled at St. Mary' University in San Antonio.

Pop Sturchio, a lively diminutive Italian man, was head of the Music Department. And I was pleasantly surprised that my high school band director, Mr. R.A. Dhossche, was the flute teacher there. One thing I wasn't too pleased about was having to repeat courses that I had already taken at U.T. The reason given was that I had been out of school too long. Pop said that, and I guess he was right! Other music teachers there were Al Sturchio, Pop's son, and Leo Green. Leo, and several other students there were musician friends I knew from dance band engagements.

Other musician friends that are St. Mary University Alumni are: Paul Elizondo, Julio Dominguez, Johnny Rodriguez, Jacinto Guzman, Ramiro Cervera, Cervando Aleman, Dan Frels, Pete Rodriguez, Maurice Dacbert, Heron B. Smith Jr., Richard Nuñez, Eddie Garza, and Ben Valdez.

St. Mary's had a superb ROTC marching band, as well as an outstanding concert band. Having acquired a new love for classical music, I naturally took advantage of volunteering as usher at the San Antonio Symphony concerts. We were permitted to do this as long as we wore our ROTC uniforms. Once the music started, we could sit and enjoy the concert for the rest of the evening.

One year, Tchaikovsky's explosive 1689 Overture was performed by the St. Mary's Concert Band at the Municipal Auditorium. The music ends with a huge celebration involving loud brass, bells, and exploding cannons. We had never rehearsed with the cannons. Approaching the finale of this sensational piece, the cannons started exploding right behind the clarinet section where I was sitting. I felt like I was catapulted out of my chair and was sure my eardrums were shattered. Some "brilliant person" had improvised the idea for cannon shots. The loud explosions of the cannons in the music were caused by shooting rifles into three wooden wine barrels. The resonating sounds created inside these empty barrels was "more real" than actual cannons.

Most of our concerts ended with the ever-popular John Phillips Sousa march "Stars and Stripes Forever," with the Piccolos marching to the front of the band. This was very impressionable!

At another concert, we ended uniquely different with a composition called "The Musicians Strike". About half way through the music, the horn section casually walked off the stage. After a while the trombones walked off one at a time, then the saxophone section casually left, and then the clarinets. The music was getting thinner and weaker. Finally, just one Piccolo was left to finish the piece to the "dramatic" end. Of course, the audience goes wild with applause and laughs. But a more dramatic and unexpected ending was the manner that Pop exited the stage. As he was taking his last bow, six band members approach the podium and literally lifted him and the podium up and carried him off the stage. This was a complete surprise to Pop, and even to some of us in the band. The applause and laughter were frantic.

St. Mary's ROTC Bandsman

St. Mary's had a fine music department but the portable wooden building and facilities left much to be desired. The music department must have been at the bottom of the financial totem pole.

St. Mary's University was an all male institution. Yet, there was one female in our graduating class that broke the tradition. As far as I remember, she was probably the first female attending at that time. When walking through the campus, she would catch the eye of not only the male students, but also a couple of the Marianist brothers.

During my college years, I continued leading my dance band or playing with other groups. Since my brother Danny had established a reputation in high school and thereafter, we continued to receive many calls. Even after I took over the band, my dad kept booking jobs. As manager, he kept us busy.

Finally on Sunday May 29, 1960, I graduated from St. Mary's University with a Bachelor of Music degree. The graduation ceremony took place at the very popular Municipal Auditorium. The graduating class walked in proudly to the majestic sounds of *Pomp and Circumstance*. I took a deep breath in overwhelming gratitude and thanksgiving to a loving God who granted me the opportunity to reach two very important goals – marriage and a college degree.

CHAPTER 15
NEW CAREER AS A BAND DIRECTOR
NATALIA, TEXAS

I was entering into one of the most exciting chapters of my life. Driving to my first teaching job I was reminiscing over many years of college and part time jobs. Now I was finally reaching my goal of band directing in a public school. As I drove into this small country town of Natalia, I had mixed feelings. I was accustomed to the big city. "What would these people think of me?" I thought.

It was difficult for a "rookie" just out of college to get hired in San Antonio. Unlike math, history, and other academic subjects, a school normally hires just one band director. Therefore, it was a more specialized field. At the annual Texas Music Educator's Convention, I had come across a job offer in Natalia, Texas, a small community about thirty miles south of San Antonio. I jumped at the opportunity with enthusiasm and drove down with great anticipation.

Mr. A.P. DeMare, the school superintendent, a tall stout ex-Marine interviewed me for the position. His height and stature appeared threatening at first, but he was exceptionally courteous. I began to feel comfortable and more relaxed. I was privileged being led around by the superintendent of schools. He took me on a tour of the campus which included the junior high and the high school. We ended up in the principal's office where he introduced me to Mr. Bill Howard, whose office was right next to his. It was going to be a humble beginning but I was excited! I say that because this school did not have a band program or even a band room. With this challenge I knew there was only one way to go, and that was UP! I knew that Lupita and I would have to move to Natalia to get established and acquainted with this new community. I was being cautious and trying to make a good impression as I met with the school board. The board, which was made up of hard working country folk, found favor in my credentials and hired me after the first meeting.

On the following Monday, Mr. DeMare showed me the makeshift band room – an old army barracks sitting alongside a dusty road, next to the Agriculture (Ag) Building. However, he promised to get me whatever I needed to get started. I could have been discouraged. There was nothing there! Trying to think positive, I reasoned, "I'm thankful to have a job." No matter what I did, it would be a FIRST!

I was excited because it was a completely new adventure for me. Mr. DeMare kept his promise! To begin with, he drove up with a truckload of used surplus instruments from Army surplus stores in San Antonio. Some were from World War II and were beyond repair. Others I put together by repairing or replacing with leftover parts. Hey, I never knew I had all this "skill!" I learned a lot with each new day, things that were not taught in college! I took the challenge head on... it was a completely new adventure for me.

In the meantime, Lupita and I were getting settled into our new home. We found a small quaint little house, about a half mile from the school which we rented from Mrs. Jewel. We were very happy in our first home and my first job. I was looking forward with anticipation to getting started. Natalia was a friendly country town where neighbors all knew each other. From the beginning, I was known as the "Band Master." I didn't know why, since I was I was just a freshman band director! This quiet little community was made up of Charlie Brown's Grocery Store, a post office, a service station, a theater, a roller skating rink, a barbershop, several churches, and a few small businesses.

My first teaching job in this little friendly town was an experience that I would never forget. My wife and I were exceedingly happy. To add to this joy, exciting news came. My wife was expecting our first baby. Through the long nine months of waiting, we got acquainted with Dr. Spock, who was considered the expert on child rearing. When the time drew near, we had her suitcase packed and ready to go. We were going to stay calm and prepared. Well, when the contractions came that night, we rushed to the hospital in San Antonio. Yep, you guessed it, in the excitement, we forgot her suit case at home behind a door. We had a lot to learn, but fortunately it was a false alarm!

In God's time, on September 10, 1961, little Ricky was born at Baptist Memorial Hospital in San Antonio. His official name was now Richard Roland. Roland Parga was a dear friend, Boy Scout executive, and member of our church in San Antonio.

Natalia was "Mustang country," and the town folks all went wild on Friday nights. That's when the stadium lights lit up and the Mustang Football Team rushed on the field. The school was the center of most activities in town, especially sports. The high school, the junior high, and the elementary school, were all on one campus. The elementary school principal, Mr. Doyle Wilson was also the high school coach.

As a side note, one of my band students who shined shoes at the barbershop in town brought me an interesting revelation. He saw me getting a haircut in the barbershop and was surprised! Later he made this remark, "Mr. Cortez, you are the first Mexican-American to get a hair cut there!" I may have broken a race barrier without knowing it. Mr. Penland, the owner had a son in the band, and we all eventually became good friends.

The pastors from the different churches began to visit us. We attended several churches, but did not find the Methodist, which we preferred. After much thought and prayer we decided to join the Natalia Baptist Church. Since I was the band teacher, the church graciously appointed me as congregational song leader. That's before they heard me sing! I accepted and truly enjoyed serving the Lord in that position. Harris Shinn was the pastor at the time. After several years he resigned and went into private business. Pastor Ralph Meeker, a tall, kindly and gentle person replaced him as pastor.

Everyone in town was excited because Natalia was going to have a band. Everyone was exceptionally cordial and extra-friendly with the new Cortez family in town. I know they had great expectations of me, and I was not going to disappoint them. I was fresh out of col-

ENDING THE GLORIOUS RACE: BY GOD'S GRACE

NATALIA HIGH

NEW CAREER AS A BAND DIRECTOR

SCHOOL BAND

lege and I had a lot of ideas going through my head. I prayed that God would guide me with wisdom and patience in every decision I made. And He did!

"I will instruct you and teach you in the way you should go,
I will counsel you with my eye upon you..." (Psalm 32:8)

The first Natalia Band

I started out with a small group of very enthusiastic youngsters. We made use of the few surplus instruments without complaining. Of course I had to do some minor repairs, and "patch work" on the salvageable instruments. The students would not be required to buy new instruments until they demonstrated noticeable interest and improvement. Being a small school we could incorporate the junior high kids into the high school band. They all had the desire to learn and I was willing to work with them. Some even came after school for extra practice. Then there were those who just came to hang around and chat whenever they had a break. Before long some of the parents started inquiring about the purchase of new instruments. I was honest with them concerning the degree of their child's progress and interest. In one year's time I had a better assessment of the children's improvement and could more easily give an intelligent answer to the parents. In most cases, parents did not hesitate to buy the instruments. This band program was a new love for the school and the community, and many wanted to get their kids involved. I was just as excited! I invited Norman Bade from San Antonio Music Company to come introduce instruments and prices to the parents. We became good friends, and he would come regularly throughout the years.

While I was living in Natalia, shocking news came that President John F. Kennedy was assassinated at 12:30 p.m. on Friday, November 22, 1963, in Dealey Plaza, Dallas, Texas. Kennedy was fatally shot by a sniper while traveling with his wife Jacqueline, Texas Governor John Connally and his wife Nellie. His death sparked an intense ten-month investigation. Even to this day there are questions about his assassination.

Most small Texas country towns take a lot of pride in their teams, mainly football and basketball. Natalia was no exception! Now all they needed was a pep band or some loud "noise" to blast out the school spirit at the football games. Mr. DeMare, who was always very encouraging, came to me with an idea." Mr. Cortez", he said, "If you can just get the band to learn a few pieces of march music so you all can play on the bleachers during the football games, that would be great."

I was glad to hear that, because we already had a few marches we had learned. The kids were excited that we were going to be part of the action at the football games. Our temporary uniform would be blue jeans and white shirts. This was simple and practical; plus, blue and white were our school colors. You noticed I said "our" school colors - I'm was really getting into this school spirit! Yea Mustangs!! Shortly after that, we added a small cowboy type bow tie - blue, with white letters "Natalia Band". We were starting to get popular at the games. However, I experienced what could have been a shocker for this new band director.

One evening as the band marched from the band room to the nearby stadium, a girl saxophone player whispered in my ear, "this guy that sits next to me has a gun under his shirt." As they filed into the stands, I observed that particular student very carefully. Sure enough, I could detect something bulky tucked inside his white shirt. I have to admit, I was a little nervous! I swallowed and I tried staying calm. Then I very casually walked over to Mr. Howard the principal, who was not too far from the band. After a brief explanation, he inconspicuously came and called the boy out. After about an hour, they both came back. The youngster grabbed his saxophone and took his place in the band. Few knew anything about this, except for a few kids in the band. This boy was a senior who had never been a problem and had a clean record. He claimed the reason for the gun was "for protection." He anticipated trouble from that rival school which we were playing that night. There had been tension with this San Antonio school in the past. That was the first and last such serious problem we ever had with that student.

However, the following year we played the same school but on their home turf, in San Antonio. Again, tension seemed to be mounting through out the game. Of course here, all their hometown fans outnumbered us. Since we were playing in San Antonio, my brother Danny had accepted my invitation to come to the game. He arrived around the forth quarter after getting off from his part-time job, as a sheriff's deputy. The timing was perfect, because he was still wearing his deputy uniform. I felt much safer as he "escorted" the band to our bus. Then he drove in front of the bus until we were out of town. There was some degree of respect, which probably discouraged any trouble or rock throwing. That somewhat dramatic event had some negative consequences!

On Monday morning, Mr. DeMare called me into his office. He wanted to know all about that "police escort" which accompanied the band bus after the football game. My honest explanation did not please him. He stood up from behind his desk, looked down at me, and with a firm convincing tone said, "It was completely uncalled for, and will give our school a bad reputation. Try to use more discretion when something like that happens." For the most part, Mr. DeMare and I got along fine. In fact, there were times when he would invite me to go bowling in Hondo, together with the Mr. Howard, and Coach Wilson.

Then there were times when he would caution me about band booster members dominating over band affairs. The band boosters were made up of band parents, including three or four school board members. Remember, "you're in charge," he would say. Fortunately, I never had any problem with any parent. We developed friendly and healthy relationships from the very beginning. The Natalia Band was improving and growing in numbers. As our popularity in the community grew, many kids wanted to be a part of it.

The Boosters became a strong supporter with many fundraising ideas for the band's needs. The greatest fundraiser was the food concession stand at the football games. With much planning, hard work, and tireless effort from all the members, the money started rolling in. The boosters suggested I could start looking into band uniforms. I began searching through band uniform catalogs and trying to decide what would be best for our band. I finally got a sale representative from Sol Frank Uniform Store in San Antonio to come with samples and pictures of different styles of uniforms. Mr. DeMare again reminded me that I was the "Band Master", and I should make the final decision.

I felt privileged that all the parents looked up to me with respect, and I never felt any pressure. I have great memories of the Natalia band parents' organization. We worked together in harmony with few, if any disputes. They supported me and the band program one hundred percent; and I owe them a debt of gratitude. There was this kindly older gentleman whose granddaughter played in the band. He was not only a band parent, but also a school board member and a school bus driver. He would tell me that he was glad that he had voted for hiring me, and would remark, "I knew you were the right person for this job." This was the typical attitude of many of these folks, who were honest, humble, and fun loving. The band boosters gave me the liberty to choose what ever uniform I liked best. Having gained their trust and respect was humbling and rewarding for me. I was told the cost was not going to be a problem.

This was indeed overwhelming for me, especially since I was learning to expect, and accept, unusual responsibilities. I slept on it, and prayed about it, with a thankful heart. When the time came, I chose a uniform that seemed to please just about every one. I did not hesitate to choose a uniform that was real classy. It was a stunning blue, gray, and white, west point style uniform. The colorful shako, with a smart chinstrap, displayed proud peacock-like feathers on the front and center. This was a sharp dazzling uniform that we could all be proud of, no matter where we went.

By this time I had already started designing half-time shows for the football games. In fact, some nights I would jump out of bed, and copy down ideas as they came to my head. Music companies sold exceptionally well-planned half-time shows together with accompanying music. But I was going to be original by designing my own half time shows. The first one would be simple by just having the students march on the field and form simple notes and chords and adding appropriate music. We were having a lot of fun and it was surprising to see the "pieces of a puzzle" come together on the field, just as I had imagined it in my sleep.

My son Ricky, who was four years old, would also have fun, running in between the ranks when we practiced on the field. During the half-time shows I was given the opportunity of introducing and announcing the band as it marched on the football field. These were proud moments, after many days and hours of rehearsing over and over, until the whole show was fine-tuned. Coordinating the music with the show routine while marching smartly in step took many hours. There were times when two or three band students were also football players. During half-time they would quickly change into their band uniform and join the band for the half-time performance. This was a necessary arrangement because we were a small school. Later we started getting more "sophisticated" with our half-time shows, doing pinwheels, and other intricate maneuvers. For one of the home games, I got a "bright" idea. I planned for the visiting band and ours to march in from opposite ends of the field at the same time. Both bands would be playing the same music. We would cross each in smart fashion on the 50 yard line and proceed with some simple maneuvers. My band director friend from the other school, agreed with the plan. Everyone looked forward with anticipation for this game, and the half-time show. All went well, and we were pleased at the applause from the fans. Well, I have a confession to make! The show went as we had planned, except for one small detail! Both bands played the same march music as they marched on the field. However, the music arrangements were in different keys! It's possible nobody noticed since the crowd was shouting so loud. I have never gotten over that! I'm glad I got that off my chest. In the meantime, the Band Boosters were busy selling hot dogs, hamburgers, and all kinds of goodies to the hungry fans.

When the band was preparing for a parade, we would drill on the streets of Natalia. We aroused not only the dogs, but also a cantankerous donkey that would respond to the music with a loud "Hee Haw." Yearly we were invited to march in parades at some of the surrounding towns, including the Peanut Festival Parade in Floresville, as well as the Strawberry Festival Parade in Poteet. Of course, the most exciting of all was the night Flambeau Parade in San Antonio, during Fiesta Week.

Longhorn Band Day in Austin became another exciting event that kids looked forward to. Once a year the Longhorn Band would invite area school bands to march, and compete in a parade in Austin. Afterwards all the bands had the privilege of sitting in a reserved section of the football stadium to watch one of the football games. During the game, the Longhorn band members would pass out snacks for all the visiting bands. This was a welcome treat. Band Day also served to attract students to consider attending U.T. in the future.

Since I was a member of the Longhorn Alumni Band, I had the opportunity to perform with this group from time to time. The Alumni Band would perform during the half-time at one game each year. At one of these games, during Band Day, my band students who were up in the stands, got a surprise when they suddenly saw me marching on the field with the one hundred fifty member Longhorn Alumni Band. There were other surprises during our trips to Longhorn Country. At one game, during the half-time, we were shocked to hear on the P.A. system that the Natalia High School Band had won first place in the Class B Category. My wife, Lupita, who was sitting behind me, grabbed my neck and almost chocked me with excitement. The kids were ecstatic!

Judy Whittington
Natalia High Drum Major

Judy Whittington, our drum major and I went down to the field to receive the beautiful trophy. These trips were always fun and challenging. The training and discipline had paid off. The kids were tired but proud as we headed home with that beautiful trophy. Another year, Judy Whittington proudly came home with "The Most Outstanding Drum Major" trophy. She won first place among all the bands in the Band Day Parade.

As the band continued to improve, it was ready for more challenging things. We entered the UIL (University Interscholastic League) Band Contests, which included not only marching, but also a concert playing contest, and a solo and ensemble contest. These highly competitive events took place at different times throughout the year. This required rigorous discipline and serious responsible individual practice. The goal was to develop well rounded musicians with a love for music, as well as to develop responsible, conscientious citizens.

Betsy Crawford, was another drum major who assisted me in close rigid inspection of instruments, uniforms etc. before leaving for any contest. With so much equipment to take, I kept reminding the kids not to forget anything. On one trip to a concert contest, as the bus was underway, I stood up to give final encouraging remarks. One student asked "Mr. Cortez, where is your coat? Wow, no coat, I was embarrassed. Then I noticed I had also forgotten my director's baton. The kids laughed, but they were understanding. I was fortunate enough to have a band director friend about my size, who lent me his coat and baton. His band was scheduled to play at a later time.

During my years at Natalia, I was working on a Master's Degree in Education at Southwest Texas State College (SWTSC), in San Marcos. I spent many weekends and long hot summers studying and doing research in the library. I was determined to get this degree to advance in my profession and to progress to a higher pay level. One of my courses involved the study of acoustics. I decided to apply some ideas that I read about. Large egg cartons make good acoustical material, because they are absorbent. I thought this would be perfect for our wooden barracks band building. Plus, it was inexpensive! I introduced this idea to Mr. DeMare, and within two days, he hauled in dozens of these egg cartons. It didn't take long to find student volunteers who would help me tack them up side-by-side, covering the walls, and ceiling inside the band room. Surprisingly, this cut down the reverberation. Some people thought it was weird, but it worked, and that's what mattered.

What encouraged me was that my Mr. DeMare would always listen and was supportive. At the Annual Teacher's Banquet, I received a beautiful band director's jacket, personalized with my name and school logo on the front. The band students were also awarded similar jackets each year. One year I was presented with a colorful blue blanket with white lettering, including my name, title, and school logo. Another year Mr. DeMare surprised me with one of those

NEW CAREER AS A BAND DIRECTOR

popular silver "Academy Awards Style" Oscars Statue.

Since our move to Natalia our family was growing, so we decided to move to a larger house just a couple of blocks away. During the time that my wife Lupita was expecting our second child, there was a parade in Natalia. The Home Making Teacher surprised me by decorating a baby stroller with blue and white streamers, and had a student push it behind the band in the parade. Anyway, we were blessed with a precious little girl on May 27, 1963. We named her Mayra Aida, after two of Lupita's sisters. She was a "pudgy" healthy little baby. Now Ricky had a partner to play with and to chase the horned toads in our backyard.

"Behold, children are a heritage from the Lord, the fruit of the womb a reward". (Psalm 127:3).

We were in our second home, and were basking in God's blessings. Eventually, we moved to two other houses while in Natalia. The thought of buying a house did not enter my mind at that time. In the back of my mind I still thought of this band position as temporary, a stepping stone to "greater" things. Many years later, the third house, a pink house at 300 3rd street was converted into what is now the Natalia City Hall. And I am proud to say, that the mayor at the present time is Ruby Vera, who was a majorette in my band, back in the 60s.

One small dark cloud started hovering over the progressing Natalia Band Program. A dispute over the ownership of the band uniforms arose. The whole situation was mundane! Mr. DeMare claimed the uniforms were school property, and the Band Boosters Club claimed ownership, because they had paid for them. Mr. DeMare argued that those monies were raised at the football concession stand, which was a school function on school property. The whole scenario was ridiculous to me. I was right in the middle of all this, but remained relatively quiet. If I recall correctly, the boosters yielded to the concept that the uniforms were school property.

I had well behaved kids in the band program. No major discipline problems! However, I did apply the "board of education" from time to time. I was well acquainted with most of the students in the band, mainly because they started in junior high then continued taking band through high school. Rey Fraga, a short but very conscientious student, who was always polishing his trumpet, is one of the few former students who has kept in touch with me throughout many years. We became faithful friends over all these years, even though we were far apart. I'm happy to say that Rey is retired from the U.S. Navy, and is presently working for the V.A. in Colorado. I still enjoy conversation and communication with him until this day. We still get together from time to time when he comes to Texas, or I travel to Colorado.

One summer, during one of my classes at SWTSC, a professor asked to talk to me after class. During a long and interesting discussion, he wondered why I was still teaching in that small town after six years. He suggested that now, with a master's degree and six years of experience, I might want to consider "greener pastures." He felt I was prepared, possibly for a larger school, which could be more challenging and more profitable. From then on, I kept pondering and thinking about this conversation, and the fact that I now had a Masters Degree in Education. In retrospect, I had been content and happy in Natalia. It had been home for me and my family for six years. Around this time, the current school board had begun making radical changes that caused strife among the teachers. This raised a red flag and further caused me to consider a change. I prayed and meditated on this idea. I discussed it at length with Lupita. Finally, I submitted my resignation to the school board on June 27, 1966.

After ending this chapter in Natalia, I had the task of deciding where I would go from here. I had to explore the field for band director positions. I entertained the idea of a job overseas. Since I had been abroad in the Navy, that sounded like a good idea. So, during the summer of 1966, while taking summer courses at St. Mary's, I started inquiring about overseas jobs with military dependency schools, as well teaching positions with oil companies. Being in the searching mode, my attention was aroused to an interesting article in the local newspaper. I followed up on a classified ad where teachers were being interviewed for jobs in Hawaii.

On May 2, 1966, I met with a representative from Hawaii at the employment office in San Antonio. At the end of an enticing interview, I had signed a contract to teach band and music in Hawaii. I was "flabbergasted" as I left the office. Had I done the right thing or did I act too hastily? I had been in Hawaii when I was in the Navy, so I wasn't completely ignorant of that wonderful place. And Lupita was equally surprised and very pleased when I came home with the good news. It was a bold and daring move, especially with two small children. But we had the assurance that God would guide us along the way.

We approached midsummer and I did not receive any further word from Hawaii. I began to worry, so I wrote to the Hawaii Department of Education in Honolulu. Their brief reply was just a small measure of assurance! A few weeks later, I decided to write to the principal who had interviewed me. I'll never forget his response "Richard, you have a contract to teach in Hawaii! Come!"

My Dad—A big inspiration in my life

Natalia High School Band Reunion—1981

Natalia High School Teachers

CHAPTER 16
THE HAWAIIAN ISLANDS
SEPTEMBER 1966

"The most beautiful chain of islands anchored on any ocean." (Mark Twain)

So, we placed a lot of our belongings in storage and got rid of a lot of winter clothes. I kept the little Rambler station wagon, which I drove to California. It was pretty well packed with a few essential items, including a television set I had won in a raffle. I drove to California with Danny and his family right behind me in their car. From Los Angeles I had the car shipped to Honolulu. I had decided to go ahead of my family, rent an apartment, and send for them later. I was glad we did that, because even after I got there, no one seemed to know where I would be assigned.

What I did know was that Ralph Miller would meet me at the airport when I arrived in Honolulu. Providentially, I had met Ralph's sister at a Baptist church in Devine, Texas, months before. She was a Hawaiian girl married to an ex U.S. Marine. Now living in Texas, she was thrilled to hear that I was going to her home state. She didn't hesitate to introduce me (by mail) to her family who lived in Kailua, Oahu, about a thirty-minute drive from Honolulu.

As that huge Boeing 747 approached the Hawaiian Islands, I could hear beautiful captivating Hawaiian music on my earphones. My eyes were glued to the little window; I begin to take in the breathtaking beauty of this tropical paradise. Coming off the ramp and into the crowded Honolulu Airport receiving area, Ralph had no trouble recognizing my white Stetson cowboy hat that would stand out as the Texan arriving. The reality of finally arriving on this beautiful island in the middle of this massive Pacific Ocean suddenly hit me! As a new "malihini"(a new-comer), I could sense the excitement, the aloha spirit, the welcoming girls in their Muumuus with the flower leis, the scent of flowers, the palms trees swaying in the breeze, the Hawaiian music, and the pineapple juice being served under a thatched roof gazebo near the landing area.

Tour groups were being herded toward big roaring buses, cabs, tour limos, and rent-a-cars. Ralph took me straight to Kalakawa Ave and Waikiki Beach to witness that world famous site. After several hours of sightseeing Ralph treated me to a super dinner. Then he checked me in to a modest hotel about a stones throw from Waikiki Beach. It was within walking distance of the beach yet more reasonable than the larger luxury hotels. The first night in Hawaii – Wow!

I was thrilled even after checking into my hotel. I could sense the sights and sounds of Waikiki in the distance. I wondered what the next day would be like. Well, the next day I wandered up and down Kalakawa Ave. I became a beach bum for a couple of days and discovered some interesting attractions. Probably the most entertaining was the Kodak Hula Show that took place right there on the sandy beach at Waikiki. Tourists gathered all around to enjoy the show and take pictures.

The Kodak Company that sponsored the show had a small grass shack booth that sold film, cameras and other Kodak accessories. After the show, the dancers would pose with admiring tourists and visitors. "Hilo Hattie" was a popular old gal that performed with the older "wahines," and she always stole the show! She would wiggle and waddle and shake her "Okole" (her bottom) in the most peculiar way. I was concerned that any moment she would dislocate a joint! Of course, there were younger girls that did a smooth hula dance using their hands with graceful movements to depict the swaying palms and the ocean waves. By the way, it a false notion that they wear grass skirts. The truth is, they wear big green tea leaves, and some wear gym shorts underneath.

One Saturday, while strolling through the famous International Marketplace on Kalakawa Avenue, a small sign attracted my attention. It was an announcement for church services on Sunday morning. It was to take place in that courtyard (a large Lanai) decorated with all types of flowers and tropical plants. I was there bright and early the next morning. Mostly tourists and visitors came, and were being welcomed by receiving a small Vanda orchid for their lapel. The makeshift chapel was made up of colorful wooden benches and a simple pulpit. The hymns were familiar, and the preaching was biblical. After the service, I met the preacher, Dan Kong. He was pastor of Olivet Baptist Church in Honolulu, and freely volunteered his time to this ministry.

After about three days, I woke up and realized I was not a tourist, and I was not here for pleasure. Plus, I couldn't afford to spend the few dollars I had in my pocket. I felt like I had a "Puka" (hole), in my pants pocket, the way the money was going. Desperate times require desperate measures – I checked in at the downtown YMCA. One weekend, Ralph Miller invited me to his house in Kanehoe, where I met his mother Phoebe, his brother Walter, and the rest of his family. He had a sister that worked at Kamehameha High School. I remember her telling me that they had just hired a band director at her school. She felt like I might have had a chance at that position if I had come and applied sooner. This was an exclusive school for students of Hawaiian ancestry. Anyway, I already had a contract with the Hawaii Department of Education.

One Saturday afternoon Ralph took his two children, (Kimo and his little daughter) and me swimming at Makaha Beach. Later I found out that this is where International Surfing meets are held. Anyway, we had a great time even though we didn't surf.

I finally found out the time and the meeting place for all new teachers. Those meetings were to take place in Waipahu, a former sugar plantation town, just eleven miles northwest of Honolulu. By this time I already had my car, so I drove out there and rented an apartment. There I met several new teachers, some fresh out of college that had contracts for one or two years.

I tried calling home regularly to update the family on my whereabouts. The day came when my wife Lupita, Ricky, and Mayra were to come. I had been attending a Hawaiian church in Honolulu where I met with a lot of very friendly local folks. The services always started out with the reading of the Word, first in Hawaiian, then in English. The Hawaiian hymns came easy for me because the language and words are very similar to Spanish. Several of the brethren had decided to accompany me to the airport to welcome my family when they came. That Sunday, several families loaded themselves with flowers, and flower leis, and were ready to meet my family with that famous aloha spirit. I clung to my flower leis, and Torch Ginger as the plane landed promptly at 3:00 p.m. The passengers all came out, one family after another. Then the pilots and the crew came out. What a great disappointment, that my family had not made it on that flight.

I was informed that another flight was due in from L.A. at 4 p.m. So, we waited for the next flight. And again, I strained my eyes as a lot of excited people stepped down from the airplane. Everybody came out, except my family. That really blew my mind! I was embarrassed and discouraged, to say the least. My aloha spirit was beginning to dwindle, and the flowers wouldn't stay fresh much longer. I felt like a steaming volcano getting ready to erupt!!! Excited visitors and loved ones from each flight would meet with embraces, kisses, and a lot of loud chatter. Soon the area was quiet and desolate again, except for "lonely" me.

A little anxious and bewildered I think I drank all the sample pineapple juice at the gazebo while waiting. I finally called home and was told there had been a little problem getting started. My mother assured me of the exact flight they were coming in, which was 6 p.m. Hawaiian people are usually pretty laid back, but these faithful Christian friends, were getting a little impatient. They excused themselves, mainly because they had to attend their evening service.

They regretted having to leave, but left me with all the flowers. By this time I was exhausted and frustrated! But now, I felt like I had enough time to go for a short nap at the apartment, and make it back to the airport in time. I carefully sprinkled the flowers with water in the sink, and hit the sack.

As soon as I closed my eyes, I heard the phone ring. It was my darling Lupita calling from the airport. I almost fell from the bed with shock! Their flight, for some reason beyond my comprehension, had arrived early. I dragged myself out of bed and hurried to the airport, which was not very far from the apartment. By this time the airport receiving area was deserted, except for my beloved carrying Mayra, and holding Ricky by the hand. They were a sight for sore eyes, as I saw them from a distance. I was exploding with mixed emotion! I had to eliminate the negative and concentrate on the positive. Tears were welling in my tired eyes, as I embraced them tightly and smothered them with kisses. It was an unusual but beautiful reunion, which I will never forget. I wasn't even interested in excuses or reasons for the delay. I was just thankful and happy to see them arriving safely.

While we waited for the meeting day with the school district, I drove the family all over the place - Kalakawa Ave, Honolulu, Waikiki Beach, the International Marketplace, Waimea Falls, and even had the opportunity to visit Mrs. Phoebe Miller, Ralph's mother. They were the family that met me at the airport when I first arrived. She lived in Kailua, on Oahu. She was a typical Hawaiian lady, very friendly and hospitable. She walked us through her yard, which was beautifully arrayed with a variety of flowers, plants, and trees, including Plumerias, Hibiscus and about three or four palm trees. She immediately fell in love with Lupita and the kids. Ricky and Mayra were having their first experience with fresh coconuts recently fallen off the trees.

The night of the teacher's meeting finally came. We all met in a large Lanai (courtyard). I was going to get a taste of a typical Hawaiian Luau, with all the alohas, torches, music, exotic plants, flowers, flower leis for all the newcomers, and tables decorated with tropical fruits. The visiting speakers were given Maile leis. Later I found out that these leis (long strings of green and leafy leis) were originally given only to the "Alii" (Royalty). After a delectable dinner, we had the introduction of all new teachers (mostly from the Mainland). Then came the guest speakers, including the superintendent of schools (for the whole state of Hawaii), and other officials and administrators from the department of education. The program ended with everyone standing and singing Hawaii Ponoi, (Hawaii state song). I tracked down one of the administrators, who told me I should report to the district office in Waipahu on Monday morning. I was anxious to see where I would work! Well, I got my answer!

I was assigned a temporary position as a traveling music teacher for three elementary schools. I say temporary, because my initial assignment on my contract was for secondary schools (middle and high school). I didn't complain, in fact I rather liked that job after I got started. For one, I was traveling and enjoying the beautiful sights. The three Elementary schools were Ewa Beach, Iroquois Point, and Pearl City. Plus, teaching elementary music was fun and the little keikis (children) were easy to work with.

After about three weeks, the Department of Education Office called and asked if I would be interested in a high school band director position on another island. I scratched my head and asked if

I could think about it. (Maybe I feared vicious "savages" who didn't welcome newcomers). The second time they called I reminded them that my contract was for the Island of Oahu. A week later I got a friendly and gracious invitation to the district office. I was introduced to a friendly Filipino gentleman who was principal of Pahoa High School on the Island of Hawaii (the Big Island). The personnel office had been persuasive but patient with me. This principal assured me no pressure would be applied. He patiently described his school situation. The band program sounded ideal. The band room was well equipped with music stands, drums, instruments, big music library, instrument storage room, private director's office, etc. The band was pretty well established, according to him. I asked him why he had left. He said, "I've been transferred to another school." He seemed sincere and honest.

After much thought and prayer, and discussing it with my wife, I decided to go for it. I suggested to the personnel officer that I would be willing to take that position if my car and family were transported. Sure enough, it was agreed! After a couple of days we were bound for the Big Island on one of those Aloha Airlines planes ("thirteen hula dancer's wide"). We were now off to a new and exciting adventure on another island. A carrier barge transported our car. Mr. Kuniyoshi, the principal of Pahoa High School was waiting for us at the Hilo Airport. He was a courteous, well-dressed Japanese man. He claimed he too was new at the school. He drove us about thirty miles out of Hilo (county seat for the Big Island), past huge sugar cane fields, and signs pointing to the Volcanoes National Park.

"He is made supreme when we are so satisfied in Him that we can: 'Let goods and kindred go this mortal life also.' And suffer for the sake of love. His beauty shines most brightly when treasured above health and wealth and life itself."

John Piper *"Don't Waste Your Life"* *(Page 170)*

CHAPTER 17
MALIHINI'S ARRIVE IN PAHOA

Finally, we arrived at the quaint little country town called Pahoa. It was a rural agricultural community that reminded me of a freshly watered greenhouse. It was plush with green vegetation and all kinds of plants, flowers, and fruit trees. Later I found out why! As we drove through the little town, I was reminded of the old country western towns we used to see in the movies. Small one level wooden structures and apartments connected side by side where passerby's could casually look through open doors while walking along the boardwalks. The women, mostly Asian, shuffled along in their long, colorful dresses and slippers - a perfect scenario for a movie.

I was intrigued! I didn't know what to expect next. Then, much to my surprise, we came upon something completely unexpected and out of place – a Dairy Queen. I was amazed to find a DQ in such a remote village in this part of Hawaii. A couple of more miles up the road, we came to the school grounds.

Three schools were on one large campus - high school, junior high, and elementary. The buildings were mainly wood with covered walkways. We drove to the school cottages, which were within walking distance of the school. They were clean, spacious, and equipped with most of the necessities, such as appliances, simple furniture, beds, bathroom, and a carport. They were surrounded by colorful huge tealeaf plants and well kept green lawns. We were assigned one with three bedrooms. The cost was twenty-five dollars per bedroom per month. These cottages were provided primarily for new teachers, mostly from the Mainland (USA). It was very economical! We would not have the usual car expenses, and clothing was casual Hawaiian style all year long. But how would the students react to this new "Malihini" band director? It would not take me long to find out.

We were given a surprise welcome from the friendly locals the second day we were in Pahoa. As we arrived back to our cottage after a short trip to Hilo, we discovered a huge assortment of local Hawaiian fruits neatly piled up on our front porch. There were mangos, papayas, bananas, guavas, avocados, and oranges. Finally we were getting a glimpse of the "aloha" spirit which was usually reserved for the tourists.

It took us a while to get use to the dark rainy nights in Pahoa. It rained just about every night! Yes, it poured hard on our corrugated sheet metal roof. It seemed like it was rainy season all year round. Now we knew why everything around grew so profusely – the grass, banana trees, papaya trees, huge ferns, and flowers of every variety, especially Anthuriums. This little town always looked exceptionally clean and freshly scrubbed.

The most incredible thing was the absence of mud. Most of the ground has its origin in lava. It is porous and absorbs the water like a sponge. The children could be playing in the yard or on the school playground in the morning, right after a hard night's rain. There were no mud puddles to contend with! Amazingly, my car never got splashed with mud, because there was none. Lava rock and pumice were predominant through out the whole island. This, together with subtropical weather resulted in an abundance of vegetation. All of the Hawaiian islands were originally formed from accumulation of lava on the floor of the ocean. We witnessed an eruption that added five hundred acres of land to the island. We were witnessing the birth of creation (at least in Hawaii). There are three major volcanoes on the Big Island: Mauna Loa, Mauna Kea, and Kilauea. Kilauea is the only one that is still active.

Some weekends I would drive the family down the Puna Area toward the ocean through roads and areas that seemed abandoned. We discovered all kinds of fruit trees and plants, including mangos, avocados, guavas, bananas, coconuts, passion fruit, etc. It was plentiful and would fall and rot if it was not picked. We would come home with a big box full of fresh fruits. (I was reminded of the abundance in the Garden of Eden). Most of it was not cultivated by anyone, but God Himself. Further down the road we did come across papaya farms, as well as colorful commercial Orchid gardens. The coconuts always fascinated the kids.

They would collect as many as they could carry and bring them home. After a few days of lying around in our yard I would have trouble picking them up. To my amazement they had grown roots that were attached to the ground. We had found ourselves on a very strange and interesting island. And there were many more fascinating and unusual discoveries to come. The rain was truly a blessing. At least for me it was!

Farming of flowers was the principle industry in Pahoa. The beautiful heart-shaped flower- with the long stem - Anthurims, grew everywhere! Some called Pahoa the Anthurim capitol of the world! It was a thrill for us to just get in the car and hit the road on weekends. We drove through forests and winding roads that led to the ocean. As we peeked through the trees we would finally catch a glimpse of the vast expanse of the Pacific Ocean.

As we got closer, we were surprised to come across an unusually beautiful black sand beach. A map told us that this was Kaimu Beach, right next to Kalapana Village. We naturally got our bathing suits on and started to wade in. A couple of local boys quickly informed us that the undertow on that beach was extremely dangerous. Now I knew why the place was practically deserted. I had hoped that warning signs would have been posted. Well, in spite of that bad news, that turned out to be one of our favorite picnic places. Picnic lunches under those serene palms, sitting on our straw mats with only the roar of the waves on the shimmering black sand beach was a dream come true.

This was better than Gilligan's Island! Ricky and Mayra played with coconuts that were all over the place. In fact, that is were I first learned to chuck and peel a coconut with my bare hands – with a little help from hard lava rocks. Then I would cut a "puka"(hole) on one end of the hard shell, which houses the "fruit" and the milk. Surprisingly, the ends are soft enough to punch a hole, apply a straw

Kaimu Black Sand Beach
Dad, Ricky, & Mayra

and then suck out the milk. Afterwards you could crack the coconut open, and get to the pulp, or the white meat.

A couple of miles down along the solitary Puna area we discovered the remains of the little deserted town of Kapoho. It was half buried in smooth but ugly black lava from an eruption several years back. It was a sight to behold! Now we knew we had to visit Kilauea Volcano, which was about forty miles up the mountain.

Back in Pahoa, the principal who described this band position for me in Honolulu was correct. All the necessary equipment for a band room was there. As beautiful and plush as this small community was, it was still an out-back rural environment. The band students represented an interesting description of the diverse make up of the community. There were Hawaiian, Japanese, Chinese, Samoan, Korean, Filipino, Puerto Rican, Portuguese, Spanish, Tahitians, a few Caucasian, and a mixture of several others, including Hapa Haoles (part white/part Polynesian mixture). Besides band, I was assigned an elementary music class and an English reading class. This was necessary to fill in my daily schedule.

Most of the people at the school looked at me as a "new dog in the neighborhood." I think Captain Cook probably got a warmer reception when he landed at Kealakekua Bay. Interestingly, the third day in the high school band class, I was to face my first serious challenge. This new "haole" (white/caucasian) was about to be tested! I could sense an atmosphere of "What does this guy think he is going to teach us?" As I was making some introductory remarks about the band program, I was distracted.

Gabriel Kealoha, a huge Samoan kanaka tuba player had made his way to the drum section. Then he began tapping a drumstick on the drum rim. I asked him to please stop at least a couple of times. Well, when he kept it up, I slowly but aggressively walked toward him through the rows of chairs and music stands. I wasn't sure what I was going to do, but I kept going! When I was about five feet from him, he deliberately threw the stick on the floor and started walking toward the door. Then in a firm commanding voice, I shouted, "GOOD! GET OUT, AND STAY OUT!"

Well, he didn't get out! Instead he plopped himself down on a chair near the door. Again, I started walking toward him. This young man had the stature and demeanor of a King Kong. Of course, the class was curious and quietly waiting to see the outcome of this classroom drama.

As I got closer to him, he clenched his fists, raised them high in the air, and shouted, "I TAKE REVENGE!" Then he stomped out of the room. I realized later I could have handled that situation differently. I confronted and embarrassed a student in front of his peers. It was similar to cornering an animal, which would only provoke him. In an effort to demonstrate that I was in complete control, I probably alienated some of the other students. In the weeks ahead it took me a while to establish a measure of control and friendly relationships. A couple of weeks after that incident, several teachers reported Gabriel as frequently disruptive and a constant problem in many classes. He was finally suspended from school.

Eventually, the kids got used to the new "haole" band director. Some would even bring speared fish to our cottage. Later, on a field trip to Kalapana Village, I was taught how to scoop up fish from under the big rocks with my bare hands. Some boys even led me into a long cave that ended up on an ocean cliff. This had been known as a favorite fishing "hole" for Hawaiian fishermen.

The important thing is that I was establishing good rapport with the students. The band participated in many activities, including a parade, all-island band festivals in Hilo, concerts, and some basketball games. Yes, after much work and practice, we were able to maintain some form of discipline and the band played surprisingly well. Some were curious about my Hispanic name and my Mexican heritage. As I got better acquainted with the customs and manner of life, the reference to haole disappeared. In fact, after the second year in Hawaii, I was considered Kamaaina (resident, or "old timer"). There were no music stores or places to repair band equipment in the remote area of Hawaii I lived in. I ordered instrument repair kits with a Bunsen Burner, corks, pads and cushions from the mainland. So out of desperation and necessity I had to do my own instrument repair. This is something I had not learned in college!

CHRISTMAS IN HAWAII

Once a year there was the Big Island Music Festival in Hilo. Bands and choirs from all over the Big Island would come into town for this big event. Each group would sit facing the center of the large auditorium. At a scheduled time each band or choir would perform three numbers. There were no judges rating these musical groups. There was no competition involved! This was a rare but pleasant experience for me. There were large bands representing larger schools, and smaller bands representing smaller schools. I rather enjoyed this concept of playing merely for pleasure and enjoyment.

Plus, the parents were thrilled to hear their youngsters perform in public. I had come from Texas where bands are very competitive and are judged at many contests during the year. Coincidentally, there were three other band directors from Texas on the Big Island. And they had no plans of returning to Texas any time soon! One school group that everyone always enjoyed was the Prince Jonah Kuhio Kalanianaole Middle School Ukulele Band, directed by George Camarillo.

At the beginning of the school year most of the teachers at Pahoa had been "polite," but few were "Texas Friendly," which I was accustomed to. The teachers that lived in the cottages (originally from the Mainland) were usually friendlier. Dr. Steurmman, our first doctor there, had warned us. He candidly told us that we would not remain very long in Hawaii. Unfortunately, "the people are very 'cliquish,'" he said. That was true, but in time we blended in very well, because we were not the typical "haoles."

We were Mexicans, or at least of Mexican descent. Since there were very few Mexicans in Hawaii, people could not label us. I could pass for Spaniard, Hawaiian, Filipino, Portuguese, or even Japanese. This proved helpful when I started driving tours. I even acquired a taste for "Poi!" (a food staple of Hawaiians). Pigeon English was common among the locals, especially in the rural areas like Pahoa.

"How's it brudda?" with the thumb and little finger sign was a common greeting among the Hawaiians.

Ricky started Kindergarten in September of 1966, our first year in Hawaii. His teacher was Mrs. Miyatake. Her husband, also a teacher, and their two young children lived in the cottage next to ours. Once a week this kindergarten class would tip-toe barefooted across the street to the band room for music classes. It was mostly a music appreciation class involving singing and storytelling relating to music. Peter and the Wolf was one of their favorites.

Our first Christmas was spent quietly in Pahoa. But we did not lack any of the decorations, ornaments, or of course a Christmas tree. We had to settle for a Norfolk Pine Tree, because that was the only kind available. Lupita treated us with a fantastic turkey dinner with all the trimmings. Nothing was left out! The walls displayed strings of colorful Christmas cards, from family and friends on the mainland, especially from Texas and California.

By this time the children has already sent Christmas greeting cards to grandma and grandpa in San Antonio. The thing they enjoyed most was a recording of our family singing Melekalikimaka (Merry Christmas) with Ricky playing the ukulele.

The band classes had pretty much settled down and we had gotten better acquainted. There was one small problem! A hole in the wall of the instrument room kept getting bigger and bigger every day. Some reliable informants provided me with names. I took a bucket full of broken sheet rock pieces from the wall to the principal. He casually dismissed it as, "That's something kids do." With this casual attitude he would ignore other problems. It didn't take me long to detect that this principal who was also on first year probation, did not want to make waves. He was an experienced principal, but this was his first position in a rural school.

At the end of one semester, I had tolerated with some degree of frustration two eighth grade boys who were determined to disrupt the class with rude and disrespectful behavior. I mentioned this to the vice principal who had been at this school for several years. Casually he asked, "Why don't you spank them?" He continued, "Bring them to my office after school."

The new principal who didn't want to "make waves" had given me the impression that spanking was not allowed. Well, I brought the two kids into the V.P.'s office after school. And with the regulation paddle that he gave me, with a brief explanation, I laid it heavy it on these two boys.

I made instant enemies, especially because I broke the paddle on the second one. They walked out with hatred in their eyes. I realized that was too hard and too harsh a punishment to make up for a whole semester of undesirable behavior. I regretted losing my cool! I was still learning in this new environment.

The Filipinos who had their own community in Pahoa, were humble and friendly. The second year I was at Pahoa, a small opportunity opened up for me. One day my principal asked if I was interested in teaching a U.S. citizenship class. The class would consist of adult Filipinos and would be taught one night per week. I accepted and enjoyed these dedicated folks who would come to class, sometimes in heavy rain. Of course they were thrilled when they passed the course and got their U.S. citizenship. A month later, they invited me and my family to an appreciation dinner at their community center. It was neither fancy nor elegant, but the small wooden building was filled with warm friendly hospitable smiles. They had a small music combo, and a long table filled with all kinds of exotic foods. There was small talk and a few speeches expressing their deep appreciation.

My family was asked to start the food line. Lupita went first as we started serving some of the most unusual and rare foods which we were completely unfamiliar with. Casually, my wife stepped up to a huge bowl filled with little black wiggly creatures. She let out a loud scream that shook the whole place. Of course, the Filipino folk got a big kick out of it, and could not stop laughing.

Afterward they explained that those little black crabs were a delicacy that taste best when they are alive and fresh. I thought to myself. "How much fresher can they get -ALIVE?" Wow! Now here comes another surprise. While we were enjoying our conversations, I had not noticed that Ricky, now six years old, was sitting in with the band playing the drums. And let me tell you, he was not just playing around! It was some kind of polka rhythm the band was playing. This was the debut to his musical career, which would come later in life. All in all, we had great fun and made a lot of Filipino friends. Since then, I have acquired a kindred spirit toward all Filipinos. I have found that most have a kind neighborly attitude.

When we first arrived on the Big Island I would take the family exploring. One of the first amazing things we saw was fuming, smoking steam vents alongside a road near Pahoa. Curious that there might be volcanic activity, we got out of the car and discovered that there was no danger. You could feel the heat if you placed your hand above these cracks. We enjoyed driving to a back road outside the fenced area of the landing strip at the Hilo Airport. The kids found it thrilling watching those huge airplanes taking off and landing. We also enjoyed picnics at Queen Liliuokalani Park in Hilo. This was a display of intricate Japanese gardening with ornate little bridges, fishponds, and rock structures which all had symbolic meaning.

Later we discovered Onekahakaha Beach Park, located on Kalanianaole Road. We immediately fell in love with this park. We made that a regular recreation area for the family. Sometimes we would meet with Chuck and Rebecca Garcia and their family after work and eat a picnic dinner there. The Garcias were originally from Colorado. Chuck was a scientist on one of the mountain observatories.

One hot summer day we spotted an ice cream vendor on the Onekahakaha Beach parking lot. He was swamped with kids swarming all around his truck. Jokingly I asked if he had another truck, so I could help him. Much to my surprise, he said he did, and gave me his number if I was interested. Well, that became my first part-time job after he repaired his extra truck. A short time after I was on a regular route through out the neighborhoods near the park. I found out why some Hawaiian wahinis (women) were so happily plump and healthy – they loved those huge banana splits. I have to admit that the ones I couldn't resist (for a quick snack) were the ice cream sandwiches.

Another trip that the family enjoyed, was the Hamakua Coast Road that led to Kole Kole Park. It was small, lush green, with small waterfalls, and picnic tables. Further up the road was the much larger Akaka Falls State Park.

This was a tropical fern forest; a wonderland of lush vegetation, tall trees with hanging vines, huge tall ferns, torch gingers, and many other exotic plants that adorned the clearly marked trails. The path, which was always refreshingly cool and exciting, would eventually take us to the Akaka Falls, a gigantic water fall cascading down a 422 foot cliff. It was awesome and inspiring like nothing my camera had ever experienced before. These are the kind of scenes you only see on travel brochures, or in movies, like South Pacific. I remembered a T.V. series about a Sailor who would sail his small boat from one tropical island to another. It was filled with adventure and a lot of natural beauty. As a young boy I would daydream, but I never expected to end up on such a spectacular island like this.

Snow capped Mauna Kea in the background

"O Lord, how manifold are your works! In wisdom have you made them all; the earth is full of your creatures. Here is the sea, great and wide, which teems with creatures innumerable living things both small and great."

Psalm 104:24-25

CHAPTER 18
VOLCANOES NATIONAL PARK

We discovered that the Volcanoes National Park was a huge attraction for most visitors coming to the Big Island. Kilauea Volcano was located in this park, it is the most active in the world. It erupts on an average of two to three times a year. The eruptions in most recent years have been exciting colorful fire fountains of lava, but for the most part are non-violent and non-destructive.

Our first couple of years on the Big Island we could not resist the unique attraction of volcano eruptions. An orange-red glow on the mountain at night would compel us to jump in our car and head for the eruption. The twenty-five miles of paved road up to the Volcanoes National Park was very convenient from our house. Halemaumau is the main vent of most eruptions. It is a pit crater located within the much larger summit caldera of Kilauea. The caldera is about two to three miles in diameter.

Cars drive in and park inside the crater. Some refer to Kilauea as a drive in volcano. The visitors then could walk up to the lookout wooden platform right on the edge of the pit. From there you could look down into a molten steaming mass of lava, gurgling and threatening to blow up, like a huge pressure cooker. Red fire fountains of lava might start shooting up as high as three feet, twelve feet, and even higher. When this crescendo began, the crowds would cheer loudly like fans at a football game.

It wasn't unusual to see molten fiery lava emerging from the bowels of the earth and spewing out through cracks along the sides of the mountain and flowing into the ocean. Sometimes sulfur fumes coming out and blowing in the air were so strong that visitors were prohibited from entering the caldera area.

Whenever there was any eminent danger, the volcanologist from their observatory would relay the danger to the park rangers who would then route the visitors out of the park. Geologist Thomas Jagger was the first man who thought up the idea of an observatory, which opened up in 1912. Needless to say, I took many pictures and movies of various eruptions during our six years in Hawaii.

HISTORY OF THE BIRTH OF THE HAWAIIAN ISLANDS

My fascination for volcanoes was intriguing mainly because I had taken a course in geology my last year in college. I was somewhat familiar with volcanic activity. I decided to take some courses at the University of Hawaii in Hilo. By doing so, I could improve my knowledge of Hawaiian history, the culture and the volcanoes. Plus, I would put myself on a higher pay scale. It would also educate me for my job as a tour guide.

In my zeal I chose to write my term paper on Hawaiian volcanoes. This was my chosen assignment for a course in Hawaiiana. It was exciting putting together a slide presentation that included pictures of past and current eruptions. Many were pictures I had taken myself. I personally narrated with sound effects on audiotape with the roaring ocean and explosive eruptions together with appropriate Hawaiian music in the background. In my narration I included the origin and the formation of the Hawaiian Islands.

"The islands owe their existence to a "hot spot" in the earth's mantle. Countless eruptions of lava, fed by the hot spot, built volcanoes that eventually grew above sea level to form the Hawaiian Islands. Each island is made of one or more volcanoes, which erupted on the sea floor and emerged above the ocean's surface after countless eruptions." [1]

The accumulation of lava over thousands of years survived the battering of ocean currents and waves. There is nothing more spectacular than to see fiery molten hot lava meandering down the mountain slopes then splashing into the ocean. As the lava hits the water it creates a huge pillar of steam and smoke that can be seen for miles around. It is spectacular, especially at night when an awesome orange-red colored cloud is visible in the sky. The type of lava that flows rapidly down the mountains is called "Pahoehoe." Then there is the slow creeping "chunky" kind called 'a'a. This also has a distinct destructive power for anything that is in its path.

Near the unique Kaimu Black Sand Beach is the picturesque Kalapana Gardens Subdivision. This subdivision was still being developed when we lived there in 1966. It was nestled in the wooded area near the village of Kalapana.

In December 1986, something unprecedented happened! Seventeen homes burned completely to the ground. This whole area experienced the destructive force of creeping lava flows. One by one the houses were being consumed by the slow moving lava flows as the owners stood and watched, completely helpless as their dream homes went down in flames. As soon as a finger of lava touched a structure, it would immediately incinerate. By 1990, fifty homes were evacuated. Some were completely consumed and some people were able to move their houses away from the area. At times the 'a'a flows crept along painfully slow, consuming everything in its path. The heights of the lava flows were not high, but they were unstoppable. There is nothing that can stop a lava flow. One man tried stacking huge rocks in front of his house, but that failed. The worldwide media was covering this colorful but tragic drama.

Jim Denny, a teacher and close friend who came to Pahoa at the same time I did, was energetic and filled with the aloha spirit. I think his enthusiasm rubbed off on me. He invited me to a Monday night teacher's bowling league when we first came to Pahoa. Later he got me interested in being a tour guide. I first started out with the McKenzie Tour Company, transporting tourists from the Hilo Airport to the hotels. This involved welcoming the visitors as they arrived at the airport. The arriving "wahinis" (ladies) would receive flower leis around their neck and a kiss (on the cheek!!). Then the work began - loading the passengers and their luggage into a twelve-passenger limousine. Later, I was assigned a route that included the famous Banyan Tree Row in Coconut Island, the city of Hilo, Commercial Orchid gardens, and ended up at the Volcano House, at the Volcanoes National Park. The Volcano House was a rest stop for all visitors. If Kilauea (about a quarter of a mile away) was erupting, the diners could witness the action through a huge picture window while they ate. This was the beginning of many interesting and exciting trips to the park with tour groups.

Halemaumau is the home of Madame Pele, goddess of Hawaiian volcanoes, according to the traditions of Hawaiian mythology. She is a dominant figure that Hawaiians revere religiously. Any and all activity that surrounds an eruption is caused by the power of Pele, according to the Hawaiians. One example that they claimed was proof of the existence of Pele, involved a lava flow that had covered a portion of a park road. Park maintenance crews tried to bulldoze the lava off the road, not once, but several times; and each time was followed by another lava flow that kept accumulating on the road. The destruction crew finally gave up and left the road alone. Madame Pele was appeased and the Hawaiians were satisfied. This was a significant interruption for tour groups that traveled that road daily. Someone suggested that if the tourists were allowed to take souvenir samples of lava, the road would be clear in record time. Of course, taking anything out of this national park is prohibited. The Hawaii Tribune-Herald once printed a story of a visiting family that secretly carried several lava rocks out of the park, and took them home to the mainland (USA). Several months later, it was reported that every single rock was mailed back. The reason given – the family had encountered numerous serious misfortunes!

Later I signed up with Gray Line Tours. Weekends and summers I had occasion to take my loaded twelve-passenger limo up the lush Hamakua Coast Road, past green picturesque Kole Kole Park, beautiful Akaka Falls State Park, then a temporary stop at breathtaking Waipio Valley on the north eastern part of the island. The whole time I was entertaining the passengers with "colorful" narration, or Hawaiian songs on the Intercom. Some of these songs I had learned while singing with the elementary music classes in Pahoa. Heading to the west, we would go past the huge Parker Ranch, one of the largest cattle farms in the world. The "paniolos"(cowboys) could be seen riding their horses on the spacious range. Another stop would be the very elegant, but hidden and private Mauna Kea Beach Hotel, owned by Lawrence Rockefeller. This architectural masterpiece was adorned with such amenities as uniquely designed swimming pools, saunas, a golfer's dream golf course, and an immaculate sparkling beach.

Many claimed that this was a favorite retreat for Bing Crosby who would lounge around this golf course unshaven and in wrinkled clothes. Most of the hotels had a special dining room near the kitchen area for all employees, including tour guides. We ate the same food as the tourists, but we had the privilege of being treated to Poi. Our all-day tour across the island would end at Kailua, Kona, on the far western side of the island. After one of these long trips, one passenger insisted that I take a break and sit with them by the swimming pool. Well, I couldn't resist the break, as well as a few sips of an icy cold Mai Tai that they offered me. After a short while, I started to say my goodbyes and aloha. Whoa! When I got up from that lounge chair, my legs got wobbly and almost brought me down! That drink was deceiving! Even a few sips, on an empty stomach can turn you "topsy turvy!"

After a good night's rest at the driver's special quarters, we would walk a short distance to a hearty breakfast at the hotel. This was a real treat since the breakfast was served on a lanai that faced the serene ocean just across the street. We would then pick up another group that would be headed back to Hilo, on the eastern side of the island. Tourists do not travel light! The baggage usually would take up all the trunk space, as well as the rack space on the top of the limo. Plus, it had to be covered with a tarp, in case of rain. For a part-time job it was fun, as well as profitable. Something novel that amazed the tourists was seeing me on my knees and drinking the ocean water at one of the black sand beaches. Of course they didn't know there was a small fresh water spring right on the beach where the salt water washed up. I was aghast when a local boy first showed me the spot where little bubbles were coming up from this fresh water spring.

A big special aloha event came on May 12, 1967. The Lord blessed our home with the birth of our little Pacific jewel, Ruby Maile. We thought that would be appropriate for our little "keiki" (child). She made her entrance at the Hilo Hospital, about a stone's throw from the beautiful Rainbow Falls. It was somewhat miraculous that Lupita didn't have a miscarriage. The road from Pahoa to Keaau, then Hilo, during her pregnancy was under construction and very rough. Needless to say, we were thrilled to have a baby in our house. Ricky and Mayra experienced the wonder of having a baby sister, and a new playmate in the family.

Back in San Antonio, my mom and dad were so happy and excited; they started making plans to come visit us. My dad even bought a new camera for the trip. Unfortunately he got sick and the plans were on hold. His situation got so serious that I decided to go visit him in San Antonio.

We enjoyed warm and encouraging conversations in the hospital for a week. When he appeared stronger and recovering, I went back to Hawaii. My mother and family kept sending me updates on his condition.

Then on April 30, 1968, I got a telegram from home informing me that he had died. I tried to stay calm, but my grief was heavy, and I felt a big knot in my throat as I tried to hold back uncontrollable tears. My dad was a godly person and I had assurance that the Lord had taken him home. As I grieved for my father and thought of going home for his funeral, my mom called me. She relieved my mind and comforted my heart when she said there was no need for me to come. She claimed that my visit the year before was so encouraging that it helped him build up new strength and faith. She was pleased that I had seen him when he needed me most – while he was still alive. As a gesture of my love, I sent him a beautiful double-orchid lei. Mom placed it around his neck in the casket.

---

[1] "Hawaiian Volcanoes"– USGS Hawaiian Volcano Observatory. https://hvo.wr.usgs.gov/volcanoes/ Retrieved April 25, 2015

CHAPTER 19
PAPAIKOU

My family back in San Antonio had encouraged my mom to take the trip to Hawaii just like she and my dad had planned. It would be a place where she could find rest and relief while mourning my dad. It was a long flight, but she was excited as she started making plans. We had invited her to stay with us indefinitely.

We were thrilled to see mom when she got off the airplane at the Hilo Airport. From then on, we took her on sight seeing tours all over the Big Island, from the flower gardens, to Akaka Falls State Park, to orchid farms, Waipio Valley, and to Kailua Kona on the other side of the island. She was in a dream world, and was taking pictures of everything. While she was still here, her brother Joe showed up. He was supposed to meet his Filipino wife here. She was returning from a business trip from the Philippines. Well, she never showed up! That marriage didn't last very long! In the meantime, Uncle Joe took in all the beauty of the Big Island, and even got to see a dramatic nighttime eruption at Kilauea.

The following year Lupita's sister Mayra, her husband Harry, and daughter Letty also visited us. Harry, a loving and devout husband, desired to treat Mayra like a queen and wanted to insure her happiness and enjoyment. Lupita was very pleased that her sister was able to come. As customary when malihinis came, we would take them on an island tour. They were amazed at the natural beauty all around.

Once in a while a cruise ship would come into the harbor, and I would be hired to pick up parties that wanted a short tour. On one occasion, a gray-haired California judge and his wife hired out a private car that I was to drive. Since they had met Lupita, Ricky, and Mayra on the dock, they insisted that the family come along on the tour. The judge said he would take the responsibility for taking additional passengers. Well, this was the beginning of an enjoyable tour, and a very friendly relationship. Our kids reminded them of their grandchildren back home. Later, they would surprise the kids with letters and gifts at Christmas time.

From time to time, tour groups came from Mexico and other Central and South American countries. They naturally requested Spanish-speaking guides. Since I was one of two tour guides that could narrate in Spanish, I would get called. This is where my bi-lingual background proved profitable, especially since this was above average pay. On one tour across the island I was called to translate for a busload of Portuguese from Brazil. When I explained that I could not speak in Portuguese, they were not discouraged. The tour escort promptly replied, "We can understand Spanish." Another time, I had to translate for a group from Monterrey, Mexico. I translated and my Kanaka partner drove the big tour bus.

Everything went well until the end of the tour. The people happily stepped off the bus and walked to their hotel entrance. The customary dollar tip from each family was completely ignored. The bus driver could not believe it. He said, "Hey brudda, there is something terribly wrong; go check da the tour escort." The tour escort had a strange explanation. She said they had just returned from Japan where tipping is not customary. As a consolation, she gave me a Mexican Olympic coin. My bus driver's aloha smile turned into fury! He vowed in expletive terms to never take another tour group from that country.

Sometime later, we had another visitor at our home in Papaikou. My Aunt Mamie came from California. She was my dad's sister and had always been very close to mom. So these two were like two high school girls on an island picnic. They loved to wear their floral Muu Muu dresses every time we went out, and they both had a fabulous time.

One warm Papaikou afternoon, I was watching the kids playing as they climbed the Plumeria tree in our front yard. Whoa, I thought I saw a familiar person walking down our street. Sure enough, I was dumb-founded when I recognized the face. It was Louis, Lupita's brother, from San Antonio. Why was he walking? How did he know where to find us, and why didn't he call? And why was he alone, empty-handed, without a single bag? I couldn't believe my eyes! Well, it turned out he had an argument with his wife and decided to get away for a while! I won't say too much, for fear other husbands might get the same idea!

SEPTEMBER, 1968 –

KALANIANAOLE INTERMEDIATE SCHOOL

George Camarillo, a robust and good-natured Filipino, became my good friend. He was band director and was well known for his popular ukulele band. He and his family had spent a wonderful Christmas with us when we were at Pahoa. One day he surprised me with this stunning comment, "Hey Cortez, how would you like to take my job at Kal (Kalanianaole Intermediate School)?" His school was located in Papaikou, right off the beautiful Hamakua Coast, about five miles north of Hilo.

George had built a house in another part of town, and was offered a job at a nearby school. His principal had told him - "I will release you, only if you can find a band director who is able to teach Spanish." Of course, he said this because George was also the Spanish teacher. He immediately thought, "What an excellent opportunity for my good friend Richard. He encouraged me – "Hey "brudda", being Hispanic, with a Spanish minor, and a band director, what are we waiting for!" When he mentioned my name to his principal, he naturally thought this was a joke, or an incredible coincidence. In my heart, I knew this was God's providence!

Having served my two challenging years of probation at Pahoa, I was ready for a transfer. Everything was falling perfectly in place! God was faithful, working things out in my life.

In September 1968, I started teaching at Kalanianaole. I was band director and Spanish teacher. Mayra was now five, so she started her first year there at the elementary school. Mr. Kurashigi, the principal ran a "tight ship", which made for good working conditions and a comfortable environment. The teachers and staff were friendly and did not treat me like an outsider (or a haole). We even had the privilege of moving into George Camarillo's school cottage, just across the street from the school. The band room was just a stone's throw from our cottage. The students were better behaved and knew the consequences for wild and unruly conduct.

However, one youngster remains on my mind. There was one good-looking Portuguese kid who always got suspended the first week of school. Either he would get involved in a fight with another student, a teacher, or was insolent with the principal. His father, a respectable looking professional, would come to the principal to defend his child's actions. He accused the school of being unfair with his son. I felt sorry for that poor boy. Occasionally, he would come and just hang around outside the school fence looking for someone to talk to. Other than that, there were few major problems. The band room was well equipped, and the students seemed eager to learn. They had a cooperative attitude, and took pride in their band.

We played on the school playground for the annual popular May Day program. May Day (May 1) is a fun day through out the state of Hawaii. Classes are dismissed, and every one is involved. All organizations and clubs contribute to this all day affair. Dancers of the different ethnic groups, in their traditional colorful costumes, would perform. Some of the dances represented were: Hawaiian, Filipino, Japanese, Chinese, Korean, Tahitian, Samoan, etc. It was like a three ring circus, with so many groups – from elementary to intermediate school children. Some were doing the dances of Samoa (using machetes or swords), others martial arts skills, while others were dancing around the May Pole. The band had a stationary site surrounded by chairs for parents and visitors. The playground was unrecognizable! There was also crowning of a King and Queen on a portable elevated stage. The court and the attendants in their regal attire would approach the stand in pomp procession. There was an outburst of applause when the King and Queen were announced. Sporadic drizzle through out the day did not hinder or dampen the enthusiasm of hundreds of kids that filled the entire playground. The band added atmosphere by playing "I'm Singing in the Rain" whenever it started to sprinkle.

Other band activities at Kalanianaole, included parades, concerts, and a Christmas concert at the Hilo Mall. At one Hilo Patriotic Pa-

Ricky & Cub Scouts in Hilo Patriotic Parade

rade, I had two functions, leading the band, as well as organizing my Cub Scout Troop.

Once a year I took the band on a concert tour to Kailua, Kona on the other side of the island. As a special attraction on this concert tour, we featured Hawaiian dances. A select group of girls in the band would perform in the typical Hawaiian dress. Most girls in Hawaii learn these dances when they are young. We were welcomed with enthusiasm at the two schools where we performed on our way to Kona. In Kailua, the kids enjoyed the comfort of the Pacific Empress Hotel, which is very close to the ocean. However, they seemed to prefer the fresh water hotel pool. Much to my surprise, some of these kids had never been to this side of the island. I was surprised, because I myself had taken tour groups the width and length of the Big Island many times.

Also, because of my "popularity" I had been chosen, or "volunteered," as Cub Scout Master at Papaikou. And, because the Den meetings were held in the school, and because my son Ricky was in the Cub Scouts, I became a prime candidate. The other male parents assured me that "the Den mothers did most of the work." They were right! In due time, I started enjoying it! I remembered the exciting times I had as a young Boy Scout. Things went well with weekly meetings at the school. There were interesting projects and goals for the boys to accomplish. The yearly soapbox derby was one of the popular events that the kids really enjoyed. Plus, we made plans to take the boys hiking inside the extinct Kilauea Iki Volcano. Now that was really exciting – hiking on the surface of harden lava flows.

Then we explored "Devastation Trail". We soon took a break for lunch in this foreboding place. Devastation Trail was located in a forest that was completely consumed by lava. The "charred skeleton" trees was all that remained. Everyone thought we should make that an annual affair. Most of these kids and parents were also involved in other activities, such as t-ball during the baseball season.

Papaikou is where Ricky first starting preparing for the "big leagues" – displaying his skills playing T-ball. All these activities did help him to work, play, and relate to other people. However, there was this chunky Kanaka kid who was bullying this smaller "haole" boy, with the funny looking eye glasses. I suggested to Ricky that he invite him to church. Much to our surprise, he accepted the invitation! We picked him up on Sunday morning, and he enjoyed being accepted by our family. After that, the boys became good friends. In my teaching experience, I found out that these bullies (in every school) are loners with anti-social attitudes. They stand out because of their awkward large stature and need to be accepted. They use their big bodies aggressively, because that is what they do best.

KINOOLE BAPTIST CHURCH

Our family had been enjoying fellowship and worship at Kinoole Baptist Church ever since we were at Pahoa. Pastor James Sanbei was a short, amiable, Japanese man. He graduated from a Texas seminary, and had a deep love for the Lord. On his way to church (on Oahu), on December 7, 1945, he was one who saw the Japanese planes flying overhead on their way to bomb Pearl Harbor. When he found out what was going on, he promptly turned around and went right back home.

But now, we were enjoying peaceable services at the church every Sunday. Sadao Tachibana and Y Ebizusaki were the two very devout deacons. When I first joined this church, the brethren claimed I was an answer to prayer. Since I was a music teacher, the Lord providentially brought me to this church, where they needed a song leader. I accepted with pleasure. Many Saturday mornings, Ricky and I would ride our bikes to church to help with building projects. The biggest project that took "like forever", was the construction of a youth building. We were well rewarded before we even started working! The men prepared a hearty breakfast before work. I can still smell the coffee, orange juice, bacon and eggs, butter (or jam) on toast, and pancakes. Each of the men contributed with their cooking skills. These were the good old days at Kinoole.

> Many years later I was very sorrowful to hear of the death of James Sanbei on July 21, 2012. I have many wonderful memories of my pastor in Hilo, Hawaii. His widow Katherine still lives in Hilo.

Once a month potluck lunches after the church service, were delectable and interesting. We were treated to delicious Japanese, Korean, Chinese, Filipino, as well as old fashion sandwiches and deviled eggs. For the most part, foods and customs are very Americanized in Hawaii.

**Richard, Ricky, Pastor Sanbei, Katherine, Mayra, Mom, Aunt Meme, Lupita & Ruby
At Kinoole Baptist Church**

On Friday, March 20, 1970 I took my school band to perform in the annual Hawaii Music Festival in Hilo. The next day, March 21, I flew my family to Honolulu for a visit to Waianae Baptist Church. This gave us a rare opportunity to visit some unfamiliar parts of Oahu, including the USS Arizona Memorial. This ship which was sunk during the Japanese raid on Pearl Harbor, is now a monument and a memorial, and is visited by many.

Several months later, Pastor Charles Mullins from Waianae Baptist Church called and invited me to lead the singing at a revival. With all expenses paid and a big plantation home to room in, I felt privileged and accepted the invitation.

Waianae Baptist Church

This time I just took Ricky as my companion. We stayed in this massive historical former plantation home. Ricky and I even had time to visit the Honolulu Zoo. The brethren at this small church were warm and very eager to hear and learn the gospel. The visiting preacher was from the Mainland. I led the singing and directed a children's choir, which Ricky also got involved in.

However, something awkward and embarrassing happened. Halfway through the week my voice gave out! I was barely able to whisper.

Yes, I knew music, but in reality, I did not have a trained voice. Leading the singing every night took a toll on my larynx. This was inevitable! I was a band director filling in as a song leader everywhere I went. During our stay there I found out that Pastor Mullins was the "last official evangelical missionary" to the state of Hawaii.

Several months later, back at Kinoole Baptist Church, I was selected as Director of Evangelism. The church deemed it important that I receive vital training. So that summer I was sent to Glorieta, a beautiful Baptist encampment nestled in the majestic mountains of New Mexico. I was there from August 6th through the 12th, 1970. Cool early-morning devotions under the trees were devoted to bible studies. Days were filled with a variety of classes in specific fields, such as New Testament, Old Testament, missions, evangelism, etc. There were periods of recreation and hiking, and plenty of delicious food in a huge sparkling dining room.

My plans were to head for San Antonio as soon as the camp ended. I thought of taking a plane or a bus, or hitching a ride with some camper going that way. However, my brother Danny came to the rescue! He drove his little Pinto all the way up to Glorieta to meet me and take me to San Antonio. It was one happy reunion with

Danny and his family, Adela, Cindy and Eddie. I was extremely grateful to Danny, not only for "escorting" me when I first drove to California on my way to Hawaii, but now taking the time and effort to bring me all the way home from Glorieta. He is a great brother! Once back in San Antonio, I was as excited as a little boy coming home after a long trip. Just to feast my eyes on the whole family was a thrill!

One day while sitting and talking to my dad, he had brought up an interesting subject. "Richy, you need to settle down somewhere and establish a permanent home for you and your family." In his mind he probably thought I was on an extended Hawaii vacation. My mind had already been set on living in Hawaii indefinitely. Of course I didn't tell him that! Later in life, I came to realize how painfully lonely it was to have a loved one leave home indefinitely. Later in the future my daughter Ruby would choose to move across the country to live in Massachusetts. I succumbed with emotion as I consented.

After a few days in "Good Ole San Antone," I flew back to Hawaii. For some reason, my flight was late! In Los Angeles I had to run across the terminal to catch my connecting flight. In Honolulu, I barely made the last flight to Hilo. Wow, that was close!

Our family was settled and enjoying a peaceful time in Papaikou. On still nights we could hear the ocean waves smashing against the cliffs and huge rocks, all the way from our cottage. By this time, we had made many friends in school - teachers, parents, the Cub Scouts, t-ball, etc. In fact, we were now considered "Kamaainas" (permanent residents) wherever we went. That meant we were privileged to local rates, instead of tourist rates. Mayra was enjoying school and Ricky had started collecting parts of a drum set to practice at home.

Ruby was now walking and enjoyed staying home with mommy. However, she was about to face a difficult crisis. A couple of weeks before Christmas, she started with flu-like symptoms. Gradually a fever began to develop. It subsided for a while, so we placed her in bed with us to keep a close watch on her throughout the night. About five in the morning we were suddenly awakened when she began shivering uncontrollably. It scared us, so we quickly wrapped her up, and decided to take her to the hospital. We called our neighbors the Shimisu's, and they agreed to take care of Ricky and Mayra. Ruby was in the hospital for two days. The doctor finally agreed to release her so she could be at home for Christmas. We were happy to have her home, even though she had lost quite of bit of weight.

We felt blessed to have the whole family together that Christmas.

In the meantime, I was staying busy with the school band, Cub Scouts, and driving tour groups. Another part-time job, which was more fun than work, was playing with the Hawaii County Band. We rehearsed once a week and had occasional concerts in the park, parades, and performances for visiting dignitaries.

Mayra, Lupita, Me, Ruby, Rick
My Malihini Family

One summer, Lupita and I decided she and the kids needed to visit the families in San Antonio. I was to stay and drive tours at the peak of the tourist season. Several friends came to bid them aloha at the Hilo Airport. On the surface, this trip seemed like a practical idea. But hey, after a few days, I started getting lonely and I missed them. I missed them a lot! I would come home and the scent of the baby and the sight of the toys filled the room. Sleeping alone, eating alone and no one to talk to made me feel desolate. I tried to stay busy, and keep my mind occupied.

Family at the San Antonio Airport

Then when the time was getting close for their return, I received a letter from my beloved Lupita. She informed me that they were not coming back! I read it twice! I got a big lump in my throat, and thought I would have an anxiety attack! This was the last thing I needed! Loads of things came to my mind. Why? Why is she doing this? Did her family influence her? I always had the impression she enjoyed living in Hawaii. After much brainstorming and scratching my head, I decided to write her a letter. I wrote what I thought was the most profound and penetrating letter I have ever written. I had to be gracious and diplomatic, trying not to provoke her. Yet, I had to be firm! I reminded her of the bond and sacred covenant which we made before God at the altar.

Her mother, God bless her soul, also reminded her of the tremendous responsibility she had, not only to her children, but also to her husband. "You don't belong here; you belong with your husband," she would say. My mother-in-law's husband had been a big disappointment. So she was wise in giving her daughter direction in marriage responsibilities. The Lord answered my prayers and my wife finally decided to return to Hawaii, together with the children. We settled down and things were going along smoothly. We were going to church regularly, and had sweet fellowship with the brethren at Kinoole Baptist church. Occasionally we would cruise over to Onekahakaha Beach Park and picnic with our good friends, Chuck and Becky Garcia. I continued with my part-time job with Gray Line Tours.

Then the "Adversary" slowly crept in again! My wife started acting very strange and peculiar. I could not understand what was going on. Things were going pretty smoothly, and now this! I was unable to comprehend this sudden bazaar behavior. She became suspicious of some of our best friends, and made unusual accusations. She started to isolate herself and would not go out very much. She even refused to attend church.

Meanwhile, I was hard pressed for an explanation about my wife's unusual behavior. We finally sought counsel from Pastor Sanbei. He tried counseling her, but with little results. He finally referred us to a local psychologist/psychiatrist team. After several visits she seemed more settled and calm. But the same behavior flared up from time to time. Out of desperation I wrote to a close confident in San Antonio. One who knew her real well was her brother-in-law. He and his wife thought maybe Lupita was homesick, and might prefer to come back to San Antonio.

Right about this time, I was informed that we needed to move out of our school cottage. Plans were to build a new band room on that lot. So here I was, sacrificing my home for a new band room. I had mixed emotions! I didn't know whether to rejoice or cry! Of course I had no choice! I was fortunate enough to find a suitable house at 123 Kohola Street in Hilo. The children had to change schools to Kapiolani in Hilo. I would drive the four miles along the Hamakua coast to Papaikou, which I didn't mind.

Our backyard consisted of a small patio, a papaya tree, and a macadamia nut tree. One day I got a call at school of an "explosion" at our home. I was shocked and rushed home to find that my wife's stomach was burned from a pressure cooker. Her doctor applied some burn cream. Later our Hawaiian neighbor explained that we had the perfect medicine for burns in our yard. This is when we discovered the miraculous medicinal properties of aloe. Lupita's skin did not blister and she healed very quickly without pain or scars. One day Ricky almost had his head crushed while he and Mayra were playing on the stone patio. As he laid on a patio bench, a stone pillar suddenly came crashing down and grazed the top of his head. At the doctor's office he asked not to be "sewed." The doctor assured him that the surgical staples would do the job.

Another incident on Kohola, involved our beloved cat "Naniloa." Seeking for a warm spot to take a cat-nap, she jumped inside the clothes dryer. You guessed it! Lost in there with the laundry, the door was shut and the dryer turned on; that was the demise of our darling pet.

Pastor Sanbei & wife

Daddy & Ruby at Kapiolani Park

Ruby Maile with Hawaiian dancers

Lupita at Rainbow Falls

Two lovebirds in paradise

CHAPTER 20
PALO ALTO, CALIFORNIA
1972 - 1973

I saw the opportunity and applied for a band director exchange position in Texas. But since there was no response after a year, I applied in California. Surprisingly, one Mr. Bruce Wolff, Band Director at Palo Alto accepted. The Hawaii Department of Education (D.O.E.) which promoted the idea of exchanges in the mainland, promptly approved my exchange. The Hawaii D.O.E. paid the two-way airfare for my family and me. Plus, my salary would still come from Hawaii.

In September of 1972, we flew to Mountain View, California. I started teaching at Wilbur Junior High School in Palo Alto, just a short distance from Mountain View. At the same time, Mr. Wolff started teaching in my place in Papaikou, Hawaii. Palo Alto was a sophisticated community, with many professionals, scientists, and was the home of Stanford University. It was quite a contrast from the rural and agricultural environment on the Big Island. There were a lot of skilled and highly motivated students at that school. But there were also major problems. I thought it unusual for a junior high school to have a full-time psychologist. And I was also surprised that the school had a teacher's governing board had more power than the principal. In fact, at the end of the school year, I observed a sad scenario when the board "dismissed" the principal with a farewell dinner. This gentleman was practically in tears when he spoke the final words of farewell to the faculty. I was discovering that California is very innovative and different from other states.

This school environment was an eye opener for me! Something else that I found unusual: Each morning a custodian would raise the U.S. flag in front of the school. No fanfare or announcement was made, in contrast to Hawaii. At our school in Papaikou, we had buglers that played to the colors at every raising and lowering of the Flag. Students everywhere would stand facing the Flag upon hearing the Flag bell. I had another interesting experience at the first school assembly in Palo Alto. I was accustomed to having the band play the Star-Spangled Banner at the beginning of most assemblies at other schools. So naturally, I did the same at Wilbur Junior High. The response was shocking to me! Students lazily lifted themselves out of their seats with much hesitation showing little respect for the National Anthem. Later in the lunchroom one teacher commented to me, "That's the first time we've heard that song in a long time." This school was definitely liberal and different from any other I had taught. The open campus policy was similar to a college or university. Teachers as well as students had the liberty to leave the campus if they were free from classes.

As Christmas rolled around the band started practicing the usual Christmas music. At one rehearsal a couple of girls asked if we could play Hanukkah music. My casual reply was, "I'll look and see if we have any in the music library." After a couple of days the same girls asked again and I told them I had not found any yet. That same day the principal called for me in his office. He sat behind a table, instead of the traditional desk. This gentle mannered man very politely asked if I was planning to play some Hanukkah music at the Christmas concert. I honestly told him we did not have any in our music library. He patiently explained that the predominant Jewish community would expect Hanukkah music at the concert. Then he suggested that a Jewish teacher on staff might be able to help me. The teacher was very helpful and he loaned me a hardback book full of Jewish songs including Hanukkah. But what I needed was a full score band arrangement. The principal then suggested that I contact the supervisor of music for the school district, which I did. The supervisor told me not to worry; he would order that music from Hoyt's Music Company in San Francisco. I finally received the Hanukkah music. It would be appropriate for the occasion even though it was a very simple arrangement written for a beginning band.

The Star-Spangled Banner still remained unpopular at that school. We also had a classy stage band that would perform from time to time. On one occasion we were invited to play at Adlai Stevenson Junior High in Mountain View. This is where my son Ricky went to school. The school responded well to the swinging sounds of the band. And when we let Ricky sing a song, the kids roared and gave him a huge round of applause. He became quite popular with his high-pitched child soprano voice.

Meanwhile we were enjoying our little duplex in Mountain View which was located about thirty-eight miles south of San Francisco. We were surprised to discover an insignificant little tree in our small back yard that started bearing almond nuts. It was small but it gave a very generous yield. We were beginning to believe the stories of how fruitful California was. One day Mayra's little friend Debbie, who lived across from our duplex, invited us to help pick apricots from her tree. We were amazed to see how apricots grew in clusters, just like grapes. What a treat that was! Surprisingly, none of these plants or trees were cared for or cultivated.

Another thing that was surprising was that gigantic dirigible hangar at Moffett Naval Air Station in Sunnyvale. This is where the Lord in His goodness led me to a part-time weekend job managing a bowling alley.

No matter where we went Ricky always managed to get involved - whether it be sports or music, he was in the middle of it. In a *City of Mountain View Parks and Recreation Department Basketball Tournament*, Ricky's team from Stevenson, was awarded first place. This was in March of 1973, when Ricky was twelve years old. It was in Mountain View where he was first baptized. Kirby Scarborough was the zealous pastor of Mountain View Baptist Church where we attended. It was a small church which met in one of the near by duplexes.

One Sunday after the service, we all walked a couple of blocks to a big church where we had permission to use their baptistery. The pastor asked Ricky if he would please assist with managing the towels for the people who were being baptized. We sat in the congregation watching the proceedings. And before we knew it, here comes Ricky wading into the baptistery. The pastor announced that he had made a profession of faith and had agreed to be baptized. Well, that was a surprise to all of us. I'm sure Ricky didn't know the real meaning of baptism at that time., and a little friendly persuasion from the pastor made this happen.

We were really enjoying this cool colorful area of northern California. We made several trips to San Francisco to visit some of my dad's cousins, Virginia and Tino Frausto. Our very first trip to see the Golden Gate Bridge was a big disappointment. It was completely enveloped by a thick fog! Of course we were thoroughly captivated by the Oakland Bay Bridge, and many others in the bay area. We also visited our cousins, Jeanie and Dan Cruz in San Jose, a few miles south of Mountain View. Another time we took a trip down to Los Angeles to visit uncles and aunts. On the way there we stuffed ourselves with strawberries, which were being sold along the road (Highway 101). Those strawberries were tantalizing, but they affected our stomachs in a very peculiar way when we reached our destination.

The folks back home were hoping we would soon make a one-way trip to San Antonio. Because my wife was not completely well, I was torn between going back to Hawaii, staying in California, or going to San Antonio. After the exchange position in Palo Alto for the school year, 1972 to 1973, I decided to stay in California; but I needed to find a job. I resigned my position in Hawaii, and notified them that I would not be returning. I reimbursed the DOE in Hawaii with the return airfare fee. After much prayer and laboring over applications, I landed a band director's position in the Pajaro Valley Unified School District. I was assigned to Rolling Hills Middle School. That was a year-round experimental school – an interesting and peculiar situation. This was very characteristic of California's progressive innovative school system. However, I could not help but notice the distinct difference between this school and the middle school in Palo Alto where I had taught the year before. The general attitude was friendlier. The staff, the teachers, and even the students provided a more pleasant working environment.

WATSONVILLE, CALIFORNIA, 1973-1974

So, I moved my family to Watsonville, a small agricultural community just a few miles south of Santa Cruz. Some called it the artichoke capital of the world. Apples and strawberries among other fruit and vegetables were visible everywhere you drove. In our backyard, cherry tomatoes were growing like weeds. And a big shady cherry tree adorned the middle of the backyard. Again, I took no credit for any of this – the Lord has blessed California with fertile ground and favorable weather, which causes plant life to flourish! The Cortez family was sojourning and enjoying new territories. Ricky started school at nearby E.A. Hall Middle School. He immediately signed up for band and was assigned to the drum section. Mayra and Ruby started at Minnie White Elementary, just a block away. At the near by church, Mayra was blessed to have a kindly lady "prayer partner." She was very sweet, and showered Mayra with praises and gifts. And, this is the year Ruby learned to ride solo on her bike, that is, after I was out of breath. I almost wore out my shoes running next to her. She was shocked the day that I was running along side of her and she realized I was not holding the bike. We were proud of her accomplishment at the ripe age of six.

Ricky and I used to ride our bikes along a levee right next to rows and rows of strawberries. One day, Ricky and his little friend Ron, came back with a large bag full of those strawberries. He claimed the farmer had given them permission to help themselves. At first I was little skeptical, but ultimately I took his word. In fact, not too long after that, he proved his honesty in a real sense. He found a small coin purse, full of money, on his newly acquired newspaper route. He showed it to me, and I explained that we needed to make an effort to find the owner. He agreed! So we went to the location where he had found it. We went to the house that was closest to where the purse was found. Sure enough, this gentle lady that came out, gave a thorough description of the purse, and the exact amount of money that was in it. She gave a big sigh of relief when we returned it. She was very grateful, especially because it was her mother's grocery money. So, Ricky was rewarded in more than one way. This was a lesson in honesty, which would remain with him for life.

Besides riding our bikes, Ricky and I would play catch on the school playground. We both liked running. Sometimes we would compete against each other. But, one day he surprised me and left me far behind. My thighs were burning when I tried to catch up. Now I knew that I was going to have tough competition with this young stallion.

Occasionally, I would take the family to the nearby beach, which was mostly long stretches of sand, with no development, and very few people. Santa Cruz, which was known for its beautiful beach, boardwalk, and seaside attractions, was about six miles down the road from us. Another activity the family enjoyed in the small town of Watsonville was the city roller-skating rink. We got pretty proficient on the skates.

When school opened, I was introduced to Rolling Hills Middle School, a very interesting school. It was an all-year-round school, referred to as 45 – 15. The children attended school for forty-five days, and were off for fifteen. Since this was done on a rotating system, it did not affect me as band director. I had students all the time. Some even came during their off days to practice and do some catching up. There was a little girl that always followed me around. Even when I was alone, she would turn up unexpectedly. Even though she didn't talk much, I had to shoo her away. The peculiar and confusing thing is that her identical twin sister did not recognize me or even talk to me when I mistakenly greeted her on the playground. Anyway, students who were slow on their academics could also come on their off days and be tutored.

The movie "M*A*S*H" was popular at this time, and the theme was one of our favorites in our band repertoire. Once again, I was learning the importance and prominence given to teachers in California. As a music teacher, I was part of the Fine Arts Department at Rolling Hills. I was also on a small committee that interviewed, and recommended new teachers for that department.

Things were going well, and as a member of the Federation of Teachers Union, I would get periodic bulletins on negotiations between the school board and the union. Gradually disputes and discussions within the school system started accelerating and heating up. After continuous negotiations with the school board, teacher meetings where held with both unions – The Federation of Teachers and the Teacher's Association. The whole thing came to an impasse. The teachers went on strike! On the second day of the strike, the newspaper printed the story on the front page. The article included some of the militant teachers' pictures picketing with signs in front of a school. Right in the middle was a brand new teacher to the district – Richard Cortez. Finally, both sides of the bargaining table decided on an outside arbitrator. After three days the dust had settled, and we were back in our classrooms. I had a band director friend who had crossed the picket line during the strike. These were called Scabs. Now he was the most unpopular teacher in his school. He had feared jeopardizing his retirement, which would come in the near future. I realized how awkward this position had to be for my friend.

I had fought the idea of returning to San Antonio. Recognizing that I was being stubborn and seeking my own will, I prayed to God for wisdom. I resigned my position at Rolling Hills Middle School after one year, and made plans to head for San Antonio. We shipped some of our furniture and valuables, and I bought a beautiful gold colored Plymouth station wagon to drive home. I knew we needed a good car for the long trip. We had a smooth uneventful ride most of the way. We did have an unexpected experience on the trip. I decided to take a pleasant sleep break surrounded by the beauty of the Grand Canyon National Park. Hey, when the sun went down it started getting cool, than colder, than much colder. We did not anticipate that! We had no coats, no blankets, and were totally unprepared. I had no choice but to continue driving into the night.

Ruby, Mayra and Ricky

CHAPTER 21
BACK IN SAN ANTONIO

Once in San Antonio, we visited all our family and loved ones. We had great reunions. We decided to stay at Mama Gollita's (my mother-in-law) house. As time went by Lupita's condition worsened. Her mental state was one of confusion. Her brother-in-law, who loved and cared very much for her, recommended a psychiatrist. We visited this doctor, and he diagnosed her with depression. He suggested we place her at Villa Rosa Hospital for rehabilitation. This was primarily a hospital for people with mental problems. The atmosphere here was very peaceful and restful. On visits we took walks along neatly manicured lawns and under shady trees. I had a heavy burden for Lupita. She had an unusual illness; I was without a job and without a home for my family. I began to get discouraged and depressed at what was going on! I had made a profession of faith many years back, but my faith now was seriously shaken. In fact, one day I started shaking. I had uncontrollable trembling, and I felt weird sensations under my fingernails. I felt like something evil had taken over my body, and my mind was unable to control it. I didn't realize it at that time but I was having an anxiety attack. I asked for my older brother Danny who came and took me to his house. I'll never forget – he was like a guardian angel. He placed me in Eddie's (his son) bed. I had calmed down a little, but I felt tired and weary. A strange fear of death had gripped me! I was falling asleep, and I was certain that I was going to die that night. The next day Danny took me to Dr. Gossett. I was in complete submission to anyone or anything at that particular time. I had never experienced such extreme depression. I truly felt I had gone through the valley of the shadow of death. God, in His goodness and mercy, put me back together again! After thirty days, the doctor released my wife from the hospital. She too had improved, so she came home. I was greatly relieved. My heart and mind were at peace. I felt like the Lord had pulled me out of a deep dark hole. I was reminded of Corrie Ten Boom's words, "There is no pit so deep that God's love is not deeper still."

My task now was submitting applications and praying the Lord would lead me to a decent band director position. The Harlandale School District called me in for an interview. In the process of the interview, the administrator asked if I knew George Aguilar. I replied, "Yes, he was one of my former band students at Natalia High School." He said, "I'm glad to hear that, because he is also applying for this job." That made my day, even though I didn't get that particular position. I remembered this student well because he had been brave enough to take up the bass clarinet in my band. It was incredibly rewarding to hear that one of my former students had taken up the career of band directing.

As it turned out, I was fortunate to get a band director's job at Harris Middle School in the San Antonio Independent School District. By God's providence, I was placed in a school very close to my mother-in-law's house, where we were staying. This was a small school, but a friendly environment. The band room was a portable building, which was separated from the main building and the auditorium. This was the first time that my son and daughter attended the same school where I taught. In fact, they both played in the band. Ricky played drums, and Mayra played flute. Ruby started out at Collins Garden Elementary School. I was satisfied that at least I had landed a job in San Antonio.

One horrible tragedy at Harris remains in my memory. One day during recess, one little boy jumped a school chain link fence to retrieve a ball. He accidentally fell in an uncovered manhole, which was covered over by weeds. He completely disappeared from sight! Firemen and rescue people searched, but no one was able to find him. A week later his body was found near the sewer plant.

While visiting the San Antonio School District Office, I ran into a friend whom I knew from elementary school. In conversation I mentioned that I was temporarily at Harris Middle School, but looking for a more permanent position. It turned out he was president of the school board. He suggested I talk to a certain administrator about a possible opening in another school. Lo and behold, before I knew it, I was being interviewed by Mr. Tom Valdez, the principal of Tafolla Middle School. So, this was the beginning of a long experience at one of the best-equipped band rooms in any San Antonio school district. I started teaching there in September of 1974.

My family was getting used to the idea that we needed to settle down in San Antonio. This was a topic that my dad was always concerned about. I thought of him on our first visit to my mother's house. I sat in his well-worn comfortable recliner, and immediately I felt a surge of deep grief and broke down into uncontrollable sobbing. It was the same mournful feeling I had when I first heard of his death, when I was in Hawaii.

TAFOLLA MIDDLE SCHOOL – AUGUST, 1974 -1988

Tafolla Middle School was cattycorner from Lanier High School.

Johnny Rodriguez, a longtime friend, was the band director there. Naturally we had a good working relationship, especially since most of Tafolla's band students would end up in his band in the near future. I could write a separate book just on my experiences at Tafolla. The band room was a band director's dream. It looked new and very clean, with a spacious practice area, two instrument storage rooms,

and a music library room. There was good lighting with plenty of windows. There was a slightly raised platform for the director's desk, and music stand, and behind that was plenty of chalkboard. The school auditorium was conveniently connected to the band room. One door would take us into the auditorium stage where we could move our equipment easily and quickly for concerts, rehearsals, and many band activities.

One week of preparation and teachers meetings were finally over. The first few days there was much commotion. The halls were filled with kids scurrying about the school, looking for their classrooms

1982 BEGINNING BAND

and lockers.

At the beginning of school, sixth graders from the elementary schools begin to converge on Tafolla. I was encouraged seeing the enthusiasm of the sixth grade beginning band students. Many were familiar with our band program since I had visited their schools. Near the end of the each school year I would give musical aptitude tests to all interested 5th graders. Plus, our band played Christmas concerts at most of these feeder elementary schools, which included Margil, J.T. Brackenridge, and Rhodes.

Beginning band was challenging but fun for me. It was somewhat tedious breaking in these future musicians. Most preferred the drums and trumpet. I had to make instrument assignments by encouraging, motivating and convincing each student, that he (or she) was best suited for a particular instrument. The size, hands, arms, and lips of a person might determine what that person might do best in. If a student had large lips, I might say that God had gifted him with generous lips to play the tuba. Smaller lips in most cases did well on a small mouthpiece, like a trumpet, or French horn, etc. If a student showed real interest in a particular "horn," I would give him (or her) the opportunity to try it out. Part of the training involved the task of learning to put the instrument together, cleaning, oiling, and general care. Now they had to know how to hold it, how to "blow" into it, and how to sit properly.

Discipline was definitely necessary when you're trying to teach thirty to forty kids at the same time. Each section was required to practice putting the instrument together, or going over the music mentally, while I would instruct another section. Good beginning band method books are very helpful. They cover and discuss music theory, rhythm, and the make up of the different instruments. My goal with all children learning music, regardless of the instrument, was to get them to enjoy and appreciate music. One motivational phrase that I tried to instill in them, as they improved, was to play "music" not just notes on the page. Music comes from the heart, an inward desire that makes it a fun thing.

Music is called the universal language because it can be heard and enjoyed in any country regardless of nationality. It is an esthetic art form that transcends all languages. It can be enjoyed by infants, even before birth, the aged, the blind and other handicap individuals. Many adults claim they are not musically inclined. Then I arbitrarily remind them that God made us all with a rhythmical body. First of all, we have a very important organ that beats perfect rhythm – the heart (the bass drum), which keeps us alive as long as the rhythm is there. When you walk (normally), your arms and feet move rhythmically without your even thinking about it. Music is primarily made up of melody, harmony, and rhythm.

One day something very awkward occurred during practice in the band room. When the six-grade beginner's band was playing, one little girl flute player in the first row begin to wet herself. She dutifully continued playing while the urine dripped on the floor under her chair. I knew I had to do something fast, but continued directing. Fortunately the girl next to her was bright and alert and was aware of the situation. I very discreetly gave her a head signal and turned it toward the restroom. She got up and very casually wrapped her sweater around the waist of her little neighbor. They walked out without drawing attention, and huge embarrassment was avoided while the band continued playing. There was never a dull moment at Tafolla!

By December this band would be prepared to play at least three or four numbers for the Christmas concert. After a concert, I might receive interesting comments. Some teacher would come up and ask - "How in the world did you get Joey to sit still for five minutes?" My most common response was usually, "You place something in his mouth to keep him quiet." In reality, most kids enjoyed the challenge, and the discipline that came with the program.

I recall a lively boy who played clarinet in the Intermediate Band (7th grade). I encouraged him because I could tell he had natural talent. Besides the clarinet, he could pick up other instruments with ease. He didn't seem to understand when I tried to explain that he had gift for music. He didn't seem to care. He was playful and wasted his time. Instead of continuing in the concert band the following year, he dropped out.

Another more positive situation was a youngster who did exceptionally well on the saxophone the first year. He very politely informed me that he could not continue the next year. I was disappointed! His mother explained that he was happy in band, but that art was his primary gift. He had excelled in art in elementary school and felt he wanted to continue with "his first love." I felt like a coach who has just lost his first string quarterback.

TAFOLLA MIDDLE SCHOOL BAND

The concert band was constantly involved in University Interscholastic League (UIL) contests – Solo, Ensemble, and Concert Band. We were the proud Tafolla Toro Band, with the colorful red shirts and black pants. We had many talented and conscientious students in this band. They were well behaved and took pride in their band. At the end of the year concert, merit awards were presented to the most deserving young musicians. Most did well in their academic work. In fact, several were members of the National Junior Honor Society.

I remember one student who joined the band with his left arm in a cast. Because of his broken arm he was unable to play the instrument he loved - the Baritone Saxophone. However, as another option, he asked to try the trumpet. He progressed well on the trumpet, which did not require the use of all his fingers. This tenacious kid, picked up the baritone saxophone (a huge instrument) the fol-

lowing year, and was a positive inspiration to the others.

His performance was outstanding with the band, and he received first place awards at UIL solo contest. This was just one example among many that made my job very gratifying. The long hours of practice, lecturing, and encouraging, paid off with very satisfying results. Some youngsters were even willing to come practice in the band room during their lunch hour. Others just liked hanging out in the band room. Many times we had sectional rehearsals after school, then they would jump in my pickup truck for a ride home. One time

I gave one of my top clarinet players a ride home and found out she lived way outside the school district.

One of the most fun things for the band kids was the annual Christmas concerts at the three feeder elementary schools. We would pile up into my Ford pickup with music stands, the larger instruments, and the music folders, and a few students. The others would ride with a counselor and teacher volunteers. We would get the elementary kids all excited by playing a march when they filed in. We entertained them with all the popular Christmas songs. We would even do some sing-a-longs. The most popular song was "Feliz Navidad." Everybody loved that!

J.T. Brackenridge, was the largest elementary school in San Antonio at that time. Mrs. Tobin, the principal, and Mr. Henry Cantu, the vice principal, always showed their gratitude and Christmas spirit by treating the band kids with cake and chocolate.

It was about this time that Juan and Belle started teaching mariachi music at our school. They would have sessions after school once a week for anyone willing to participate. This idea became very popular and spread not only to high schools, but also to middle schools.

Several of my versatile band students later became reputable mariachi musicians.

I was surprised one day when a school counselor came in and asked me for a favor. There was an older and bigger boy who was quiet but had a subtle manner of taking advantage of smaller kids in the classrooms. I was given the "opportunity" to work with this supposedly troublesome boy. It wasn't uncommon for behavioral problem students to be "dumped" in some elective as an alternate measure. Since band is an elective, the counselor approached me with "accolades" for the band program.

He felt the discipline learned in band might be able to help this boy. I took the challenge and was pleased that this man had confidence in me. This boy liked the drums so I thought it might come easy to him. I was wrong! After explaining that he had a bass drum in his chest (heart), that beats a constant rhythm day and night, and that even when he walks he walks in rhythm. I gave him some rhythm lessons using the bass drum. We played it repeatedly so he could get the feel of it. I clapped and beat the rhythm by stomping my foot over and over and over. I tapped him on the shoulder repeatedly while he was playing the bass drum. I would play the snare drum while he beat the bass drum. It seemed like an impossible task for him to get a steady rhythm. Then I got him to play along with a march record. After many weeks of individual lessons he started to "get the beat." I took a chance of having him practice with the beginning band. Lo and behold, he dove right in like fish into water. He became enamored with that bass drum and would not move away from it. He was now a serious and responsible musician playing in the Intermediate Band. From that time on, there were no further complaints with his behavior.

There was an occasion when the counselor brought another interesting student and asked if I could help. Rosie was a cute little sixth grader who could not get adjusted to middle school life. Being accustomed to the secure elementary school atmosphere, this new school was alarming. The long hallways lined with lockers on both sides, changing and scrambling to different classrooms, and different teachers for each class were just overwhelming for little Rosie. So, she would quietly hide in restrooms or behind doors or where ever she could find a little refuge. Sometimes she would walk home and hide in the garage. Out of desperation her parents placed her in a private school. That did not solve her insecure problem. She was brought back to Tafolla with a new strategy in mind. Asked what her favorite subjects were, she replied, "band and office." That's where I came into the picture. I was asked if I was willing to take her in. After some consideration and feeling sorry for this troubled kid, I took the challenge! She was very cute and eager to learn. I gave her the opportunity to play the instrument of her choice - the clarinet. She was a slow learner, but I was just pleased that she was coming to school regularly. The rest of her time was spent running errands for the school secretary.

After some months went by, the Solo and Ensemble Contest was approaching. All the students were selecting and diligently practicing their music. Well, little Rosie was not about to be left out. She persuaded me into starting her out on a solo. I thought to myself, "I'm supposed to encourage her!" To leave her out while everyone else was learning solos would be devastating, especially now that she was beginning to like school. So the day came that all the kids had been waiting for.

Contest day was filled with excitement. Each student would play his or her solo individually before a judge. Some got top ratings; others did fair. Yells and screams of joy could be heard when some got their medals and written critiques. A few were disappointed for not doing better. But the greatest disappointment was when Rosie got her written results. Her judge was merciless with his criticism. He wrote strong and harsh comments with red marks all over her music. One remark that was most painful read, "She had no business entering the contest." I tried to comfort her by saying that it was her first contest and that next year would be better. My decision to let her play in that contest and the consequences that followed has always been on my conscience. Had I made the right decision? There was one consolation, SHE STAYED IN SCHOOL!

We were able to lend out school instruments for beginning students for the first year. If they progressed well, I would let the parents know and recommend that they buy or rent an instrument. One day after school, several students including a band student with his trombone were waiting for the bus on Buena Vista Street. A car stalled right in front of these youngsters. They were willing to help this husband and wife who were pushing the car on a hot summer afternoon. In a gesture of kindness, the lady agreed to take care of their books while they helped push. When the kids finally returned, the lady was gone and so was the trombone. It was recovered in a downtown pawnshop a year later.

My principal Mr. Abbott, a tall, mild mannered man, was a great supporter of the band program. If any band related complaints ever came to his office, he would simply direct them to Mr. Cortez - "That is HIS department." he would say.

Mr. Abbott, I'm sure, felt privileged to have our school chosen for a pilot multilingual program. Qualified students from all over the district would be bussed to Tafolla every day. This was an intensified foreign language program, where students would learn one of five foreign languages (Spanish, Japanese, French, Latin, and German). Before long these select students were competing against college students and doing real well. Always looking for mature responsible students, I was able to draw some of these to the band room. This was somewhat of a boost to the band because these were top students from throughout the city.

The Tafolla band parents club deserves a lot of credit for their hard work and long hours preparing and organizing fund raisers for the band. For about three years our school hosted the All-District Solo and Ensemble Contest. The food and drinks sold by the band parents during these events was abundantly profitable.

At one of our school band concerts, we featured a small combo, consisting of Coach Al Rhodes on electric guitar, Joel (a special education student) on drums, and Mr. Harrington on piano. The students went wild, mainly for two reasons – Coach Rhodes would twist his electric Guitar around the back of his neck, while his body would shake, rattle, and roll. And two, Joel who was supposed to be mentally slow, surprised everyone with fantastic rock and roll rhythms on the drum set. After this, he became very popular in school.

When I first went to Tafolla, it was regarded as a junior high school, and the grades went from seventh through ninth. A short time later they changed it into a middle school, and the grades went from sixth to eight. Unfortunately, there would be no graduation ceremonies for the eight graders at the end of the year. There would simply have an awards and promotion assembly.

It was customary for the graduating class to go on a field trip at the end of the school year. That had been discontinued because of a tragedy. On one trip to Landa Park in New Braunfels, two students drowned in the lake while riding the paddleboats. One boy accidentally fell in. When he failed to come out, his friend jumped in to help him. He too failed to come out and drowned. Other kids that watched claimed they were entangled in heavy seaweed and unable to free themselves. One of them was a saxophone player in my band. This was an extremely sad time for the whole school. Many of their friends were grief stricken. Graduation was a mournful occasion as the drowned students who would have graduated were recognized.

CHAPTER 22
RARE MOMENTS AT TAFOLLA

As a teacher in a school environment I could always expect the unexpected. Another year before graduation something extraordinary occurred at Tafolla. Nearing the end of a school year, four astute eighth-grade boys had a bright idea. Since they felt deprived of a graduation ceremony, they put their heads and their money together. On the last day of school they arrived in front of the school in a large black shiny limousine. As the morning crowd gaped in awe, the four stepped out, wearing black tuxedos (long-tailed), white bow ties - the complete outfit. This brought a "moment of dignity" and amazement to this school, which was on the west side, located in a lower economic area. They naturally impressed everyone in the school as they marched regally from class to class in their dazzling apparel. The lunchroom crowd was surprised and stared in astonishment as the four young "gentlemen" stepped in line to get their meal in their elegant attire. After school they were promptly picked up by the same limo. This was a rare moment, never to be forgotten at Tafolla Middle School.

Another one of those rare moments at Tafolla involved a vice principal whose office was broken into and partially burned. He claimed this happened because his office was easily assessable to breaking in. The fact was this V.P. was very unpopular. Everyone knew him as the grouchy school disciplinarian. This man's attitude was harsh, bitter, and very demanding. He had no love for kids! During lunch in the cafeteria, he would shout into his megaphone, or blow his whistle as loud as he could for the kids to leave when they were finished. He did not have any children of his own, and he claimed, "This is just a job!"

Wednesdays were always very special at Tafolla, mainly because the cafeteria serves Mexican food on that day. There were very few absentees on that day. It was not unusual for the counselors to schedule testing on that day knowing the majority of the children would attend.

Most of the teachers at Tafolla were considerate and compassionate.

Some would voluntarily tutor weak or slow learners after school or during their free time. There was good rapport among the teaching staff. Teacher's meetings were never popular but were part of school life that had to be tolerated. There was always good communication and discussion of common problems during lunch in the teacher's lounge. I had many friends, but I have to admit, much of the time I was cooped up in the band room. There was the arrangement and management of music, instruments, music stands, lesson plans, and private sessions with students who needed tutoring.

One year Mr. Abbott cautioned the teachers to be extra diligent because we were to have a high-level administrator hovering over us for one year. The school district introduced a new plan. There would be three administrative assistants from the district office assigned to three schools. We were "privileged" to have one assigned to our school. She came and opened her office on the second floor and would roam about at will. She was respectable and the symbol of authority. On one occasion, she reached the top of the stairs on the second floor, turned left and spotted a teacher just as he was about to "tee off." He was practicing his golf swing right outside his classroom. It was quite embarrassing to the principal who was right next to her. He would have preferred the earth swallow him at that moment.

While eating my lunch in the teacher's dining room one day, this lady administrator came and sat next to me. Her face looked familiar, and I came up with the proverbial remark, "Pardon me, but you look vey familiar." Her immediate response was, "You SHOULD remember me Richard, your band played at my wedding." Wow, what a surprise! I had played for a lot of weddings in the past! Then, I finally remembered. Years back, a beautiful gal had married a young postal clerk, whom I had worked with at the post office. I thought, "What a small world!"

Another time a student came running frantically to the band room. As he tried to catch his breath he quickly explained that a student and a substitute teacher were fighting. I ran from the band room to the choir room, which was just at the other end of the hall. Sure enough, the young male substitute was grappling with this combative student and trying to get a hold on him to take him to the principal's office. I grabbed one of the student's arms and he pulled but did not attempt to fight me. He tried to wrestle himself free from the substitute by pulling, kicking, dragging his feet and cussing. This went on from the second floor all the way to the first floor. We released him right in front of the office. At this point, he deliberately dropped himself on the floor throwing some kind of tantrum just as the bell rang. By this time the principal, vice principal, and a couple of office staff tried to pick him up and calm him. It was between classes so the hall was full of students, who curiously slowed down, gawking and wondering what the ruckus was all about. It was sheer pandemonium, that's what it was! Later I found out this student had a nervous condition that would flare up easily when provoked. Of course, the substitute was not aware of this. Mrs. Hernandez, the regular music teacher and choir director, was out that day. Everyone liked her, and she did a super job with the kids, and the choir. I never saw that substitute again.

Tafolla Concert Band
Director Richard Cortez

THE MYSTERY OF THE BROKEN TOILET PAPER DISPENSER

The choir room and the band room were on the second floor and were separated by a long hallway. In between was a back-to-back girl's and boy's restrooms. Several times I had noticed that the toilet paper dispenser in the boy's restroom was broken and just dangling. I was sure the janitor would fix it, without question! Then one day a girl came out of that girl's restroom crying hysterically and could hardly talk. A friend of hers explained that there were "peeping toms" looking into the girl's restroom. To get a clearer picture of what they were talking about I went to investigate. Sure enough, the boy's restroom toilet paper dispenser was broken again! And this time, there were footprints on the wall leading up to loose tiles on the ceiling. Lifting one tile the snoopers could look down into the girl's restroom.

About this time the bell rang, and a girl surprised everyone by running and screaming toward her boyfriend in the hallway. She proceeded to slap and beat him, accusing him of being one of the peeping toms. This was the beginning of an interesting and curious investigation! The boy who was attacked by his girlfriend in the hallway was not about to take all the blame. Bruised and ashamed, he had to appear before the principal. There, he was "persuaded" to name two other curious peeping toms. All three were interrogated in the principal's office, separately, and collectively. Finally, one was bold enough to admit that the whole thing was his idea. This peeping tom episode would be the topic of conversation at Tafolla for a long time. The custodian who was responsible for that restroom later mentioned to me that he too had been baffled by the frequency of those broken toilet tissue dispensers. It had been a mystery to both of us! But the mystery was finally solved.

RHODES DRIVING SCHOOL – 1981 -2001

Al Rhodes, one of the coaches at Tafolla, owned a private driving school. Both he and his wife Janice operated Rhodes Driving Schools. They had six schools throughout the city. I couldn't resist an attractive offer that Al made me. He asked if I would teach teenagers Driver's Ed. in my spare time. I could do this on weekends and summers while teaching full time. The first thing I had to do is complete a course in driver education in San Marcos, Texas. When I first started teaching I had to use my own car. Later, cars were provided as the company grew. In spite of the visible "Student Driver" signs on the front and rear of my car, we were still rear ended at least three times.

Rhodes Driving School Instructors

Fortunately no one was ever hurt, but it gave the students the experience of calling and responding to the police and getting the paper work done. For safety's sake, I would take first time beginner drivers to practice on a school parking lot, or some other available area. Then gradually I would "promote" them to more busy streets. The "panic" brake on the instructor's side came in handy many times. I had picked up lots of tips at the instructor's licensing school in San Marcos, Texas.

Ben Ramon was the first instructor at Rhodes to break me in as a "rookie." We became good friends after that. I instructed beginning students on the necessity of checking under the hood- the fluids, belts, and tire pressure. I recall one "slow" student who was going on her last lesson in my car. She kept reminding me that she had not driven on the expressway. I said, "Okay, we will do it!" As I glanced at the rearview mirror inside the car, I could see the two boys in the rear seat motioning frantically with their hands, "Don't do it, don't do it!" Well, we entered the expressway, stayed in the right lane and took the very first exit to satisfy the student and comply with expressway driving. The big challenge for most student drivers was parallel parking. After teaching youngsters in the car for several years and suffering hair loss, I decided defensive driving in the classroom might be better.

So I started teaching adults who took the class to have driving violation tickets dismissed. They would also get a ten percent discount on their auto insurance. Most came in with long faces, knowing this was going to be a long boring six hours. Plus, some felt this was unfair punishment for such a "small thing." They gave every excuse under the sun to justify their situation. Some would put the blame on the officer or the judge. I would simply ask, "Is this the first time you've broken the law?" Most of the time I would get dead silence. There were always some that felt the need to defend themselves.

Some acknowledged their guilt. All kinds of excuses were given which were common in every class. On the road we all break the law, either intentionally or unintentionally. Once in a while we get caught!

The six-hour defensive driving class was practical and beneficial! To keep those in the back row awake I would target them with surprise questions. Once I made the mistake of asking a friend to wake up his neighbor sitting next to him. His reply was "You put him to sleep. You wake him up!" For the most part, I kept them well informed using auto crash films and having open discussions. Of course, the bloody scenes where usually the most popular. I had to struggle with those large reel to reel movies. I was very content and continued there even after I retired from public school teaching. All together I remained with Rhodes for twenty years.

THE 80'S AT 208 W. LIGUSTRUM

The 80s were exciting and eventful years. Our homestead was now at 208 W. Ligustrum Street. The Lord providentially brought us to this house. After a couple of days of searching for a house with our realtor, we were getting a little discouraged. In the late afternoon of the third day, we left the realtor and drove off in our own car. As we drove on Ligustrum Street, we noticed a "For Sale" sign on a house. It read "For Sale by Owner." Lupita didn't think it was a good idea to stop there since we didn't have an appointment. Though we were a little tired, we were encouraged to stop for just brief information. Lo and behold, the lady was a realtor and she graciously invited us in to look around. We immediately fell in love with this house. It was perfectly designed for our size family with a spacious master bedroom, a large bedroom for Mayra and Ruby, and a back bedroom for Rick. This was the beginning of a new era for the Cortez family.

Ruby started going to Woodlawn Hills Elementary School. Mayra was now part of the flute section at Longfellow Middle School and enjoying her new school. Rick was testing the Band Director's nerves as a drummer in the Jefferson High School Band. Rick claimed Mr. Van De Putte shouted louder than anyone he ever knew. Rick also got his kicks performing with the school's top notch Jazz Band. So, we as faithful and loyal band parents transported Rick to school every Friday evening. From there, the band together with the cheerleaders and pep squad were bused to Alamo Stadium. Oh, by the way, the football team also went along on separate buses, because it was FOOTBALL SEASON! This routine took place EVERY Friday evening during the football season. In fact, the football fever accelerated throughout the whole state. Some people questioned the benefit of thousands of dollars being pumped into football and other sports every year. Were the Academic subjects being sacrificed for sports? The justification by coaches and other sports figures was that sports events, especially football and basketball, brought in huge profits that benefited the schools.

Here are some "small" ways which this intense football fever affected my family. All our children, Rick, Mayra, and Ruby, were proud members of the Thomas Jefferson Mustang Band at one time or another. So, year after year, for many years, we drove them, cheered for them, and transported them back and forth from the school to the stadium. That did not include other activities such as contests, concerts, and parades. Then, tired and sleepy after the football games, we would all drive home amidst shouting and screaming from cars and buses. No matter who had won or lost, everybody shouted, "WE'RE NUMBER ONE!"

A couple of times I rode on a band bus with a band director friend. On the way back after a game everyone was shouting, "WE'RE NUMBER ONE!" I thought it strange, because this team never won any games. One night we drove Rick clear across town to Highland High School where he would perform with the All-City

Band. As we arrived there Rick discovered he had forgotten his music at home. So, dutiful daddy had to boogie on home clear across town to bring his music before his group played. Fortunately, the All-City Band was last on the program.

Rick had also picked up weight lifting and bodybuilding during his senior year. One day the coach saw him in the hallway and commented, "You should be out their on the football field hitting someone." Those were the magic words! He was now gripped with that football fever. His interest and enthusiasm persuaded the band director to release him from the band to play football just for the football season. The coach was in agreement! I admired Rick's zeal but reminded him that most of the football players had been playing since junior high school. And most had the experience of four years in high school football. In spite of this, he was not discouraged. He wanted to be part of the team! Well, he trained hard and had great expectations. True, he didn't play much; but the few times he played, he went in like a wild animal. At least that's what his playmates claimed. And I'm telling you, we would go wild in the stands when he was called to play. This football experience had both positive as well as negative effects on Rick.

We were equally proud to see both Mayra and Ruby marching and playing their flutes in the band, even though they were four years apart. Even though I was part of the educational system as a band director, I often questioned the money and hundreds of hours spent at cheerleader and pep squad camps. Band I could justify because it was a useful aesthetic art form. So, I was naturally surprised when Ruby decided to drop band and join the "distinguished" Jefferson Lassos (A glamorized pep squad!). She wanted a different experience, so she joined up her senior year. What I could not understand was, why did it take a whole summer (at camp) to learn a "few" routines, and how beneficial was all that yelling that goes on? I know it's fun getting together with your friends every day, and generating school spirit, and supporting the team.

I realize there was value in some of these extracurricular activities. The camaraderie, discipline, and teamwork, were worthy, and motivated some students to stay in school. That extracurricular activity might be the only reason a student might come to school. I discovered that when I was teaching in junior high schools. One "privilege" we received from Rick being on the football team was having our house decorated (inside and out), with colorful spirit signs, banners, and streamers right before a game.

BABES AND TOTS DAYCARE

On April 21, 1978, Lupita opened "Babes and Tots Group Daycare Home" for children, ages infancy through 13. There was a great need for child daycare centers after World War II. Mothers working outside the home became a new "phenomena." It took me a great deal of effort to acquire the daycare license for Lupita. First, I had to make an official request before the city zoning commission. Neighborhood surveys were taken and reviewed. The commission rejected our request, but I had the option of appealing that decision before the City Council. I decided to go for it! I was a little nervous as I entered City Hall that day. With carefully prepared and convincing statements the City Council approved. What a relief that was! For several years Lupita demonstrated her love for children and became very successful in dealing with the little ones, as well as the parents. Some toddlers became so attached to her that they bulked when their mothers came to pick them up after work. Babes and Tots became a family affair with our teenage children contributing and helping. We all became very fond of all those little ones running around the house, or bouncing in their cribs.

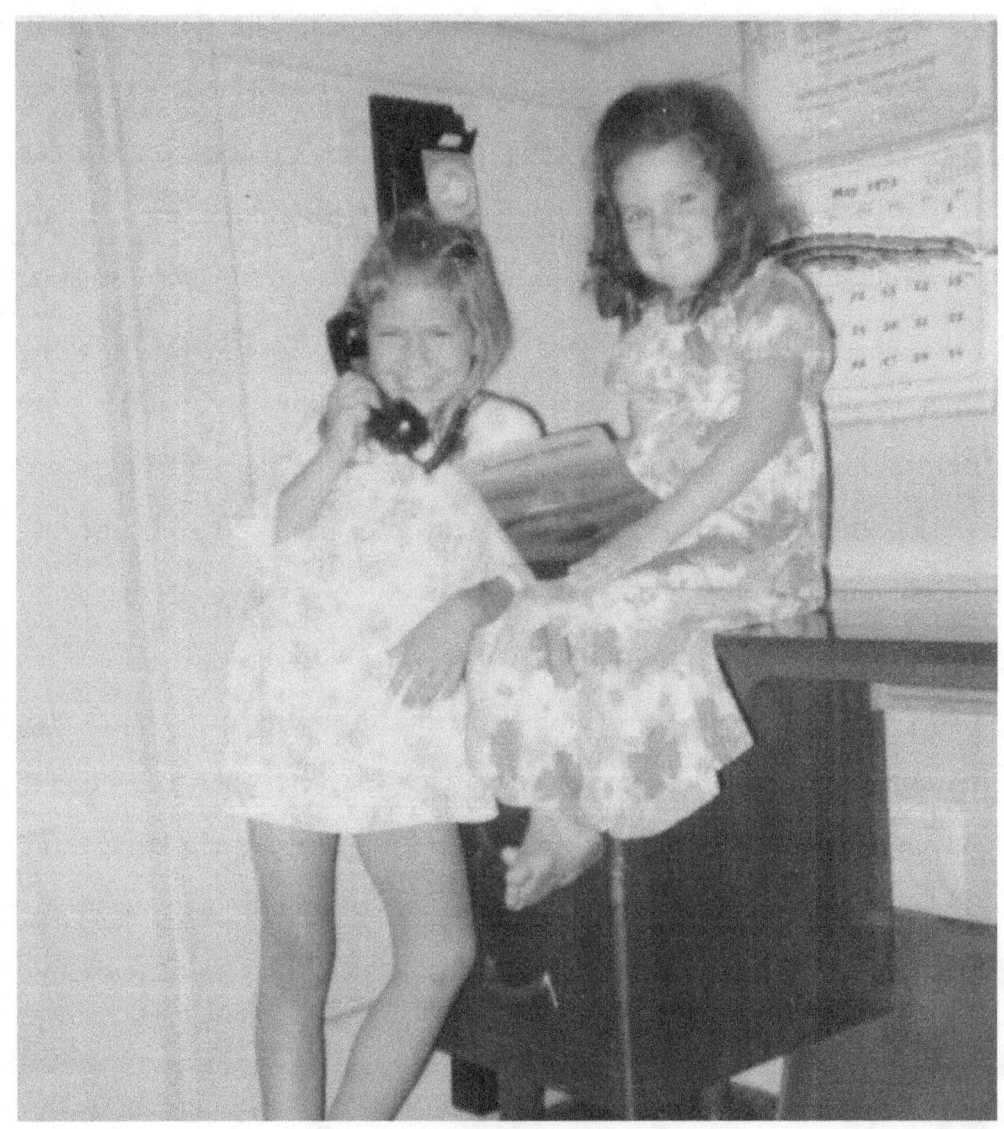

Mayra & Ruby

CHAPTER 23
CAMPING TRIPS

In 1980 we were still living at 208 W. Ligustrum, right around the corner from Vangie, Rudy (her husband), and their family. By this time our family had made several camping trips to Garner State Park. We had great times, swimming, hiking, climbing, and exploring. We used to rough it out when we first starting going there. We would sleep in our own tent, cook on our Coleman stove, and sometimes cook the meat on the grill. These times in the woods, when we really bonded with our kids. It was a wonderful time of living, learning, and growing. As time went on, we decided on the more comfortable screened shelters, with concrete slab floors. One night, we had an unexpected sudden cold front that blew in. So, out of desperation, we quickly set up our tent outside. That was a good idea because we were much warmer in the tent. However, as the years passed, we went for the more "luxurious" cabins, with beds, linen, appliances and dishes. At Garner, we discovered a cave (a big crack between huge boulders). To get to it we had to climb a "mountain" and walk along a very narrow ledge. The greater the risk, the more the kids enjoyed the challenge. Of course I was the valiant "fearless" leader. There was no way I could back out! Our brood was at an age where they enjoyed the outdoors, trips, camping, and swimming.

CAMPING WITH RICK AND EDDIE

On another trip to Garner, Rick, Eddie (his cousin), and I were getting ready to sack out after several long days. We had brought army cots to sleep in at night. Rick complained that he was hot and planned to sleep outside the tent. I warned him of dark heavy clouds that had been hanging around. "That's okay dad" he said. Then he stepped out of the tent carrying his cot. It was like a brewing storm didn't faze him. Around 5 a.m. in the morning we were awakened by strong winds, lightning, a crescendo of thunder, then suddenly heavy rain pouring down.

Eddie and I laughed as Rick quickly scrambled and fumbling to unzip the door to the tent to bring in his cot and blankets. After a while we were not laughing. A powerful storm was sweeping through the campgrounds with rain and whipping winds. We knew we had to get out of there fast– real fast! We quickly threw all our gear, our clothes, shoes, blankets, and folded cots into Rick's pickup. We struggled and were fighting against the torrential rain and wind as we tried to break down our tent. I'm sure we brought it down in record time! We quickly jumped into the pickup and drove off as fast as we could. We knew that park was known for getting flooded during heavy rains. We had our fun, and we laughed all the way home.

BASTROP STATE PARK

I recall another time when Rick and I took a trip to Bastrop State Park, east of Austin. We found a good camping site to set up our tent, and started unloading our stuff from Rick's pickup truck. As we drove the pegs into the ground and were stretching and setting up our tent, Rick sneezed. And he sneezed again! In fact, he seemed to be having a "sneeze attack." I knew he had a problem with allergies, and I was getting concerned. As we looked around, we discovered the culprit! We were inside a forest of pine trees. I told him we would stay over night and would have to go somewhere else if that problem continued. Thank God he seemed to have gotten over it by the next day. The next several days we spent the time just lounging around, reading, snacking and swimming. These types of trips with my son were fun, and made me feel young. Plus, these experiences created a stronger bond between the two of us.

HIKING IN GRAND CANYON -1980

That same year (1980), Rick and I decided we were ready to take on the Grand Canyon. I was a young 53 and Rick was a strong, healthy

Richard with his 150XLT Lariat Ford Truck

19. This was a trip to remember! We had long conversations on this rare and much anticipated trip. Driving through New Mexico, the "Land of Enchantment," we acknowledged why it derived that title. It was awe-inspiring! We had decided that Carlsbad Caverns would be a fun side trip on our way to the Canyon. The entrance to the

Cavern was typically commercial with souvenir shops, snack bar and lunchroom. Then we were ushered to an elevator. Wow, this was getting more interesting! We descended three stories under ground. It was a weird feeling, to say the least! Getting off the elevator, we entered into a huge dining area, like a food court in a big city mall. Next we tagged along with a group that was lead by a park ranger. He was going to be our tour guide through the caverns. Right about this time we begin to feel cool; and as we go farther in, it got colder and damp. But our eyes were wide open as we experienced this magnificent under ground wonderland. We were carefully trekking from one huge room to another gigantic room, with spectacular stalactite and stalagmite formations on the walls and ceilings. Exciting colorful lights were reflected off the hanging stalactites, which gave the appearance of chandeliers. Many were strategically located throughout the walls and ceilings, and bounced off the structures in a magical fashion. The path we were walking on was kept safe with railings in most places. There were some climbing rails along the ridges, and also very narrow holes and cracks where we had to crawl through. We were led through many awesome compartments of the caverns. Then came one of the intriguing points on the tour – all the lights were turned off! You could not see your hand in front of you. Total darkness– that was eerie! After the Caverns, we continued north toward Grand Canyon.

As we were getting closer to Grand Canyon National Park, we stopped at a quaint trading post (general store) right inside the little town of Flagstaff, Arizona. A cup of hot coffee warmed our bodies in that cold remote outpost. Before leaving, Rick went to the restroom while I waited in the car. Two young Indian boys (around 18 or 19), who appeared friendly, approached me. They offered me a fairly good backpack for five dollars. It sounded like a good deal to me, so I bought it, and they left. A short while later, three other Native-American Indian lads approached me, and asked about a backpack that was stolen. They naturally claimed the one I had was theirs. Just then, Rick comes out of the store with his shoulders looking much broader as he looked down from the store porch, and asked, "What's happening?" Then these three casually backed away from the car saying "We were just asking him a question." I was reminded of the cowboy and Indian movies I used to watch on T.V.

After some friendly farewells, we drove off. As we reached that spectacular Grand Canyon National Park, we circled around portions of the rim. The Canyon is known as a marvelous wonder of nature. But I knew that the rain, the Colorado River, the wind, erosion over the years, and other contributing factors had formed these huge depressions. It was all part of God's design in creation. The Visitor's Center was a beehive of activity with people scrambling in and out and buying all kinds of stuff. There were calendars, maps, pictures and souvenirs.

I was impressed at the number of visitors from so many different countries. We could overhear conversations in French, German, Russian, Spanish, and countless others. I got a hold of a good booklet that had a lot of valuable information for hikers going into the Canyon. So, when we got back to our tent, I got excited and started reading up on suggested supplies, equipment, and snacks to carry in your backpack. That night I eagerly stuffed my backpack with dried fruit, small cans of beans, fruit, celery, and all the other recommended supplies. In the cool brisk morning before sun up, I could see heads popping out of their tents like groundhogs. Men, women, children, all excited to start the day, going to the bathroom, showers, or preparing breakfast. As I was entering the men's shower stalls, I saw a young girl coming out, her hair rolled up in a towel and wet clothes under her arm. I looked at her with a puzzled look as we both looked up at the "Men's Shower" sign at the entrance. She just shrugged her shoulders with a casual "oh well" and walked away.

As we reached the rim where we would start, it was time to get our stuff out of the car. As we were getting our backpacks out of the car, Rick felt the load of my backpack, and said, "Wow dad, you've got to be kidding, that's entirely too heavy." So he dumped it all back in the car, except for the water. Later I was thankful he had done that! I started on the trail with a bottle of water in one hand and a stalk of celery in the other, and that was it! From the starting point, it was indeed a sight to behold – the majestic mountains all around, and the IMMENSITY of this huge Canyon cut out in the middle of this desert, and the small meandering Colorado River way down at the bottom of this huge depression. We found out later that this river was much larger than it appeared from above. I marveled at God's incredible creation, as the warm sun was beginning to rise in the horizon.

We followed the path that consisted of gravel and a curious zigzag trail. This zigzag pattern will be our greatest challenge when we struggle to get out later on. As we started on the trail, four tired and weary hikers were coming out - dragging their feet. Their only comment was - "NEVER AGAIN!" Right then I felt energetic, and was really enjoying the sights. Then Rick suggested we should go a little faster, because the mules where coming close behind us. And unfortunately there were no "super scoopers" out there. Some people preferred to ride the mules instead of walking. Those animals are surefooted in their walk and kept a very constant and steady pace. So sure enough, they caught up with us and we had to make room for them to pass. We just had to be extra careful were we stepped from then on. At one point along the hike, I had to get off the trail briefly to respond to my bladder. I thought I was well hidden behind some brush, until a park ranger a short distance away shouted "STAY ON THE TRAIL!" Then Rick promptly responded with "HE'S TAKING A P..." Then the ranger shouted back, "OKAY!" There were small rest shelters along the trail, but I don't remember seeing any restrooms. It was thrilling, finally hiking inside the famous Grand Canyon. As we zigzagged down to what seemed like an endless trail, I hung onto my water bottle and occasionally took a bite of my celery stick. We saw experienced hiker couples and young guys, who were lean and tan, and confident in their stride. We knew they had been here before! The trail finally took us to a plateau, or butte, that extended beyond a huge rock formation.

From that point we were able to experience the tremendous expanse of this amazing canyon. The sky was wide and blue with huge red rock structures and steep cliffs that surrounded us. With our binoculars we were able to make out a small boat with people riding the rapids along the Colorado River far below. It was truly a spectacular sight! Shortly after that, we reached one of the rest shelters and took a much-needed break. It was beginning to get late, so we decided it was time to turn back. Some hikers continued to the bottom of the Canyon where there are sleeping shelters, restrooms, water, and tent areas. Obviously we were not prepared to spend the night there. Not with one water container and a stalk of celery! Anyway, we were satisfied to have gone this far. So back we go zigzagging up the trail. After a while, dark, threatening clouds appeared above the canyon. We thought it best to "step it up!" As we picked up the pace, I was thankful Rick had dumped out all those cans and heavy stuff from my backpack.

We were surprised by the feel of thunder reverberating off the canyon walls. The thunder was accompanied by small flashes of lightning and strong winds that blew against our tired bodies. Rick, who was a few steps ahead of me, urged me to hurry so we could get to a shelter before the rain came. Suddenly the sky opened up, lit up with streaks of lightning and a torrential downpour pounded on our weary bodies. We finally reached one of those small wooden shabby shelters. But what a disappointment! It was packed to capacity with other hikers. Since we were already soaking wet, our only option was to press forward and upward. Plus, it was beginning to get darker. As we pushed our bodies through the storm, we heard a faint airplane motor flying somewhere above us. (The next day we heard of a plane crashing in the Canyon that night.) The weight of our heavy wet clothes clinging to our bodies made it hard to move, much less climb. My knees and my legs were beginning to weaken as Rick tried to encourage me. He would point to the top of the cliff shouting, "Look dad, we're almost there, see the lights of the cabins up there." Sure enough, but the zigzag trail leading to the top made it much further. We finally reached the top, dragged ourselves to the campsite. After a quick hot shower we retired into our tents. I was "dead tired" as I crawled into my sleeping bag. Then my body started trembling uncontrollably. I didn't want to tell Rick, but this went on for about two hours. I curled into a tight fetus position, covered my head as I struggled to keep warm. I was totally exhausted, and finally fell asleep late into the middle of the night. When we woke up, it was six o'clock in the evening of the next day. We had slept all night and all the next day. It had been an exhilarating experience, to say the least! We ate and relaxed as we made plans for our trip home the next day. The next morning our thrill was dampened when our car refused to start. Fortunately, the park rangers are prepared for stalled cars affected by the high altitude. A park mechanic came and got us started.

Driving home through New Mexico, we were enjoying "the land of enchantment" while munching, and talking about that incredible and memorable hike in the Canyon. About this time a highway patrol car passed us going the opposite direction. Oddly, the trooper kept staring at us. Then Rick realized we were speeding. There was a wire fence in the median so we felt like he wouldn't bother us. Rick continued and at the next crossroad he turned left. A short distance ahead we stopped at a small cafe for a cup of coffee. While we are relaxing, guess who came through the door? A patrolman with his dirty boots and shiny badge walks in with a smirk on his face. "Do you own that car parked outside he asked?" We were "busted!" All in all, it was a trip that Rick and I will never forget. This type of adventure experiences created a stronger bond between me and my son.

CHAPTER 24
UNIVERSITY PARK BAPTIST CHURCH

Joe Riley, Woody Thames, Richard Cortez,
Charles Martin, & Pastor Bob Canion

We enjoyed many happy years at University Park Baptist Church (UPBC). One year, Rick coached the girl's softball team. I wouldn't mention this, except for the fact that they had a group of real special teenage girls from the church. And they had a tough coach. Rick trained them hard! And the player he leaned on the hardest was his little sister. Ruby was small, petite, and very "lady like". But Rick insisted that the coach's sister must do better to set a good example.

Sometimes she would come home crying because Rick was so demanding of her. After much repetitious workouts, training, shouting, and shaping up, Ruby finally became an outstanding shortstop for the team. Not only that, all the rigid training paid off for the whole team. They brought home the City-Wide Church Championship. They were awarded a huge trophy, about four feet tall. I had never seen one that big! After much celebration, we thought it was all over.

We found out differently! One morning, we woke up and found the front of our house completely enveloped with a curtain of white toilet paper. There must have been at least seventy-five or more rolls hanging from that tall tree in our front yard. I thought of families that could have benefited from all that tissue, but I had to accept the traditional symbol of victory. Rick's team was very thorough with everything they did, even in the middle of the night.

Rick and I also played with the UPBC's men's softball team. It was fun working out and playing with a bunch of faithful brethren from our church. The Christian attitude and team spirit was exemplary. We won some and lost some. One night, fun turned to tragedy. One guy from the opposing team dashed from third base to steal home. Rick was catcher as this runner slid into home plate. His shoe struck Rick square on the shin of his left leg. The bone cracked so loud it was heard in the outfield. Needless to say, this put Rick out of commission for quite a long time. God had provided a close camaraderie within this team of Christian brethren.

LAKE OF THE PINES

Another memorable, exciting camping trip was with the UPBC young people. The youth department planned a weeklong evangelistic trip to Lake of the Pines in east Texas. Several adults were involved in what was a very well planned trip. We loaded our yellow bus and a couple of vans, and hit the road heading east. Once there, we located a nice area that would have pretty good shade most of the day. We pitched our tents according to specific groups.

Each group was responsible for certain duties on assigned days, on a rotation system. This would include duties: serving, washing dishes, making the beds, and keeping your tent and surrounding area clean. The groups, labeled by numbers, not only worked together, but also competed against each other in games. This went on throughout the whole week.

Our main goal for the trip was to walk through a small country community and introduce ourselves. We would hand out Christian literature and bibles. Then we would ask permission to have children's backyard bible studies. To attract the attention of little children out in the country, a couple of our people dressed up as clowns. Several families with little children were enthusiastic about the idea and gave permission to use their backyards. This was great and unusual summer fun for many of these country kids who passed the word to their friends. Many bible-related activities were enjoyed by all; coloring, storytelling, games, among other things. Meanwhile, back in our camp, after hearty meals, we had our own games, group bible studies, and discussions on the backyard activities.

In spite of busy days, we also found time for individual leisure, rest and meditation. We also went hiking and even killed a snake. Later a park ranger informed us that we had killed a good snake, the kind that eats bugs and rodents. We had a hilarious week, except one of our vans had a blow out on the road coming home. We had several youth leaders, but the principal "captains" were Claude McHorse, David and Kaye Cooke, and Charles and Patsy Martin.

During our years at University Park Baptist Church, three families were sent out by the church to begin a new ministry in the area of Leon Valley and further west. One of their first meeting places was an education building at the corner of Bandera Road and Grissom. With much growth and development in this area, this ministry began to progress rapidly. They moved to at least a couple of other locations. The ultimate result turned out to become what is now Crossroads Baptist Church, located at the corner of Guilbeau and Tezel.

Christmas was a time of big musical productions at our church. There was much practice and preparations. We had a good music and choir director who had the gift of putting on good performances. We also went Christmas caroling for homebound elderly, nursing homes, and other families. Of course during this season there was always the pressure of having to work long hours, shopping for gifts, sending cards, preparations for church functions, parties and dinners.

I have to admit there was little time for reverent meditation on the Word of God. Our main concern was on giving and receiving. We were accustomed to reciprocate and exchange gifts with the persons that gave us the previous year. We might give benevolent gifts to the poor. Some never considered that "God's presence far exceeds earthly presents." That included me!

"Every good gift, and every perfect gift is from above, and comes down from the Father of lights..." (James 1:17)

We had an exceptionally competent Minister of Music and Administrator at UPBC. He excelled as leader in the youth department. Besides being song leader, and choir director, he was a very conscientious administrator for the church. He performed in all these ministries diligently and quietly, and was admired by all. We had a well-organized adult choir that would present inspiring cantatas on special occasions like Easter and Christmas. I have to admit that many Sundays I received a greater blessing from the music and lyrics sung in the choir than from the preaching.

The time came that I would walk out of the Sunday service disappointed and spiritually empty. Not wanting to discourage others I hesitated to mention this to anyone. As time went on I was becoming very saddened and disillusioned at the decreasing number of people and more empty pews every Sunday. It was very obvious looking out into the congregation from the choir loft. The situation got worse every Sunday and it became apparent to some of the faithful brethren. Meetings were held; motivational speakers were invited to address this declining problem. Special seminars were presented together with films on Sunday evenings. Several pragmatic efforts were applied, but with few results.

Finally, we found the "solution." We consolidated with a vibrant church group who had out grown their small church building. They had the people and we had the large building! Both congregations took a vote and a unanimous agreement was reached. It was agreed that our pastor would step down and their pastor, who happened to be a well-known evangelist, was retained. Our building was now filled, and everyone appeared happy.

The scripture states in Proverbs 14:12: "There is a way that seems right to a man, but its end is the way to death", and in Proverbs

16:2: "All the ways of a man are pure in his own eyes, but the Lord weighs the spirit."

Not to go into much detail – strife and conflict began to emerge in the leadership of the church. This happened a few short years after the merger. Some accusations were made and an "inquisition" type meeting took place. Embarrassment and shame began to create divisions among some people. The Adversary began to raise his ugly head. Eventually our new evangelist preacher suggested that our church administrator be released. He wanted to fire a man that was revered and loved by the entire "original" congregation. He had been faithful in teaching by word and example to many of the different age groups for many years. An outbreak of discord was about to take place!

There were no signs of reconciliation when a general meeting was called. God was not honored, and men acted and reacted in the flesh and in their emotions. I could not comprehend the harsh temperament of "Christian" men and women whom I knew and worshiped with. Plus, I was a deacon and was right in the middle of it all. But I just listened in amazement!

The new "renowned" pastor made accusations against our church administrator, and asked that he resign. This is where the heat was turned on! The so-called "victim" who had an impeccable record and had lived an exemplary life was about to be fired. I was getting sick to my stomach, so I walked out. This was painful for me! It was like a bad dream. This conflict caused the church to split right down the middle. After much heated arguments, both men agreed to resign, and many left the church. A young man was assigned as interim pastor. Later Dale Cruz was hired as full-time pastor. After a short time he was dismissed! The church could not tolerate his preaching of the Doctrines of Grace.

My mother and I started visiting other churches where we had friends. By this time she was in her early eighties and needed a walker to get around. I didn't explain all the details to her. She just knew that she missed her Spanish Sunday School Class with teacher Mr. Dan Hernandez. Dan was a gentle and compassionate person who loved the Lord.

We finally ended up at Hillburn Drive Baptist Church. The preaching of Jose Maldonado impressed us. It was different from what we were used to. Biblical truths were being preached with power, with authority, and with clarity. We discovered this was a Reformed Baptist Church, and were introduced to the Doctrines of Grace for the first time. My mom and I were enlightened and encouraged, so we started attending both morning and evening Sunday services.

MY MOM SUSTAINED IN FAITH, DESPITE DECLINING HEALTH

My mother had diabetes, an enlarged heart (which she boasted about), arthritis of the knees, and high blood pressure. But she never complained and had everything under control with medications. She was happy and content, had a good appetite, and loved getting out of the house. Her walker did not slow her down. I would drive her to church, to doctor's appointments, and to the grocery store in her car.

She enjoyed her doctor's visits. I mentioned to her heart doctor one day that I was concerned about her eating too much. Sundays after church we would usually eat at Bonanza Buffet Restaurant. She would eat her steak, salads, desert, ice cream, etc. The doctor surprised me when he said, "She is 82 years old, let her eat whatever she wants. She has already lived a lifetime. Let her enjoy herself."

One day I noticed that the inspection sticker on her hardtop gold Chevelle had expired. For that matter, her auto insurance had also expired. Right then she gave me the assignment of taking care of all that paperwork. Eventually, she turned the car over to my name. (Forgetting that in her will, she had assigned it to my brother Danny).

One of her doctors started her on Coumadin Therapy to prevent blood clot and a possible stroke. Blood was drawn every Friday to gauge the effects of the Coumadin, which is supposed to thin the blood. Unfortunately, the count was fluctuating irregularly. For some unusual reason, that doctor gave the assignment to another colleague.

At this point my mother was thinking clear and was cognizant of everything going on around her. That's why it surprised me when she ended up at Humana Hospital. Three days later, on November 21, 1990 the Lord took her home. She was 83 years old. I wasn't satisfied with the doctor's treatment and lack of answers, especially in regard to the Coumadin, which was so unpredictable.

The cause (or causes) of her death were Pneumonitis, Intraventricular Hemorrhage, and Coumadin Therapy.

Amidst the uncertainty of her death, the Lord gave me an extraordinary peace and comfort while mourning. When the family met in a near by room, I had to return to her room to retrieve something. A nurse was attempting to close her mouth with a towel as I glanced to the bed where she laid. I saw a body, a "shell," but it wasn't my mother anymore. Her life, her soul, her warmth had vanished. I was content to know that she was in her eternal home. I was truly thankful that she had lived a long happy life. She enjoyed the blessings of her children, grandchildren, and great-grandchildren.

Dale Cruz, who was the pastor at University Park Baptist Church, preached a beautiful gospel message at her funeral. The church was filled with loving family and friends. Her grandson, Bill Cortez read a beautiful poem and a men's quartet sang "Amazing Grace." I was grateful to Pastor Jose Maldonado and deacon Ruben Robles who had shown so much love and compassion for my mother while we attended their church. A week after the funeral, Ruben surprised me! He told me that my mom and dad had been in his parents' wedding, and was nice enough to show me a picture of the wedding and bridal party. My mom had enjoyed the services at Hillburn Drive Baptist Church, but she always missed her Spanish Sunday school class at University Park Baptist Church.

"Behold, how good and pleasant it is
*   when brothers dwell in unity!*
It is like the precious oil on the head,
*   running down on the beard,*
On the beard of Aaron,
*   running down on the collar of his robes!*
It is like the dew of Hermon,
*   which falls on the mountains of Zion!*
For there the Lord has commanded the blessing,
*   life forevermore*

Psalm 133

"In my distress I called upon the Lord; to my God I cried for help. From his temple he heard my voice, and my cry to him reached his ears. Then the earth reeled and rocked; the foundations also of the mountains trembled and quaked, because he was angry."

Psalm 18:6-7 (ESV)

CHAPTER 25
NEWLY WEDS

MARRIAGE OF MAYRA & SAM CERDA
JUNE 4, 1983

(Front Row) Mr. and Mrs. Augustine Cerda
(Second Row) Richard, Mayra, Sam, Lupita

In 1982, in God's providence, Mayra, my oldest daughter met a quiet and serious young man by the name of Sam Cerda, They met at San Antonio College in the Baptist Student Union. Eventually it was apparent to both of them that God had planned this meeting and their eventual marriage. They have enjoyed 28 years together with the added blessing of four children: Caleb, Benjamin, Dorothy, and Samuel.

Sam & Mayra happily married

My wife and I enjoyed watching their family grow. Their visits were, and still are, very special. We were privileged when they came to live

Richard, Gilbert, Rudy, Danny
Lupita, Sophie, Vangie, Adela
At Mayra & Sam's Wedding

with us. I had the distinct pleasure of seeing Benjamin come into this world right in our house. What a blessing it was to gaze at the miracle of a new infant being born. This was a new and awesome experience for me. Since then I developed a special bond with Ben, who is now a mature Christian serving the Lord.

Dorothy was also born in our home with the assistance of a midwife. However, her's was somewhat of a frightful experience. On November 11, 1993, as night fell at 208 W. Ligustrum, Mayra was keeping us in suspense as the contractions begin. Tired after several hours of anxiously waiting, Lupita and I finally decided to take a little nap. Ruby, who was still single at the time, was supposed to call us if anything happened, or if Mayra was ready to give birth. After a short deep sleep, I heard a rumble outside our bedroom.

Mayra, Sam, Grandpa, Ben, Caleb, Dorothy, Samuel

As I opened the door, half asleep, I was shocked to see two EMT firemen (including Ernest Estrada) rolling Mayra in a gurney down the hallway. The mid-wife along side, holding the infant in place to keep it from coming out. The baby was breached, so there was urgent need to rush them to a hospital. In the excitement Ruby had failed to wake Lupita and me. We quickly rushed to my car and followed the ambulance to the hospital and hurried up to the maternity ward. After a short wait we were allowed to enter a room where Mayra sat on the bed smiling, and holding a beautiful little baby girl. A brave mother had just undergone a C-section. We got to see little Dorothy for the first time. Later I could say that she "hit the ground running," because as a tiny little toddler she never stopped running.

Fast forward, now at 18, she has blossomed into a beautiful and gracious young lady. She is an accomplished pianist, and gives lessons. She designs and sews her own clothes, is a promising cook, and she went to college to learn American Sign Language. Most of all, she recognizes that "Charm is deceitful and beauty is vain, but a woman who fears the Lord, is to be praised." (Proverbs 31:30 ESV). In spite of her unique entrance into this new world, the Lord in mercy had blessed the Cerda family with a little princess.

She diligently sought to serve the Lord, but continued to pray and trust the Lord would prepare her for marriage. Meanwhile behind the scenes, David Luciano was seeking counsel from Pastor Tim about marrying Dorothy. David, a respectable and courteous gentleman, had already become acquainted with Sam, Dorothy's father, at a church Men's Retreat.

Seeking favor in the eyes of the Lord, Dorothy's faithful prayers were answered on December 4, 2013, David appeared at her grandmother's door at ten that night, and graciously made a proposal of marriage.

That "memorable" night, Charity had called her cousin Dorothy to go outside and observe a very spectacular star display in the sky. As Dorothy stepped outside the front door in her pajamas and robe, lo and behold, there stood David.

Before this, their relationship had been somewhat casual. David had started to make more "intentional" short-stop visits to Devine on his way back from work in Laredo. Long discussions, which began on the front patio of my house, led to a final decision on the wedding date. It was decided that Saturday, April 26, 2014 would be the best time.

NEWLY WEDS

David & Dorothy at their wedding

MARRIAGE OF RICK AND BELLE – JAN. 8, 1985 @ UPBC

Tyreka, Michelle, Belle, Rick (Baby Steven), Michael, Tabitha

Rick and Belle knew each other in high school. As time went by, they developed a harmonious relationship. On January 8, 1985, Belle discovered she was with child. It was confirmed in the doctor's office. As she and Rick came down on the elevator, she cried. Rick proposed they get married. So, they headed to the courthouse where they obtained a marriage certificate. Shortly after, they met with Judge Mike Machado who performed the marriage ceremony with his secretary as witness. Next came the task of giving the news to the parents.

They first went to Belle's mom, who was not very happy to hear the "good news." Then they drove to our house on Ligustrum, but we happened to be out. Ruby was the only one home, and her only comment was, "Rick, you're in trouble!" When Lupita and I finally came home, they broke the news to us, and added that we would soon have a grandchild. For a moment I was speechless; I was totally unprepared!

This was a "first" for my wife and me! I guess I had mixed emotions. Suddenly a spontaneous surge of affection came over me. We hugged and congratulated them and cried. I think we all cried! After the emotions had settled down, I suggested they get married in church.

On February 8, our Pastor Bob Cannon performed a short ceremony at University Park Baptist Church. Determined to do things right, they took their solemn vows before God. John Lopez, Rick's good friend was best man and Monica, Belle's younger sister was maid-of-honor. Present for this small ceremony was Belle's father, Richard Albidress and his girlfriend, Sam, Mayra, Ruby, and me and my wife, as well as Rick's son Brandon. (Time has passed and my grandson Brandon has grown and developed into a mature God fearing young man whom I respect and admire.)

After the ceremony, we all decided to celebrate at Mi Tierra Mexican Restaurant. Nothing fancy, but in a festive and flamboyant atmosphere, a new chapter began in the Cortez family. The Lord in His goodness and mercy has sustained Rick and Belle through various trying times. But by God's amazing grace, they have overcome and recently celebrated their 27th wedding anniversary. Plus, they have been blessed with four beautiful children, Michelle, Michael, Tabitha, and Tyreka.

Purchased Duplex On Babcock Rd. - Aug. 1986

A couple of years before my retirement my interests turned to real estate investments. I fell in love with a very attractive duplex on Cincinnati Avenue. I drove by it several times a week and was convinced that would be a good investment. Plus, it was very close to St. Mary's University. I envisioned making profit by buying and then renting it. I finally contacted the owner who showed me around the property. The roof and the foundation and the inside appeared in good condition. The necessary papers were prepared. After my credit was approved, the contract was written up. I brought it home, examined it, and signed it.

After church the following Sunday, I took the family to Luby's Cafeteria for lunch. Providentially, I came across an old friend who would launch me into an exciting new venture, or maybe I should say "adventure." He was a Christian friend and fellow musician from junior high and high school band days. I remembered him as a boy who lived his faith by example. In conversation, he mentioned he was now involved in real estate. I took this opportunity to mention the contract I had just signed. He suggested I not take any action but to bring the contract to his office the next day. Little did I realize how Louis Garcia, my old and faithful friend, would enlighten me in my newly found financial practice. He saw and heard all the beautiful details of the duplex that I was in love with. Then he showed me another similar duplex on Babcock Road, near Fredericksburg Rd. It was an excellent and ideal location! This I could buy for ten thousand dollars less than the one for which I had signed a contract. I had a dilemma! Louis, who had much experience in real estate, said, "Not to worry, let me see your contract." In it, he found several loopholes! As a result, I was released from that obligation. What a tremendous relief that was for me!

Wow, I was really excited! Now I was convinced that my meeting Louis at Luby's that Sunday was definitely providential. I was deeply grateful for my old friend who was giving me a tremendous lesson in real estate. I was getting a duplex that was a much better investment than the one I had previously chosen. I had a lot of faith in Louis, because he had Christian values that were part of his life. We developed a closer friendship that would continue for a long time. My faithful and benevolent God was opening an enormous opportunity. He never has forsaken me!

"Many are the plans in the mind of a man, but it is the purpose of the Lord that will stand." (Proverbs 19:21)

It didn't take me long to learn the ropes of renting. I was excited! It was challenging and profitable. Wow, but now I had the unpopular title of "landlord." I was committed to being honest and fair with all my tenants.

To avoid miscommunication, I made the rental agreements very clear for everyone to understand. I soon found out that just being practical and reasonable does not work with some people. In general, most of the tenants I had over the years were honest, clean, and cooperative. But some, I still cannot forget, like this young innocent looking widow who came and pleaded with me to rent to her and her little daughter. The first couple of months she paid on time, and seemed quiet and settled. But shortly after that, neighbors were complaining of loud Saturday night partying, drinking, and screaming stereo music.

The little innocent looking "widow" turned out to be a "party animal." One Saturday night a beer bottle broke a neighbor's window. Of course no one knew anything about that! After continuous warnings, I asked her to leave at the end of her contract month. When it appeared that she would not leave at that time, I sent her an eviction notice with a sheriff's deputy.

When the deputy arrived, she had already left. The apartment was filthy with beer bottles, cans, and trash. Plus, there was a hole in the wall as big as a softball. The deposit usually covers some of the damage and clean up, such as this. I still had to pay some money out of my own pocket!

In another rare case, my life was threatened! A clean-cut African-American young man rented an apartment. Since he rode a wheel chair, I built a temporary ramp in front of his unit. He paid his deposit and rent, and was living peaceably, as far as I could see. After a couple of months a robust, husky gal moved in with him. He said it was his wife who had just reconciled and was back with him. I had no objection! I like it when married couples reconcile after small quarrels or arguments.

However, after three months, she calls me on the phone and asks for the deposit because her "husband" has left her and skipped town. I tried to reason with her on the phone that the deposit usually is refunded to the person that paid it and rented the apartment in the first place. She was not satisfied and became very angry. She demanded that I bring her the deposit or, "I will tear up your apartment." She sounded serious, and I knew she meant what she said.

On the way there, Lupita warned me not to go inside the apartment. I should have listened to her! When I went in, this girl confronted me in the kitchen. She had a demonic look on her face and a stick about three feet long with a metal hook on the end. She kept pointing it at me as she blurted out vile and profane language. I wasn't about to provoke her! I knew she was on some kind of "high."

I did try to reason and rationalize with her, but she kept insisting that as "wife" she had a right to the deposit. Realizing that we were not getting anywhere fast, I started to exit through the kitchen door.

Well, she blocked it with her big body and pushed her big bosom against me. As I tried to squeeze through, she accused me of pushing her. When I finally made it outside, my wife and a few other onlookers were standing by. I asked Lupita to call the cops.

In the meantime, this mad woman followed me to my car, while two of her friends urged her to leave. I looked in my wallet and told her I would give her the last twenty-dollar bill I had. She grabbed it and left. The police came about a half hour later, but no charges were filed, and fortunately no one was hurt. "The LORD will keep you from all evil, He will keep your life." (Psalm 121:7)

In an other case, two industrious young men who claimed they were interior decorators, rented one of the units. After a few weeks they offered to paint their bathroom. It sounded like a good deal, especially since they would provide the paint, labor, and all the equipment free. Well, they did a good job, which they called modern psychedelic. They painted the whole bathroom, including the tub, and lavatory - solid black. It blew my mind when I first saw it! Of course, I had to redo the whole thing when they moved out.

Then there was that young couple with three children. He was a Pentecostal preacher and she was a very neat stay-at-home mom. Every time I showed up, she had something cooking on the stove.

And she would not let me leave without a warm taco or one of her home cooked meals.

This showed me there were people out there that were responsible and thoughtful. In the meantime, I was enjoying the challenge and profit of renting properties. Even now, I am convinced that property is the best investment a man can make, if he stays well informed and manages efficiently.

AUGUST 24, 1987 – MOVED TO 8519 BRISTLECONE STREET

With retirement approaching, we had a new vision. Lupita and I decided to rent our Ligustrum house and move somewhere else. Once again my friend Louis Garcia was ready to help us. He found us a beautiful home in Northwest San Antonio, outside Loop 410. This was the Wildwood II Subdivision, just past Leon Valley. It was a little bigger than what we had expected, but Louis got us a really good deal that was hard to turn down. The combination of red brick and wood on the outside, with a huge oak tree in the front of the house was very appealing. The sliding doors from the kitchen led to a covered patio over looking a spacious back yard. The Lord was faithful and continued to meet our needs. This home would be the starting point to a variety of adventuresome activities, including trips in Texas and other far away places.

1987 - MAYRA AND SAM MOVE TO MASSACHUSETTS

Mary Enriquez, Mayra's high school friend, was beckoning her and Sam to come to Massachusetts where there were good paying jobs in abundance. After much meditation and prayer, they decided to take the step of faith and head east. Upon arriving they were warmly welcomed by a loving and thoughtful Christian family. The Scannings immediately invited them to stay in their home in North Attleboro, until they could get settled. This was the beginning of a new phase and a completely different environment for Sam and Mayra. They were now in the land where our nation was born.

NOVEMBER, 1988 - LUPITA AND I VISIT SAM AND MAYRA

After retirement in 1988, my wife and I decided to visit Mayra and Sam in Mansfield, Massachusetts. This was a most exhilarating experience! We had traveled to California and the west coast, but never to the east coast. We purposely arranged to arrive at the Providence

Rhode Island Airport. This was a smaller airport, and a shorter route to Mansfield. Plus, we avoided the bustling Boston airports and the heavy traffic. Pastor Becker (the Cerda's pastor) greeted us and drove us to Mansfield. The thing that impressed us the most at first was the array of colors. Fall foliage in New England is awe-inspiring! The trees were bursting with leaves of a multitude of colors – reds, yellows, browns, etc. For newcomers, it was a refreshing sight, driving on streets and roads, that were lined with beautiful tall trees on both sides.

Mayra had recently given birth to Caleb, so this first trip was real special. Plus, it gave grandma the privilege of bathing the newborn in the kitchen sink. We were retired, relaxed, and really enjoying our loved ones in a completely beautiful and different environment. We visited many historic places including Sturbridge Village and Plymouth Plantation. I was thoroughly fascinated visiting the land where our forefathers first landed and struggled to ultimately form what is now the United States of America. The Native-Americans, the Pilgrims, the freezing winters, and the fight for independence were vividly displayed for visitors. All this was unfolded before us as we had read in our history books.

The commuter train from Mansfield to Boston was a rare and unusual experience for us. This was an extraordinary ride through the beautiful countryside that rolled past unique little towns enveloped in fiery-red maple trees.

In Boston, we visited the popular Faneuil Hall and the Quincy Marketplace with its quaint cobblestones, bright banners, combined with special events, food, flowers, fashions and fun. Here too, we would experience the cold attitudes and habits of the local Bostonians, who live on the "fast track," with their noses in a book much of the time. I couldn't help but miss the "friendly" Texas atmosphere.

One day we headed toward Newport, Rhode Island to visit some most phenomenal and dazzling homes. Guided tours led us through the elegant massive and opulent Newport mansions built by the Vanderbilts, William Shepard Wetmore, and other tycoons around the 1800s. We were amazed to find out that some of these extravagant mansions were considered summer homes or places for social functions for the very wealthy. Today, these exclusive historical abodes sitting along the coast are preserved for visitors and tourists to enjoy. Unlike Disney World castles and palaces, these mansions are the "real thing."

DRIVING RUBY TO MASSACHUSETTS – DEC. 1989

In December 1989, I drove my daughter Ruby to Massachusetts. She had decided to venture far off to see another part of the world. She would be joining Sam and Mayra (her sister), who had discovered a plentiful job market in the Northeast. So we jam-packed every inch of her little brown Celica and hit the road. I was the "volunteer" driver. I never felt real comfortable about this trip, but the little "birdie" wanted to spread her wings, so I obliged!

It was December, the off-season for tourists, so we got reduced rates at most hotels, including one in Nashville. We spent one night in a motel in the Smokey Mountains National Park, and it was practically deserted. We stayed briefly, enough to enjoy our first snow. From there we drove off through the colorful and breathtaking Blue Ridge Mountains. The variety of colors along this mountainous range was spectacular. You could see the strokes of God's paintbrush all along this picturesque drive. We couldn't resist stopping off and taking pictures along the way. Ruby said she had the urge to visit and talk to people who lived in those colorful quaint houses on the grassy hills. They reminded us of the pictures one sees on calendars. However, for the most part there was silence in the car. I had a strange hollow feeling in my stomach, and words would not come out. Ruby was a very special person in my life. And here I was, taking her further and further from home, clear across the country. It was very awkward for me, and I was forcing myself to "enjoy" the trip for her sake.

Driving through the state of Pennsylvania at night was scary! It was a black, murky night enveloped in thick dense fog with dangerous curves. Visibility was very limited, and I went the wrong way at a fork in the road. We finally decided to stop and spent the night at a small motel in a remote area. My goodness, the next morning we noticed we had been driving through a treacherous mountain pass. The Lord was with us, and we were thankful for His mercy. We took a deep breath, ate breakfast, and continued on our journey. "He who dwells in the shelter of the Most High, will abide in the shadow of the Almighty. I will say to the Lord, My refuge and my fortress, my God in whom I trust." (Psalm 91:1-2)

We reached Washington D.C. during the rush hour traffic (which is all the time). We just aimed the car toward the tall Washington Monument. Once we got there, we were in close proximity to some of the other famous monuments. It was getting late as we drove around, so we determined to come back the next day and visit inside these historical monuments. We were not going to miss this once in a lifetime opportunity.

However, we found it's impossible to park anywhere in Washington, D.C. We managed to find a motel in German Town on the outskirts of the Capital. The next day we drove back to D.C. and started by visiting and climbing to the top of the Washington Monument where we got a view of the Mall that led to the Capital. There was a great panoramic view of the whole city of D.C. We paid our respects to Abraham Lincoln at the very dignified statue erected in his memory. The Jefferson Memorial was equally impressive. We drove past the White House, the Capitol, the Supreme Court and others.

We finally got on the road that would take us to Massachusetts. We were squashed in the car, packed with "stuff" to the ceiling, but we were warm and getting closer to our destination. We started to feel relief and excited. Mayra and Sam were equally excited when we called and told them how close we were and the approximate time of our arrival.

We finally arrived at the Taxi Inn Restaurant, right below their apartment. We were all thrilled as we reunited with hugs and laughter. Ruby and Mayra were gripped with uncontrollable laughter the whole time we were unloading the car. There was an overflowing of joy and emotion. That tall climb up those stairs was not a laughing matter for me, as I huffed and puffed. The next morning we were introduced to the couple that operated the Taxi Inn Cafe where we had breakfast. What a thrill it was riding the train from Mansfield to Boston again. I thought this was something San Antonio needed real bad. We walked down town to the museum and the Boston Harbor. I was surprised to see many working people commuting to their jobs in Boston by riding a ferry from the other side of the harbor. We were in for a lot more fascinating tours in Massachusetts.

On my return trip to San Antonio, I ran into a little problem at the airport ticket counter. Realizing that two-way tickets are cheaper than one way, I had bought round-trip tickets when I first started in San Antonio. When I attempted to use one ticket of the round-trip ticket deal, the alert ticket agent was not about to let me get away with it, and charged me the higher price on a one-way ticket. That's when my two loving, protecting daughters came to the rescue of their Papacito. They disputed the unfairness of the higher charge, and the girl behind the counter explained that she was just following established Airline policy. In the end she gave me a break, thanks to Ruby and Mayra.

SECOND TRIP TO MASSACHUSETTS - SEPT, 1990

Lupita and I were drawn back to visit Massachusetts for a second time. The Northeast was exciting, colorful, and historic. One day Sam decided to take us on a scenic drive through the picturesque state of New Hampshire. We eventually ended up in Maine, the most northeastern state in the U.S. The cool breezes on the beautiful beaches in Ogunquit, Maine were truly a far cry from Texas. We roamed around all day, and enjoyed a picnic lunch on the beach before heading back to Mansfield.

On a cold Sunday morning after a night of snow, we drove to church with Sam, Mayra, and Ruby. The brethren all huddled together to keep warm. It was a close-knit family atmosphere that made me and Lupita feel right at home. The church was characteristic of the New England "puritan" style. That included the architecture of the church, both inside and out. The hard narrow wooden pews made it difficult for anyone to fall asleep. During the morning break we would go up to the kitchen, located in the loft, for coffee, cocoa, and sweet bread. We enjoyed warm fellowship with the brethren on this cold winter Lord's Day. The beloved Pastor Becker, a righteous man, could belt out the gospel louder than I had ever heard. He and his wife Jessi were exceptionally warm and cordial. They made us feel right at home around their fireplace, drinking hot cocoa during a cold wintry night.

One real special event was my reunion with a former Navy buddy who lived in Hingham, Massachusetts. Tony Muzzi and I had not seen each other since we played in a Navy band on the Island of Guam in 1947. That was forty-two years ago. Tony, in his typical friendly Italian spirit was really excited, and invited Lupita and me out to dinner. The bad news was that his first wife had drowned in their backyard swimming pool. The good news was that he had now remarried to a wonderful lady, who was somewhat of a "fortune teller." We reminisced back to our time on Guam over a great dinner while our wives got acquainted. Tony was a good-natured guy who played string bass in the band, even with a broken arm in a sling. When overseas, he would always remind me that I was welcome in his home, and that I could even date his sister when I returned stateside.

Lupita and I especially enjoyed Mansfield in the winter. This snowy winter wonderland remains indelible in my memory. Some wintry mornings we would trek through the snow and head for the Colony Diner located just around the corner. It was a typical cozy New England cafe with its frosty windows, and a chubby good-natured waitress. The eggs, wedged potatoes, giant hot biscuits, and coffee, were a delectable treat. After breakfast, Lupita and I would wrap ourselves up with coats, scarves, and gloves and walk to the nearby library. That was another unique building where we would take refuge from the cold. There might be soft snow flurries, but we were really enjoying every moment of it.

One cold night we drove to Boston in Sam's car. Driving through town when there was little traffic, we came upon this well-known park. We didn't realize how cold it was until we saw giant life sized ice sculptures of horses. They were beautiful works of some artist. More incredible, these ice statues had been there for two or three days without melting. These are just a few of the highlights from our unforgettable trips to Massachusetts.

SAYING GOODBYE TO MASSACHUSETTS

My last trip to Mansfield was to help the Cerdas and Ruby prepare for their final trip back to San Antonio. They had enjoyed cold winters and the snow was beautiful. However the cost of the long winters was high. The operating fuel alone was a great expense. That was just one of the main reasons the Cerda's decided to move back to San Antonio.

Sam's car was to pull a small trailer that would carry all their belongings. The trailer was indeed small! But Sam was determined that every thing would fit okay. We loaded the trailer, and Sam arranged and rearranged everything several times. It became obvious that one of the most valuable items, their big beautiful mattress would not fit into that small trailer. It would have to be shipped separately. A friendly neighbor that had seen Sam struggle trying to fit everything in the trailer came to help. He seemed to have the solution!! It was like putting all the pieces of a puzzle together. He took EVERYTHING out and started fitting and squeezing things into place, one by one. It was starting to get dark as Sam finally tied a rope over and around the tarp. Sharon Sirici, an intimate Christian friend of Mayra, had been kind enough to invite us to dinner that night. We were ever so grateful. The next morning she was the lone person that sadly bid us goodbye. She was one of many faithful Christian friends that had close bonds with Sam and Mayra. It was truly emotional seeing Sharon standing there on the sidewalk waving goodbye until we drove out of sight.

Sam, Mayra, and Caleb, were to ride in their car, and I would drive with Ruby in her car. Of one thing we were certain - we would not rush! We were finally on our way back to San Antonio. It was a very long drive but we made several stops to eat, to enjoy the scenery, and to take pictures. It was a most memorable trip!

CHAPTER 26
MARRIAGES AND MISSIONS

MARRIAGE - RUBY TO TIM CONWAY
JAN. 29, 1994

A bitter-sweet experience was the giving away of my youngest daughter Ruby Maile. Ruby was not only my daughter but she was a special friend. As a young Christian woman her desire was to wait patiently upon the Lord for the man that would be her husband. So to this end we often prayed together.

We were happy at Free Grace Baptist Church, even though we were just a small motley group. Because our church was so small, I would kid her with remarks like, "It will be a miracle of God for a handsome "eligible" young man to walk in through that door and propose to you." The day did indeed come that *prince charming* came into her life! This happened through an interesting chain of events. Tim Conway, a young engineer from Michigan came to live in Texas and joined Community Baptist Church (CBC) in Elmendorf.

My son Rick, a member of the same church, quickly recognized the godly qualities of this intelligent young man. So after much discussion, Rick arranged a blind date at the Black Eyed Pea restaurant on Bandera Road and 410. Ruby and Tim met there for the first time. Immediately they both recognized this was "love at first sight." That's what I say! But they prefer to say, "We both realized this would be my spouse for life."

Lupita and I were a little puzzled when this young man drove up our drive way on a motorcycle. This was his first visit. The little we knew of motorcyclists was not very favorable. We now realize all this was providential, according to God's plan for these two. Even so, I still had a big lump in my throat and a tear in my eye when I walked her down the aisle to "give her away" in marriage. It was a very emotional moment for me! University Park Baptist Church was filled to capacity with family and friends. I had the privilege of saying a few words after some hymns.

Then Pastor Pat Horner performed the marriage ceremony. After that, he did what Tim had suggested – to preach the gospel without a time limit, which he did.

Ruby and Tim's Wedding

In the meantime, Gilbert Jr. (one of the photographers) was scanning throughout the whole congregation with his video camera. Later the video showed that a great number of people were dozing off during the long sermon. The reception in the church fellowship hall was filled with wide-awake guests, enjoying plenty of good food, people renewing friendships, and old relatives getting reacquainted.

I am happy to say that Tim is my pastor now, and they have four beautiful children (Charity, Grace, Joshua, and Joy) that make this old grandpa very happy. This is brief, because their life story would be the subject of another book.

Grandkids—"Children's children are the crown of old men." (Proverbs 17:6)

Charity, Dorothy, Ben, Tabitha, Michael, Caleb, Michelle

Grandpa, Ben and the Frog

Ben's Graduation—April 24, 2010

Caleb's Wedding—March 2012

Thanksgiving 2013 at the Butterbaugh's home

At the Conway's in Elmendorf, Texas

AGUA CALIENTE, CHIHUAHUA, MEXICO

Brethern at "Agua Caliente" Conference

I had the privilege of making several trips to Mexico with Tim, Ruby, and the family (Charity and Grace). Our destination was a Mission Conference in Agua Caliente, where Andres Galaviz is the missionary pastor. The trip took us past the Big Bend National Park to the border town of Presidio, Texas.

From there we entered into the small Mexican border town of Ojinaga, in the state of Chihuahua. After the usual inspection and identity routine at the "Aduana," we continued driving into Chihuahua, the largest state in Mexico. I was waiting to be impressed. But all we experienced was a long hot day's drive through dry desert with no human habitation in sight.

We could see huge mountains in the horizon. At last we entered the mountains, where the fun would begin. The narrow road curves through treacherous mountain passes that would take away your breath. Dodging long log carrying trucks kept us all wide-awake. Our first stop was the city of Cuauhtemoc, a colorful town, not too different from any south Texas town, except for the Spanish billboards, culture, and language.

There we met up with another group of brethren who were also attending the Conference. We had sweet fellowship while eating some hearty hamburgers at the town's popular "burger joint." Then we all continued on to our destination further up in the mountains. After a total of seventeen hours of driving, darkness was approaching. Tim suddenly turned into a pile of rocks along side the road. Tired and weary, I asked, "Where are you going Tim?" He answered, "This is the road to Andres' house". A four-wheel drive vehicle would have been more appropriate as we went bumpiddy-bump through this unmarked and undeveloped "road".

Several other families had already arrived at Andres' house. His faithful wife Rhonda is a registered nurse and serves the Lord by providing medical assistance to the weak and sick in that remote mountainous area. It was a humble dwelling but well built, and had a spacious living room with concrete floor. This would be our place of worship, eating, fellowship, and sleeping for the next several days. It was indeed a blessing being there (what seemed like the top of the world).

Conference at Agua Caliente, Mexico

It was wonderful and rare experiencing the bond of Christian love with so many brethren whom we had never met before. We ate together, sang hymns and worshipped together. Then blankets and sleeping bags were spread out on the floor, from wall to wall. It was a time of rejoicing and being thankful. The sisters put to work their individual gifts in the kitchen, and prepared sumptuous meals. During the daytime, we had time to do some projects around the house. When I was there we helped build a fence around the property.

On previous trips Tim, Brother John Systma, and other men had developed a system of channeling water from a natural fresh water spring to a tank that would supply the whole house. Other projects were a shower attached to the side of the house, an outhouse, and ultimately a church building. We also had time to wander off and explore the beautiful mountainous sites that surrounded the house. One favorite spot we liked to hike to was, "Aguas Calientes." (natural warm water spring). That is where Andres' mission site derived that name. It was a great warm relief just sticking our feet in there. Some of us even enjoyed taking a dip into this spring that remained warm even in the wintertime.

Ruby, Grace, Tim and Charity in the desert in Chihuahua

One morning we got in our cars and traveled about three miles away. In about six vehicles we carried all the equipment, including chairs, songbooks, and sound equipment. The microphone and huge speakers were connected to a pickup truck battery. We set up chairs under the shade of a big tree surrounded by tall mountains in the distance. The gospel was about to be preached in a beautiful and picturesque outdoor setting. When we started singing, the music seemed to reverberate from the mountains all around. Native Indian families starting trickling out of the crevices and slopes along the surrounding mountains. Some sat on the rocks to listen while others started coming down. It was an inspirational and encouraging sight!

Another day we took the gospel message to the backyard of one of the church members. The homes were humble dwellings, but the people were faithful brethren who loved the Lord. Meal times at Andre's house were always a delight with the women preparing warm hearty dishes as the men sat around the table in lively conversations. Here we were, thousands of miles from home on top of huge mountains, sharing eternal thoughts with brothers and sisters of like faith.

What a joy that was! On one of these occasions I translated for Tim as he preached in English. But it was Rhonda who did most of the translating for the different preachers. These mission trips were sponsored and supported by Community Baptist Church. Tim always had a great zeal for missions. He had made several trips when he was single. He had been sent by his company to help develop the bleachers inside the new Alamodome in San Antonio. While here, he visited CBC. There were many things there that attracted him, including the Doctrines of Grace, which were being preached with unusual power and clarity.

Plus, this church had a heart for missions in Mexico. So, after seeking God's will, Tim left his job in Michigan and moved to Elmendorf, Texas. To get him started, John Systma, a church elder, gave him a job on his ostrich farm. To give him the opportunity to use his engineering skills, John assigned him to develop an incubator for ostrich eggs. After much research, Tim came up with an innovative incubator that was practical and would be very helpful to ostrich farmers. This became a profitable product for the Elmendorf Ostrich Farm. The incubator was now being marketed through out the country. Eventually the Systmas sold the ostrich farm, and Tim got an engineering position with the Miller Curtain Company.

At this time, Tim and Ruby were married and had two children, Charity and Grace. I always enjoyed the Mexico mission trips with the Conways. I too had a desire to serve the Lord in the land of my ancestors. A land where I knew the language.

TORREON MEXICO – JULY, 1998

I had another opportunity to attend a Conference in Torreon, Mexico with Tim and Ruby. It was indeed a blessing to meet and hear Mexican preachers expounding the Word of God in Spanish. We had the pleasure of staying with a couple of single sisters from the church. They were very hospitable and really enjoyed the cute Conway children. During these trips to Mexico, I had the pleasure of meeting and bonding with a brother who was humble and faithful in truth. Ruben Covarrubias lives in Chihuahua, Mexico, but we still try to stay in touch by way of encouraging letters and e-mail.

MARRIAGE OF ADELA TO DAVID BUTTERBAUGH – JULY 31, 1999

I had the distinct pleasure of giving Adela away in marriage. She is a very special niece whose father Rudy, had passed away. She and I had built up a close relationship ever since she was attending Crossroads Baptist Church. She finally moved her membership to my church, Free Grace Baptist (FGBC), after hearing much gospel truth. In fact, Adela and I spent much time discussing our faith, and what was being preached in our churches. One Sunday evening, we were even asked to leave an ice cream parlor with our cones in our hands. (It was closing time!) We enjoyed sweet fellowship at FGBC, especially since my sister Vangie (Adela's mom), was also a member of the church.

In time, our good buddy and brother-in-Christ Eric, introduced Adela to his brother who lived in Florida. It wasn't long before David Butterbaugh flew to San Antonio while Adela (and the whole family) waited at the airport. This was just the beginning of a romance that inevitably ended in a proposal of marriage. That's when Adela asked if I would give her away at the altar. Naturally I was excited and felt privileged! I even thought to surprise her with a Mariachi band at the wedding reception. I contacted one of my former Tafolla students who played with a fine group. Later, I found out that Adela was not too crazy about Mariachis. Other than that, it was a beautiful wedding.

The day came when the newlyweds decided to move to Florida. I was to help with the move. It was unbelievable the amount of stuff

Hurry up Uncle Richard!!

that Adela had to move. In fact, they had to hire a huge U-Haul truck, plus a small one to squeeze in all her belongings.

Eric drove the huge fully packed U-Haul truck. I was the "co-pilot" who read and slept much of the trip. David, Adela, Vangie, and their precious cat "Bobo" traveled by car. We had loaded both trucks by the sweat of our brows, and left a trail of pennies all the way from San Antonio to Florida. I think that huge jar of pennies was Adela's collection from her childhood days.

A couple of years later I had the pleasure of visiting them in Florida. We did much sightseeing, including Miami. However, the most exciting part of that trip was attending an R.C. Sproul Conference in Orlando, where I got to hear and meet well respected and loved preachers such as John MacArthur, R.C. Sproul, Al Martin, and D. James Kennedy.

Uncle Richard gives Adela away

David & Adela with family

Sam Cerda Family

Tim Conway Family

CHAPTER 27
GRACE, GRACE, GRACE

Free Grace Baptist Church (1991-2002)

The teaching and preaching at Hillburn Drive Baptist Church included biblical truths that were edifying. The pastor was Joe Maldonado. The brethren were warm and cordial. Then one Sunday, another church group started a ministry in a small trailer next to the church building. It was a small group of about five families. Pastor Ken Billings preached the Spanish service. This got my attention because both my mom and I liked Spanish.

I started visiting with this group and was truly blessed by the articulate preaching, and hymn singing in Spanish. After several weeks of praying and asking the Lord for wisdom and direction, I could sense a peace about joining the "Iglesia Bautista de la Libre Gracia." I felt a little awkward telling this to Pastor Joe Maldonado, whom I had a lot of love and respect for. But he was very understanding!

It was a cold December winter as we huddled around a potbelly stove to keep warm. We sang hymns then listened to Pastor Billings preach on "Las Parabolas" (The Parables). The cold weather in this small enclosure seemed to draw this small motley group closer together (literally!).

By January 1991, we had moved to a larger and more adequate building at 423 Pleasant Road. We cleaned, painted, installed an AC unit, and generally improved the condition of the building. By this time, Sam, Mayra, Caleb and Ruby had already joined us. We enjoyed fellowship luncheons under a big tree in the backyard of the church. We did such a good job of sprucing up the building that before long the owner hiked up the rent. We were compelled to search for a new place to worship.

The Lord in His goodness led us to a beautiful, clean, air conditioned building. Balcones Heights Community Center, right off Fredericksburg Road, had all the conveniences with a fully equipped kitchen, appliances, bathrooms, tables, and chairs. We were happy and we gave praise unto the Lord for His generous provisions. We enjoyed sweet fellowship in worship, praise, and prayer. I was privileged to lead the singing as the church was growing. By this time the Lord had added new church members, including the Steve McConnell family and the Jim Smith family. Pastor Billings had gone from preaching in Spanish to bilingual, and finally to all English. This was done for the benefit of the children and young people who didn't understand Spanish. Because of strict regulations and raise in rent by the city of Balcones Heights, we were compelled to move out. Sam and Mayra offered their home in Leon Springs for the church to meet until we could find another place. We met in a large playroom, and even used a long concrete porch for Sunday school. The porch was also convenient for serving food after the services. Later, we moved to a portable building provided by Village

Parkway Baptist Church on Culebra Road.

After about a year, providentially an opportunity opened up and we found the building that we would purchase. We were blessed with a beautiful building located at 1801 Thorain Street. It turned out to be an answer to our prayers. We were even blessed with a $90,000 interest free loan from a church in Pennsylvania, where Bob Carr was the pastor.

One Sunday I made friends with a young Air Force Lieutenant who was visiting our church. Eric Butterbaugh was to be stationed at Kelly Air Force Base for four years. He joined our church and Pastor Billings asked if I would help him find an apartment. After searching we found something he liked which was in close proximity to the church and the base.

Just as important was the beginning of a solid friendship with a brother in Christ. In spite of the difference in our ages, we had similar things in common, mainly our belief in Jesus Christ. Even though we were brothers in Christ I regarded him as a son as well. We built a bond of friendship and brotherhood in Christ that was to last for a long time.

We had long winded conversations on just about every subject and always agreed that Christ alone was the hope for our future. We never failed to pray no matter where we went. We supported each other and became somewhat accountable to each other. Eric became like one of our biological family and was loved by everyone. He devoured Lupita's cooking and showered her with praise after each meal. One conversation piece that kept coming up from time to time was the subject of marriage. As an older married man I had much to share on the subject. As a single man, Eric had a few disappointments, especially after attending a couple of church related singles' conferences.

Many years have past and we are now many miles apart, but my good brother and I have kept in touch through out his military career. Today he is a retired Lt. Colonel, happily married to his dream girl Kate. They have four handsome young boys (one set of twins), and a beautiful baby girl. The Lord had providentially brought Eric and I together, and we still remain close in spirit.

I can't go further without mentioning my niece, Adela. She, Eric, and I spent many nights chatting outside the church after the Sunday night services. One night, shortly after I had left and Eric was also driving away, a man came out of the dark and approached Adela. Eric drove around the block and came back as the man was leaving. Apparently he was harmless, but Adela was really frightened.

Another night after spending time with them, I was on my way home and I discovered that my bible and a couple of songbooks were missing. I remembered placing them on the trunk of my car while we talked. I returned and found my books strewn on the access road near the church. At least one car had run over them. Some nights after church we would end up at Jacala, our favorite Mexican restaurant on West Ave.

Lisa Porter, our church pianist, was a quiet, unassuming, but talented young lady. Since I was song leader, I appreciated and enjoyed working with her. One day, the Lord providentially sent us another talented pianist. Paul Emslie was tall, debonair, and an accomplished musician. I introduced Lisa to Paul, and no, these two didn't compete against each other. In fact, they fell in love! Before long, the inevitable happened! They decided to make music together and ended up walking down the aisle to the sound of the wedding march. It was exciting seeing how the Lord had brought these two young people together. With their combined talents and being of one mind, spirit, and faith, their service would now be for the kingdom of God. Today they are happily married and the Lord has blessed them with seven beautiful children. "Behold, Children are a heritage from the Lord, the fruit of the womb is a reward."(Psalm 127:3)

The Lord opened up an opportunity to bring the gospel to the jail. This became one of our ministries at Free Grace Baptist Church. Christ once said, "When I was in prison you visited me..." Eric and I would always apply hand sanitizer then pray in the car. Every Saturday evening we would join Pastor Billings and a couple of other brethren for the jail ministry at the Wakkenhut Jail in downtown San Antonio.

Pastor Billings would preach in Spanish, I led the singing, and Paul Emslie played the keyboard. The meeting room would get full of Hispanic prisoners from Mexico and Central America. There was scripture reading, singing, preaching the gospel, and then face-to-face witnessing.

On March 26, 2000, I made a profession of faith in Christ Jesus as my Lord and Savior, and was baptized by Pastor Billings. I confessed and repented before the Lord.

ATTACK ON U.S. BY TERRORISTS:

SEPTEMBER 11, 2001

On September 11, 2001, at 8:45 a.m. on a clear Tuesday morning, Flight 11, an American Airlines Boeing 767 airplane loaded with 20,000 gallons of jet fuel, crashed into the north World Trade Center Tower in New York City. The impact left a huge gaping hole near the 80th floor and literally ignited the whole area with an immense devastating inferno. Eventually, it was determined that this airplane was hijacked by terrorists. Not since Pearl Harbor had their been such devastation by evil forces on the U.S. Mainland.

At 9:03 a.m. that same morning, United Airlines Flight 175 crashed into the south World Trade Center Tower. It was finally recognized that these surprise, premeditated, suicide attacks were by an Islamist militant group, Al-Queda. There was fear, confusion, and sheer pandemonium in lower Manhattan and New Your City.

At 10:10 a.m. American Airlines Flight 77 smashed at a high rate of speed into the Pentagon Building in Arlington, Virginia. This Islamic hijacker maneuvered the plane so that it plowed right through the building and exploded. There was mass destruction and confusion as hundreds ran out of the buildings.

At 10:10 a.m., hijacked United Airlines Flight 93 made an attempt to return back to Washington, D.C., with intentions of crashing into the U.S. Capitol Building or the White House. At this point, some of the passengers foiled this plan by attempting to overpower the high jackers. In the confusion the plane took a nosedive and crashed into a field in Shanksville, Pennsylvania. All the passengers were killed, including the heroes who prevented the plane from returning and crashing into another Federal building.

At 10:28 a.m., to add to the most horrific event on U.S. soil, both

World Trade Centers collapsed, causing panic-stricken crowds to scramble as debris, smoke, and heavy dust came flying through the air. All together, 19 terrorists had caused massive destruction and the deaths of 2,996 people.

GRACE ANNE GOES TO THE HOSPITAL

On March 25, 2002 a colonoscopy test was scheduled for my granddaughter Grace. I felt real sorry for her. She was seven-years old and seemed so small and fragile. The colonoscopy which was taken a month earlier, was ineffective since Grace had not completely cleaned out her stomach as required. A more difficult procedure would be necessary.

On Sunday April 28, Ruby, a concerned but prayerful mother, took her to the hospital after the morning church service. I joined them Monday morning as she was being prepared for a colonoscopy. The little princess was exceptionally brave through this whole "scary" process. She just shed a couple of tiny tears when the friendly anesthesiologist was reminding her how easy the first colonoscopy was. This did not sit too well with Grace, who kept her eyes constantly glued to Ruby, even as she was being wheeled away to the operating room. This whole drama ended when a marble size polyp was successfully passed through "normal channels." God granted much grace to both Grace and Ruby through this unusual ordeal.

Me and Lupita at Fatty's

Pastor Tim's birthday dinner at Tomatillo's

Grace Community Church at the Hackberry location

CHAPTER 28
GRACE COMMUNITY CHURCH
OCTOBER 20, 2002

My eleven years at Free Grace Baptist Church with Pastor Billings and the beloved brethren was glorious, edifying, and fruitful. There was sound biblical teaching and preaching that led me to the truth of the gospel and salvation. I have beautiful blessed memories and great love for those faithful saints. The Deacons were: Leo Lopez, Ramiro Nava, and Steve McConnell.

But now my desire was for more evangelism and outreach. There was a church that was very involved in evangelism and street ministry. I felt that in this type of ministry I would be able to serve the Lord more effectively. After much thought and prayer, the Lord gave me a peace about moving to this church. I transferred my membership to Grace Community Church (GCC). The church was strategically located on Hackberry Street, on the Eastside of downtown San Antonio.

Grace Community Church — 2005

This was an inner city ministry comprised of five families who had a great zeal for evangelism and outreach. The meeting place was a two-story white historic building. Shortly after the church opened, thieves broke in and robbed its antique glass doorknobs, the unique fireplace mantle, and a beautifully designed front door. We knew we had come to the right place! God had providentially brought us to bring the gospel to this dark part of town. The goal of this small body of believers was to spread the word of God throughout the Eastside, which was infested with illegal drug traffic, drug addiction, alcoholism, and prostitution. Then there were the outcasts, homeless and derelicts. But after going out in the neighborhoods and distributing tracts and bibles, we met a lot of decent, honest hardworking families.

Another ministry that we were involved in was serving food, handing out tracts, and sharing the Gospel under the West Commerce Street Bridge at Medina Street.

GCC Bridge Ministry—with Tim, Freddie, Heather and others.

Our goal was to spread the bad news as well as the good news to everyone. The bad news is that we are all sinners, and the good news is that there is salvation only through Jesus Christ. We were making the church and Christ known in the neighborhood. Tim Conway, my son-in-law, and brother in Christ, is the pastor of this motley group.

Serving the Lord alongside my daughter Ruby and their four children was an added blessing. Tim, whom the Lord had called out of a successful engineering career, was now pastoring and preaching to a small group of zealous and spirit-filled families. Their first meeting place was in the home of Freddie and Trisha Garza. Community Baptist Church (CBC) in Elmendorf had anointed Tim and sent him out to shepherd this flock. Now the Lord had called this small group to meet and worship at 315 North Hackberry Street.

On one occasion, while alone outside the church, a demon-possessed woman cursed Tim and called him names unsuitable for print. A short time after that she started coming to the services quite regularly. Others like her came mainly for the meals and clothing that we distributed. These were answers to prayer, because they were lost souls that needed to hear the gospel. Before long, the Lord answered our specific prayers for an African-American elder.

Charles Wilson and his wife Stormi came and were indeed a new blessing to our fellowship. Soon after that, Chip and Tress Hewitt came and we knew the Lord was answering our prayers. Chip, who was in the Air Force, had been transferred to San Antonio. Tress, an excellent and enthusiastic pianist, became our church accompanist.

Sunday school activities and meals after church service attracted many children. With permission from the parents, we had several vehicles that would pick them up from their homes. We saw this as an excellent opportunity to have Vacation Bible School. One warm summer the church (mostly women), planned and organized ideas for bible studies, arts and crafts, games, snacks, drinks and music. Leadership skills for different activities began to emerge with much enthusiasm.

Bosom Buddies Eddie Karisch & Richard

Tress Hewitt demonstrated huge energy and was skillful at leading games and songs, accompanied by her husband Chip on the guitar. Pastor Tim probably had as much fun as the kids during VBS.

During one of the outdoor games on the parking lot, little Abraham who was too little to participate, kept interfering and disrupting the other kids. To help out, I put him on my shoulders for a camel ride. Suddenly, his older brother Carlos tackled me from behind and threw me off balance. We flew forward right into the asphalt parking lot. Abraham cried but didn't even have a scratch. I got up and later discovered a serious gash in my left knee, scraped and sore elbow, and a bruised rib.

Vacation Bible School (VBS) - 2005

Over all, VBS was very successful. Cars and vans would pick up the children at their homes. We were pleasingly surprised at the large number that showed up. The children were inviting their friends and each day new faces kept showing up. As a result of VBS some new families were introduced to our church.

Samuel Kim devoted much of his time and talent painting and decorating the inside of the church with curtains, new blinds, etc. His wife, Hannah had a young lady visitor from South Korea who turned out to be a very gifted pianist. Phoebe was attending college here, and soon got very involved in serving as piano accompanist for the congregation. She was very talented and had a remarkable ear for music.

Member families were assigned to clean the church on Saturdays. There was good teamwork in cleaning, mowing the lawn, painting, and sprucing up the building both downstairs and upstairs. Sometimes needles and other drug paraphernalia were found in the backyard of the church.

One weekend we held services in a big tent on the parking lot when our visiting preacher was Paul Washer. Unbeknownst to Paul Washer, his wife Charo was miraculously saved during the tent meetings. A short time after the meetings, Paul called Tim from his home to give him the good news.

While in San Antonio, Paul accompanied Tim on a trip to one of the local crack houses on the Eastside. They were exposed to a smelly, filthy den of sin, with its occupants just lazily hanging around. The gospel was proclaimed to those who would listen.

The house next door to our church was vacant and boarded up. But that did not keep homeless and derelicts from crawling in and doing drugs, or sleeping there on cold nights. One Sunday morning, we were given the shocking news that a Saturday night fire had completely consumed that house of ill repute. The flames reached one side of our church building and caused extensive damage. Fire, smoke, and water damage made it impossible for us to meet there any longer.

For the first few weeks after that, we had to meet on the church parking lot. After the services, we enjoyed the regular fellowship meals under the big pecan trees. I must admit it had a pleasant picnic atmosphere. We did this for a couple of weeks while trying to decide what course of action we should take. One day, Tim and Ruby were inquiring about meeting facilities at one of the near by hotels.

Providentially they met Mark Outing, who was promoting his hamburger restaurant and probably thought they were tourists. In conversation, Tim explained the need for a meeting place for our church. Mark, a professing Christian quickly and graciously offered his restaurant for us to meet in since they were closed on Sundays. "Fatty's Hamburgers and More" was a bright yellow building located at 1624 E. Commerce. This would be our temporary meeting place, and no one was complaining.

We knew that the church is not the building, but the body of believers that meet in it, with Christ as the head. This was indeed a blessing; and not too long after that Mark and his family joined our church. The furniture sal-

Chris Connell & Richard at Fatty's (Mark's Outing)

vaged from the fire was placed in storage. Our upright piano was donated to Iglesia Bautista Particular de la Gracia Soberana; whose shepherd is Pastor Joe Ortega, a faithful righteous friend of our church.

With the sale of the old building on Hackberry, our church was able to purchase a two-story house on Pine Street. God was providing and guiding our ministry. This building, which we call the Men's Grace House, was originally designed to house men who were in college, working, looking for work, or for visitors in transit from out-of-state. Lost men off the street that showed interest in learning

Brethren at Fatty's Restaurant

the Word of God were also admitted. James Jennings took on the responsibility of managing this new ministry. There were some young men who came from unstable homes or had lived in an adverse environment. The men had to be pursuing a useful endeavor, and were required to attend the church meetings, including Sunday worship services.

Just recently a Women's Grace House was opened on the Eastside, close to the church with similar goals as the Men's Grace House. This house is designed as temporary housing for women off the street, which might include women of ill repute, ex-convicts, battered and homeless ladies who desperately need help. Alex Giuffre and Krystal Herbert are the two compassionate and capable Christian young ladies who oversee and share the gospel there. Each Sunday we would convert Fatty's Restaurant into a church setting.

After the morning services, we serve a fellowship meal to people off the street, and to all visitors. With much faith and prayers, the Lord began to bless our ministry. We still meet at Fatty's after eight years. In the meantime, God in His goodness continued answering our prayers. He had brought us Martha Smith, an accomplished pianist to fill the void that Chip and Tress left after they moved. We love to sing those inspirational hymns. Now we had a pianist, but no piano. Without hesitation the Lord provided the church with a large electric keyboard.

Desiring to encourage my grandchildren towards an appreciation for music, I accompanied Ruby and her four children to an initial interview with a prospective piano instructor. This was Martha Smith. She had recently graduated from University of Oklahoma where she earned a Master's Degree in Piano Performance and Pedagogy. She was not completely unfamiliar to San Antonio since she had family members here. We were pleasantly surprised to find that Martha's studio was actually located in the King Williams Historic District.

It was her aunt who graciously allowed her to set up a piano studio in her elegant home. After interviewing the four Conway kids we were very pleased with Martha's obvious God-given talents to teach children. Her pleasant disposition was an added blessing. Before leaving, Ruby and I invited her to our church and gave her the address and meeting times. Much to our surprise, she showed up at church the following Sunday and has been with us ever since!

It didn't take long to recognize the Lord's perfect providence in having our paths cross with Martha the week before. Not only had Ruby been praying for a good Christian piano teacher for her children, but also our church had been praying for a pianist. Martha turned out to be God's answer to both those needs. In addition to musical gifts, she was kind and compassionate toward the weak and the needy. One opportunity arose was when I was volunteering for the Meals on Wheels program.

Martha was willing to help me deliver hot meals to lonely and needy elderly. It was indeed a blessing to see the grateful faces of these frail elderly persons when we came to their door. Since our initial meeting six years ago, the Lord has given Martha a well-established piano studio with many students. She has been successful in presenting piano recitals which everyone enjoys, especially the parents. She continues to be a blessing to our entire church family.

Through our Sermon Audio GCC page (*www.sermonaudio.com/gcc*), an internet audio ministry introduced by Matt Haney, our outreach has expanded, and we have visitors from all over the United States, as well as from abroad. James Jennings, another gifted young brother in our church initiated the "I'll Be Honest" (*www.illbehonest.com*) ministry. Through this amazing new technology the Lord has allowed our church to reach many parts of the world with powerful sermons, testimonies, and the light of the gospel.

Through our website (*www.gccsatx.org*), "I'll Be Honest", and Sermon

Rick, Ruby, Papa, and Mayra
"I have no greater joy than to hear that my children are walking in truth." (3 John 1:4)

Audio, the Word of God is being transmitted through out the world in many foreign languages. We have been blessed with very sound capable leaders. At that time, Tim Conway and John Systma were the GCC's elders. Matt Haney and Carlos Munoz were the deacons. Even though two walls were torn down inside Fatty's to accommodate the church, there are still people standing during Sunday services. This is a problem as well as a blessing. The Lord continues to grow us. This small body of believers has fervor for spreading the Gospel to lost souls locally and throughout the world. We have a passion to be an aggressively God-loving, Bible-saturated, Spirit-filled, and racially diverse church. GCC's Mission Statement also encourages "knowing and proclaiming the excellencies of Christ for the glory of God and the joy of all people." We are reformed in that we believe in the doctrines of grace and at the same time we are very evangelistic and mission-minded.

Pastor Tim Conway, who has always had a vision for missions and evangelism, continues to pursue God's plan for the spreading of the Gospel wherever the Lord leads. His preaching reflects the passion he has for lost souls throughout the community and throughout the world. His hope for establishing churches and spreading the gospel has taken him to the far reaches of the world.

Currently, we can boast in the Lord, who has opened up opportunities for us to spread the Gospel in places far and near. Some of those missionaries and/or ministries we are praying for and supporting, include: churches in Corpus Christi, Laredo, Austin, Nuevo Laredo, Mexico; Guadalajara; Mexico City; China; India; Papua, Indonesian; Papua, New Guinea; Brazil; Turkey; Egypt; and Men's Grace House (San Antonio) and Women's Grace Houses (San Antonio and India).

Our church is blessed with many young people, both single and married, that have great zeal and compassion for spreading the gospel. Small groups meet regularly for bible studies, street preaching, and taking tracts and food to the homeless, the home bound, and ministry in a nursing home. John and Ciara Dees are a young couple, part of our ministry team in Guwahati, India.

Martha Smith and Amy Mozingo are just a couple of our young sisters who have traveled to India to share Christ and His love. Charity Conway, my granddaughter, after graduating from high school (homeschool), thought seriously and prayed for God's direction. She finally responded to a great need in Guwahati, India. The Wilkinsons, who were one of our missionary families in India, had a great need. Matt was the missionary pastor and Leanne was expecting her sixth child. That's where Charity came in! She was to homeschool some of the children, as well as being a loving, caring nanny. Weekends she devoted time to fellowshipping and encouraging the young girls at the Ladies Grace House. Leanne and Charity found time to go out shopping and handing out tracts to the rickshaw drivers and merchants. Charity lived there with the Wilkinsons from October 20, 2012 to February 2, 2013, then went back to help them as they planned their return to the U.S. This was from April to August of 2013.

The faithful God whom we serve and worship, has been answering our fervent prayers. One has been the building of a small church in Corpus Christi, Texas. Dan Sem and Mark Summers were ordained as elders. Before the ordination service, many of us were privileged to witness several baptisms in the Gulf of Mexico.

At the same time we were praying and supporting another faithful group of our brethren in Laredo, Texas. God, in His time, will establish a church there. Michael Mireles, Daniel Perez, and Bobby Barientes took their families there with hopes of building a church in that border town.

Later Daniel Alcala responded to God's calling to join that motley group. The brethren meet in Michael and Debbie's home. Currently, Ves Chancellor has been assigned as interim pastor until an elder is selected. Tim, with his inexhaustible vision, pictured God opening another church in Austin, Texas.

A small group of spirit-filled brethren are now serving the Lord with regular church services, plus going out evangelizing on the University of Texas campus. Tim and other brethren are leading prayer meetings and worship services on a weekly basis. It is through the passion and zeal of our faithful elders, Tim and John, that these ministries have become a reality. We continue to follow the commandment of Jesus in Matthew 28:19 "Go therefore and make disciples of all nations, baptizing them in the name of the Father, and of the Son, and of the Holy Spirit."

The most devastating and destructive Typhoon Haiyan, hit the Philippine Islands on November 8, 2013. Dan Sem, one of the elders at the Corpus Christi church led a team to bring aid as well as the Gospel to the most badly hit parts of those islands.

The team was made up of John and Judy Systma, Sam Patrone, Mack Tomlinson, Sarah Wynter, and Jeremy Vuolo.

Jeremy is 26 years old, and is a recent member of our church family. He aspires to go into the ministry as the Lord leads him. In the meantime, he continues as a spiritual leader and a soccer player with the San Antonio Scorpions Soccer team.

Richard Cortez Family

Because I was created by God and for His glory, I will magnify Him as I respond to His great love. My desire is to make knowing and enjoying God the passionate pursuit of my life."

John Piper *"Don't Waste Your Life"*

CHAPTER 29
THIRTY YEARS OF TEACHING

I have been privileged to serve as educator and band director for thirty years. It has been a very rewarding career. In this position I discovered that band students usually excel and are more conscientious than the average student. My personal slogan is, "A boy who blows a horn will never blow a safe." Generally, they are more self-disciplined! I also observed that no matter the size of a school, whether in a large city or a small country town, and regardless of the economic conditions, there are students who emerge with exceptional innate motivation, intellect, and talent. It was extremely gratifying helping students find and develop their gifts and talents. Most would not pursue music as their career. My major goal was to help develop character that would be useful to the students throughout their whole life.

Youngsters in Hawaii and California are not too different from those in Texas. I found that middle school students are the most challenging. They are coming out of childhood into adolescence. This is an exciting but sensitive transition, which affects their physical bodies, as well as their minds and attitudes. They want to feel grown, but still cling to childish behavior.

Middle school is like an exploratory plateau where youngsters are "groping" to see where they fit in a growing and demanding society. At this age, some may develop an independent spirit, and even rebel. Of course, there are some who are more conscientious and more responsible than others. A stable home environment many times may provide encouragement toward academic goals. Some youngsters excel in spite of their parents who have limited education.

Teaching for many years had been a very gratifying experience for me. Everyday I learned right along with the students. There is never a dull day and no two days are alike. My love for children and for music was mingled with compassion and patience. A teacher has to be friendly and have the respect and confidence of the students. However, they must not get too familiar! Familiarity breeds disrespect. Students will call a teacher by their first name if the teacher allows it. Band is a very disciplined organization where uniformity, respect, as well as quick response to commands is absolutely vital.

In San Antonio, about eighteen percent of the students came from one-parent families.[1] Many students look up to male teachers as father figures. I thank God that He gave me grace and divine guidance to recognize the needs of so many children. I also saw other teachers that devoted much of their time and effort beyond the school hours to help and encourage struggling students. It was a distinct privilege devoting my life to serving, working, and relating to youth of all ages. I now believe all this was providential and an answer to prayer! In all situations and environments (including the Navy), I was committed to use my God-given strength and gifts to perform responsibly and honorably.

As a Seabee in the Navy, I learned discipline and respect for those in authority, in spite of adverse conditions. As a teacher, I considered myself a servant to those under me, even though the majority looked up to me as a symbol of authority. With love and respect for my kids, it was gratifying to hear "Sir, yes sir," "No sir," etc., which I heard for thirty years in the classroom. Above all, my goal was to live an exemplary life with the gifts God has blessed me with.

"And whatever you do in word or deed, do all in the name of the Lord Jesus, giving thanks to God the Father through Him." (Colossians 3:17)

SUBSTITUTE TEACHING AFTER RETIREMENT

In June 1988, I finally decided it was time to retire my baton. My climatic emotional finale would be at Tafolla Middle School. My memories there are indelible! I was sixty-one years old. My eardrums were asking for relief from banging drums, loud horns, big and small, and squeaks from the reeds; day in and day out, for many years. I had noticed one retired band director friend wore a hearing aid. Years earlier, I had known another band director who had suffered a nervous breakdown.

We had settled into our beautiful new home at 8519 Bristlecone which we purchased the previous year (August 1987). We really didn't want such a big house, but my friend Louis Garcia got us a good deal for $61,812. My overall health was holding out and I thought now was a good time to retire. Now I could relax and reminisce over the first exciting years at Natalia, the beautiful aloha years in

Hawaii, and the glorious fourteen years at Tafolla. I submitted my resignation to the San Antonio Independent School District in the summer of 1988.

"Once a teacher always a teacher!" I ended up in the classroom again. But this time it was substitute teaching in the elementary grades. I guess I did this to stay busy and to experience teaching in the lower grades. As I suspected, it was less stressful in elementary than in secondary where I had taught for so many years. The Northside School District welcomed me since there was a great need for male substitute teachers in the lower grades.

It was surprisingly satisfying - the way the little kiddos responded, with innocent but genuine affection and respect toward their teachers. It was rewarding, even for a new substitute teacher. Plus, the position was profitable, considering I was a retired teacher with a master's degree. However, being called at 6 a.m. and told to report to school at 7:30 a.m. was not too appealing.

However, I found out I could choose the school or schools I preferred, and could designate the hours that I was available. After teaching at several schools I decided I was content with Eduardo

Villarreal Elementary. The working environment was pleasant. Plus, my niece Rebecca was a teacher there. So, I made myself available to this school, and they would call me regularly.

DEFENSIVE DRIVING – AFTER RETIREMENT

After retirement I continued teaching at Rhodes' Driving School. There was plenty of work there, especially during the summer. Lupita finally convinced me that I didn't need that job any longer where I had to drive across town, at times in rain or shine. I finally resigned, and Rhodes presented me with a beautiful plaque commemorating twenty years of service.

After retirement, Lupita and I enjoyed weekend trips to Corpus Christi, Fredericksburg, Bandera, and other parts of the Hill Country in Texas. Corpus was always quiet and very relaxing. We enjoyed walks along Shoreline Drive. I always enjoyed jogging along the seawall sidewalk. Sometimes we would take an ice chest full of food and drinks.

If the motel had appliances, Lupita would cook and we would eat inside while enjoying the view of the Gulf from our patio. Other times we enjoyed exploring and trying out different restaurants.

Trips on the sightseeing boats in the harbor were always refreshing. As our faces felt the salt spray, we could spot fishing boats coming in from their day's catch. The Texas State Aquarium is huge, educational, colorful, and had an immense variety of touch pools and sea life exhibits. One could easily spend a whole day there. Being an ex-Sailor, the USS Lexington (a retired aircraft carrier), was always alluring to me. Lupita was not too keen on climbing up and down those narrow ladders on the ship.

Fredericksburg is a small, quaint, and very relaxing town in Texas. It has an array of souvenir shops, restaurants, and sidewalk cafes. It attracts many visitors and tourists. But my favorite place to hang out was the Nimitz War Museum. Admiral Nimitz, who was the commanding officer of the Pacific fleet during World War II, was born in this quiet country town. The array of World War II memorabilia on display together with weapons, films, pictures, wall plaques, videos, and books, is especially appealing to veterans. Hearing a recording of the "Day of Infamy" speech by President Franklin Delano Roosevelt brought back sober memories.

TENNIS

Since I had retired from band directing and driver's education training, I decided to take up tennis. Raymond Rimkus Park in Leon Valley had good courts and was close to my house, so that's where I first started. The only person there at that time was a young lady with Sailor (her dog) that loved to chase the tennis balls. Since I was just a beginner she would give me tips as we played. Sailor was also helpful and enjoyed chasing and returning the balls that went out of bounds. I thought that was clever, except for the fact that the balls would get all soggy. If we stopped to chat, Sailor would just sit beside us and start whining, hinting that he wanted to play ball.

Jim and Carolyn Gabriel, who were closer to my age, started coming, together with a retired preacher. Eventually others came, including Pete Salas, Joe Gonzales, Joe Claussen, Jerry Roemer, Peter Guillao, Jo Jo, Vicky, Ted, Barry, Don, Velia, David, Beth, Bob Eddie, Gene Murphy (the legend), and others. We adopted the title of Raymond Rimpkus Rabble Rousers. If I got up early enough, Lupita would drive me to Los Jalapenos Cafe for tacos before going to the park. Most of the time, Lupita would walk around the marked trail at the park while I played tennis. If I stayed too long, she would just drive over to Los Jalapenos for coffee. This went on for several years. Over time, she would just sit on a park bench and smoke until I finished. She was exceptionally patient, having to wait for two or more hours.

Many new "old timers" begin to converge on the tennis courts in Leon Valley. I soon found out they had left their privileged Robert E. Lee High School tennis courts. Most of them lived close to the Leon Valley. They were experienced and very competitive. But now, because there were so many players and only two tennis courts, we had to wait our turn to play. Players started coming from all over, both men and women. But it was great fun! Some of us played for fun and for exercise. Then, there were one or two who went home sulking if they lost. You always have a few "poor sports" that ruin the game. Occasionally tempers would flare, but for the most part the majority of players were pretty cool. At least once I experienced a physical encounter, which is not worth discussing further. Hey, this is supposed to be a non-contact sport!

I developed a real friendly bond with a great bunch of guys and gals on the court. At the suggestion of Mayra, I brought two of my grandsons, Caleb and Benjamin, to break them in on this great sport. After a while, Caleb finally lost interest, but Ben seemed more interested. At first he had a hard time concentrating and was easily distracted by things going on outside the courts. In time he improved and his speed and technique were capturing the attention of the older players. In fact, he became very competitive with anyone he played with. Jo Jo, a Filipino friend, noticed Ben's potential and began giving him private lessons. His style and his serve were greatly improved and everybody liked him. However, the day that the Lord saved him, he left the tennis courts for good. He recognized that the game had become an idol. "Therefore if anyone is in Christ, he is a new creation, old things have passed away, behold all things have become new" (2 Corinthians 5:17). Like everyone else, I was surprised, but I had greater love and respect for him. I knew the Lord was truly doing a work in his heart and his life.

MOVED TO 6415 HONEY HILL – FEBRUARY 2007

For close to twenty years we had thoroughly enjoyed our home on Bristlecone Street. But now Lupita and I had decided that it had become too big for just the two of us. True, the four bedrooms, and all the amenities, including a spacious yard, front and back, had many memories of our grandchildren running all over the place. With age creeping up on us, we were ready for a smaller home. Facing reality, a smaller home with a smaller yard would be more practical. A young energetic realtor by the name of Rob Kuffel read our minds and knew exactly what we wanted. He surprised us by going beyond the call of duty. He not only suggested how we could improve our house if we were to sell it; in work clothes he would come and help me scrap and paint the inside of our Bristlecone house. In fact, Rob not only helped us sell that house, as well as the Ligustrum rental house, but he found us an ideal garden home.

After several days of helping me with manual labor, now he wanted to show us a beautiful neighborhood called Summit North. The first house he showed us was on Honey Hill Street. This street is one long block with beautiful huge shady trees. It's a quiet "no through" street with little traffic. Another benefit is that it's located one block from a small shopping center.

The second house we saw was perfect for us. The layout and the design were exactly what we needed. It's a garden home at 6415 Honey Hill, with a small yard, front and back, and surrounded by huge shady trees. We fell in love with it immediately! I had benefited and been blessed by the real estate investments that God had permitted me to enjoy. Now, at this new season of our life, I could afford to pay for this new house in cash. The Lord had been good and merciful to guide and provide for my family and me.

THIRTY YEARS OF TEACHING

[1] Eighteen Percent of families are single parents in San Antonio.: http://www.mysanantonio.com/news/local_news/article/Census-figures-illustrate-the-changing-family-1849194.php

"Now to Him who is able to do far more abundantly than all that we ask or think, according to the power at work within us, to Him be glory in the church and in Christ Jesus throughout all generations forever and ever. Amen."

Ephesians 3:20-21

CHAPTER 30
LETTERS & ALZHEIMERS

LETTERS THAT ARE AN
IMPORTANT PART OF MY LIFE

January 1, 2009

Happy New Year, Beloved Brethren,

As a new year begins, I rejoice, and I am exceedingly thankful to a good and merciful God. On December 5, 2008, I reached the incredible age of eighty-one. What is more incredible is that the Lord has sustained me with a strong and healthy body and a sound mind. More importantly, He has changed my life, and given me a new heart. "For by grace you have been saved, through faith, and that not of yourselves; it is a gift of God, not of works, lest any one should boast." (Ephesians 2:8).

This year was one of the happiest of my life. My tennis game improved, and my relationship with Lupita, the wife of my youth, is more loving and intimate. As we grow older, our brainpower is slowing down, but our love for each other increases. Extraordinary concern and care toward each other is sweeter with each day. Lupita's every moment is to serve me and to pour out praise and affection for me. My response is to show compassion, and graciously try to persuade her that she should praise and worship the God of all creation, instead of her husband.

Of course, my constant prayer is for the salvation of her soul. I am convinced that it is only by God's grace and mercy that our marriage has survived and reached the fifty-year goal. If the Lord lends us health and breath, we hope to celebrate our anniversary on August 28, 2009. Praise the Lord!!

I am constantly reminded of our vow before God - to love and to cherish... in sickness, and in health... till death do us part. Thank God for His amazing grace! But, all this has come about as a result of God's pouring His marvelous blessings on us. He, the supreme sovereign God, who left His throne, and came to earth as a man, to "save His people from their sins."(Matthew 1:21). He is now the source of my spiritual life. It is by His life that I live. Christ is the sustenance of my life, and the hope of glory. All my true joys come from Him, and in times of trouble, He is my consolation.

"There is nothing worth living for but Him, and His loving kindness is better than life." I love my wife, my children, and I adore my 12 grandchildren, but it is Jesus Christ, who sacrificed His life on the cross for me. "..the life I now live in the flesh, I live by faith in the Son of God, who loved me and gave Himself for me." (Galatians 2:20)

My sincere thanks for the love, friendship, prayers, and the sweet fellowship of the brothers and sisters that congregate to worship in that little yellow building on the Eastside of San Antonio. That little corner of the world is like a small piece of heaven for me. The grace of our Lord Jesus Christ be with you all.

-Love Richard

LETTER TO DR. KALTER OCTOBER 2, 2009

Dr. Kalter,

My wife Lupita, and I recently celebrated our 50th wedding anniversary. But, now she has the behavior and intelligence of a child. She constantly battles with hallucinations, loud talking and babbling with "old women, etc." She bangs plates, and pans, and strikes the table, as if to strike back at these invisible images. She is not able to cook anymore. She is lost in her own kitchen, and cannot distinguish a spoon from a fork or knife. She does not bathe. Physically, she appears to be okay.

Her behavior is like that of a person with some form of dementia. One major concern that I have is that she has not seen her doctor nor taken her medications in nine years.

I am feeling depressed and desperate. Rodolfo Rodriguez, my wife's brother-in-law, highly recommended you. His wife Gregoria (Gollita) Rodriguez, was your patient for several years. She is now bedridden with dementia.

I've called your office several times, left messages, but have gotten no response.

I'm hoping and praying you can help me.

Sincerely,

Richard Cortez

ALZHEIMERS STRIKES OUR HOME
DECEMBER 2009

"In this you rejoice, though now for a little while, if necessary, you have been grieved by various trials..." 1 Peter 1:6

On December 8, 2009, Lupita was diagnosed with Alzheimer's disease. This was to become the most difficult trial of my whole life. It took me a while to realize this problem was serious. At first I thought she was "putting on." I'm afraid I wasn't as sympathetic or patient as I could have been.

Our favorite place for walking was Raymond Rimkus Park in Leon Valley. Years before she had enjoyed walking around the park by herself while I played tennis. At times, she would just drive to our favorite little café, El Jalapeno, for coffee and tacos. Or, she would sit patiently under a tree on a park bench and smoke while waiting for me. But now, years later, I would walk her slowly along the path at the same park. Gradually, she started slowing down more and more. The walks were slower and shorter. The Lord gave me unusual patience. I did it lovingly, but holding back tears.

At the beginning, she enjoyed going out. If I casually said, "Want to go for a ride?" She was happy to go wherever I took her, no questions asked. I chose her clothes, shoes, dressed her, and brushed her hair, with no complaints. She was totally submissive, as a small child. And I was there to respond to her every need.

When riding in the car, I would be distracted when her little fingers would start digging through the glove compartment, the center miscellaneous box, or the side pockets. She even attempted to open her door a couple of times. This was testing my tolerance and my patience. Otherwise, she enjoyed riding as well as walking. I would find reasons to take her to HEB or Wal-Mart, mainly to help her get exercise by walking, and because she enjoyed it. After a couple of falls at home, she would hold firmly to my hand. Walking hand-in-hand everywhere we went sometimes attracted glances and comments like

"Look at that loving couple!"

Going to church on Sunday morning was a special and pleasant trip. We usually stopped for tacos at Taquerilla Vallarta with David Gonzales, Eddie Karisch and other brethren. Taking a small cushion for her comfort at church seemed to help. She appeared content for the most part. However, at times she would get restless when the sermon was too long. She would start squirming, and sometimes would stand up. I would gently pull her down! I was pleased that she would stay at church as long as she did, from 10 a.m. to 4:30 p.m. So it didn't surprise me if she stood up and walked out when the afternoon service was too long.

I would just follow her out. I was deeply grateful for the love and patience shown by the brethren toward her. They knew she was not well and they greeted her with smiles and hugs. Depending on her mood at the time, Lupita's response might not be very friendly.

She had one obsession, which I thought was a little quirky at the time. Every morning she would water the sidewalks, front and back. I suggested she water the plants instead. That didn't seem to register! When I hid the garden hose, she continued the "ritual" with a water bucket. She would help me make the bed, even though her actions were a little awkward.

After all, she was accustomed to doing this for so many years. Like other minor chores I used to help her with, now she was on the helping end. It was sad to see her gradually losing control in the kitchen, which was her domain. She would put dishes, pans, and glasses in the wrong places; then I was unable to find them. I would get frustrated when things completely disappeared. I would search for days and sometimes never found the items missing. Like the case of the missing scissors – I ended up buying six pairs to replace the lost ones.

Later, some things would show up in the most unlikely place, maybe in another room. Being ignorant of the impending mental problem, I would get impatient. I became real concerned when she could not tell the difference between the range and the refrigerator. She couldn't tell the difference between a fork and a spoon, or a glass and a plate.

By 2010, we still enjoyed our slow walks in the park in the cool of the evening, and reminiscing as we went past the tennis courts.

Through all this, we had developed extraordinary love and patience for each other. I had fresh appreciation and adoration for her with each new day. She seemed to enjoy all the attention I was giving her. The exceptions were when bathing and changing her Depends.

I would have been better prepared with a course in self-defense at this point. She suffered from incontinence and bladder control, which resulted in accidents from time to time. It was only by God's grace that I was able to efficiently and promptly manage what could have been awkward situations. Even though I was her husband, she still maintained her dignity as a grown woman. Each change of Depends and clothes would turn out to be a tug of war.

I would literally get on my knees to pull her slacks down, pleading and praying while she pulled up... her hands tightly gripped like her life depended on it! I was a "caregiver" before I even knew what that meant!

Alzheimer's disease is a slow death, and I thought I would be prepared when the time came, but I was wrong! However, recognizing the gift of love from Christ, now gave me the opportunity to pour out much needed love and attention to my dear bride.

I was demonstrating unconditional love and affection to make up for the past years of being insensitive while pouring myself into my jobs. A man can pursue his job and career to the extent that he neglects his first love. Now that I was retired and relaxed and facing this crisis, I felt like I had fallen in love again. In fact, my wife's illness brought us so much closer together that nothing could hinder us from demonstrating the tender intimate fondness and love that we had for each other for so many years.

Lupita's doctor had graciously recommended her for hospice care. The word 'hospice' shocked me at first. But this organization, called Odyssey, turned out to be a very capable and caring health-group that only takes terminal patients. At this point I had some degree of relief. Now Lupita would be monitored on a weekly basis. As a caregiver, I was warned of stress and fatigue that would result if breaks and rest periods were not taken. I was in constant prayer for wisdom and direction. My close faithful brethren and my family provided much prayer support and encouragement since Lupita was first diagnosed with Alzheimer's. I had determined to care for her in our home instead of placing her in a nursing home. My sweet loving daughter Ruby did a very timely act of mercy. She announced to the church that a position was available for someone to help me with Lupita for three or four hours a day. This would give me time and opportunities to relax on the tennis court, buy groceries, or run errands.

My two daughters, Mayra and Ruby, were immensely helpful through this difficult trial. This went on for close to three years, and my two daughters kept directing me to God's Word for relief and peace.

The Lord providentially sent me a precious young lady from our church. She turned out to be a tremendous blessing. Alex was prompt, caring, patient, and very compassionate. She quickly became familiar with Lupita's habits and personal needs. She even found

Alex, Papa, and Lupita

time to read the bible and share the gospel with her. Her original assignment was just to look after and protect Lupita while I took a morning break. Admitting this was completely new to her, Alex surprised me when she started cooking, doing the dishes, washing clothes, and making the beds. Then, she graciously took on the humble task of changing my wife's Depends, after watching me do it a couple of times. This routine usually started out in the morning when Lupita got up. The bed was usually wet.

After the change of Depends, the wet clothes and wet linen would have to be rushed to the washroom and placed in the washing machine. This young lady took on these chores with a loving attitude. I was absolutely astounded and impressed! She was performing way beyond my expectations. Arriving at 8:30 promptly every morning, she would appear with a quiet attitude and a warm smile. If Lupita was still asleep, she would prepare my breakfast, which might consist of bacon, eggs, beans, tortillas, coffee, oatmeal, etc. I mention the details because this was surprising and very meaningful to me. All I could say to myself was, thank you Lord! We would pray together at breakfast and chat about the activities for the day.

Then, she started preparing the meals for lunch. She was gentle and thoughtful and quickly sensed the hurt that I was experiencing. I was convinced the Lord had providentially sent us this saint to meet a very desperate need. Alex faced Lupita's unpredictable behavior with patience and affection. Her humble spirit and her trust in the

Lord brought a sense of peace and comfort.

I found the bible an oasis of strength and solace. Romans 8:28 opened my eyes to a new reality. "And we know that all things work together for good to those that love God, to those that are the called according to His purpose." This simple, but profound verse reminds us that God is preeminent above everything and everyone on earth. He deserves honor and praise above everyone else. The loss of a loved one is huge.

But the supreme sovereign God, creator of heaven and earth, and sustainer of life has a design for each one of His creatures. As mere mortals, we do not comprehend it all. But as a Christian, I do not question the integrity of this awesome God. It is this gracious, loving God who brought me relief and extraordinary comfort during the most difficult struggle of my life.

This God, the Master of my soul, is the one who gave me a new life. His amazing love for me was manifested when He gave His Son to die as a substitute for me. The wrath that God poured on His Son Jesus Christ, was the wrath that I deserved.

The following letters explain much of the initial "shock" and emotions which I communicated with some of my loved ones, including my daughter Ruby, my son Rick, my brother Gilbert, and others.

A LETTER FROM RUBY DECEMBER 30, 2009

Daddy,

In case I don't get a call over your way before you leave for mom's appointment, just wanted you to know that I/we are praying for you about all that the Lord has brought to pass concerning mom's health condition. I feel very burdened to pray that God would be glorified in all this...from showing Himself mighty in mom's life to filling you with peace that is beyond comprehension...so full that there would be no space for any fear to creep in. God is perfectly good and wise in all that He does...you know that. And because "God is love" every detail of this situation has God's love behind it and is meant for you to see and experience that love in a very real way. I do hope that you can walk through these days with a clear sense of God's love and His power that is strong enough to carry you through your weakest moments. Look to Jesus, Daddy; His might to save...not just mom, but you too. He will save you from fear, anxieties, and burdens that are too heavy for you to bear on your own. Lean on the everlasting arms of God and He WILL uphold you. May you find that much needed shelter under the safety of His wings during this storm. His grace He promises will be sufficient...for in your weakness He is strong. May you find rest in your Heavenly Father's providence, be that what it may, as you consider that our life, from before the foundation of the world, has been predetermined down to the smallest detail. Nothing can stay the Almighty hand of God...but we can come as His dear children, His "treasured possession" and cast our burdens upon Him for He cares for us...He cares for you. The Creator of heaven and earth is bending His ear every time we come to Him on behalf of mom's spiritual and physical needs. So as you pray in faith, and as you leave your burdens at His feet, may you press on with confidence in God's perfectly righteous and holy wisdom trusting that He will act upon His good pleasure according to that which will bring Him the most glory. May your life be a demonstration of faith in a God who is worthy to live and die for. "Worthy is the Lamb that was slain!"

Bearing this burden with you,
Ruby Maile Conway

LETTER FROM JANUARY 24, 2010

Hi Gilbert and Sophie,

Friday night (12 a.m.) Lupita fell from her bed. I put her back in bed and kept a watch on her all night. The pain on her right shoulder persisted all through the night. In the morning, she had a hard time walking, so I called an ambulance. The ER doctor at Luke hospital took x-rays and found she had broken her right collarbone. She is home now but she refuses to put on the sling, and continues to want to move her arms about as usual. She has medicine for the pain, and will probably need it tonight. I plan to take her to our primary physician this week for a check up on dizziness. Keep us in your prayers, during this trial.

Love,
Richard.

"Only one life 'twill soon be past, only what's done for Christ will last."

LUPITA - RECOMMENDED FOR HOSPICE CARE

February 8, 2010

When her primary physician, Dr. Carlos Hernandez suggested we place her on Hospice, I could not hold back that nervous "Cortez cough," and a big lump in my throat. I was stunned to hear that! "This word is mostly related to death," was my first thought! The doctor graciously explained the benefits. The reality of my faith in God humbled me as I faced this unusual devastating news. With much fervent prayer I placed the whole situation in the hands of my Lord, who is sovereign and totally in control. He will heal her or take her, in HIS time. The hospice medical team (Odyssey), consisted of a nurse, a social worker, a chaplain, and a home health aide. They came to the house and checked her vitals, and made sure she was comfortable at least once or twice a week. All this special attention was comforting, plus Medicare covered it.

Me and My Beautiful Bride

CHAPTER 31
CARE GIVER AT HOME

February 22, 2010

Hi Ruby,

I received your very emotional e-mail to Tim. You have the right to cry from time to time! You're only human! (I hope I said that right!!). It runs in the family. I broke down myself today, while reading Mom a mother's day card that you sent her several years back.

Anyway, I'm going to "unload" on you now! I understand now why some say that sometimes the caregiver breaks down before the patient. This evening mom and I decided to go get some things from HEB, to avoid the cold and rain tomorrow. Mom's reckless driving of the grocery cart is not that big a deal, nor her improper bagging of the groceries. As we are going out the door, I'm trying to help her button her sweater. She pulls away in a defiant manner and takes it completely off and puts it over her shoulder. She quickly puts it back on when she felt the cold wind outside. I'm trying to remain calm as she trails behind me in the parking lot. Now I'm searching for my maroon Toyota Camry.

It's getting colder, then I realized I should be looking for a silver "rental car" which I was driving at the time. There it was, two rows away. Now we are in the car and the usual struggle to find her seat belt. I reach clear across to grab hers and lock it in place. Then we drove up to gas up at our neighborhood service station. I stopped on the wrong side of the pump. This car has the gas tank on the opposite side of my own car. As I repositioned the car, mom had already loosened her seat belt and was ready to step outside. I let out a loud "silent scream", but patiently asked her to stay in the car.

I stick a cold hand in my pocket to pay with a $20 dollar bill. (It's one of those pay-first gas stations). The $20 bill is not there! It's not anywhere! Desperately I looked in the car console, the floor, inside the grocery bags, but found nothing. So I took another dollar bill from my wallet to pay for the gas. When I came back to the car I found the lost $20 dollar bill on the ground, just slightly under the car. I put it in my pocket and I drove off. When I rounded the corner at the Jack in the Box, I heard a little banging sound on the outside of the car. Then it dawned on me. It was the gas cap dangling on the side of the car. In my anxiety I had driven off without putting gas in the car!!! I rushed back to the station and the clerk said, "It's still open." I'm sure she saw the big "Idiot" sign on my forehead. And that was exactly the way I felt. Later as I gained my composure I was reminded of one of my favorite verses, Philippians 4:6 ("Don't be anxious for anything...") I have to admit that I will need a lot more strength (and faith) as I experience this progression in mom's illness. I know you and many others are praying for us, and I am eternally grateful.

Well, my dear - I feel much better now, after letting it all out!!!
Love you,
Dad

April 11, 2010

Hi Ruby,

I just got through cleaning the stovetop on our range. I could not help but think how I used to fuss at mom for cleaning and scrubbing that thing every night, and turning on the burners. Now she does not even notice it! In fact, she can't even tell the difference between the stove and the refrigerator. That is sad, real sad! I placed an unusually beautiful rose on our dinner table about five days ago. Now, it is droopy and withering. (Isaiah 40:7-8)

Mom's life is withering and her health is deteriorating, and I'm seeing this happen before my very eyes. Her communication is completely garbled. Her nurse calls it "word soup." I'm just guessing at what she is trying to say! She carries on long unintelligible conversations, and I just agree. Once in a while, she will drop some surprising remarks like she did to this lady at church - "You are really fat!" At church she dropped a cup of coffee on the floor during the service. That was partly my fault! The Spaghetti Warehouse after church was fun! Her usual thing is to wipe the table with her bare hands, then tears the napkin into little pieces. She ate half the Spaghetti, then lumped the remainder into a napkin. Again, that was my fault! You don't take a "two year old" to eat Spaghetti in a restaurant. Now my concern is that her appetite is diminishing and she is losing weight.

I find myself stumbling, dropping things (including food), forgetting, and generally fighting back frustration. Like a mother is not trained to know everything about her baby, a caregiver husband, like myself, is not trained for this type of situation. Mayra has reminded me of this, and she is encouraging me by filling in marvelously with much love and support. She brings food, she cooks, washes clothes, and dishes. She mops, and arranges mom's clothes, shoes, etc. And the best thing is, she relieves me and sends me to the tennis court with Benjamin. When I call her from the tennis court she encourages me to stay out, and not hurry home. She is coming twice a week. Praise the Lord for thoughtful, loving, daughters like her and you.

When riding in the car, mom's hands are constantly in motion. She is always piddling and poking into the console, the glove compartment, the floor, etc. She will grab gum, cough drops, or whatever. Then she will attempt to open the window to throw out the wrappers. Or, for no reason she will undo her seat belt or open the door. It's a little disrupting for the driver, to say the least. I can't say this goes on all the time, but when it happens, it is nerve wrecking.

On Friday, April 2, God answered a specific prayer. I was able to give her a shower. I prepared the shower bench, the towels, soap, and the adjustable shower extension. I had her clean clothes where I could reach them quickly. I was thoroughly confident of myself. But mom was not going in the shower without a "fight." She kept repeating, "I already did. I already did. I don't need it!" She was very upset and you would think she was being tortured. She even called me a few choice names that are not suitable for print. I finally and insistently removed her clothes.

The next skirmish was to get her into the shower, where there is water, slippery soap, and my beloved who is resisting with all her strength. Carefully but firmly I was able to place her right leg into the tub. She pulled her left leg out of the tub several times. All the while I pleaded and repeating "I love you baby, I'm not going to hurt you, you're going to feel much better." It all seemed so useless. She preferred to stand instead of sitting on the bench. I asked her to wash herself with the soapy wash towel while I manipulated the shower cord. All was going well until I started to wet her hair. Immediately she went "berserk" and grabbed the shower extension from my hand, and water sprayed all over the place. Yes, I had a lot to learn! Also, if I didn't hide the clothes she was wearing before, she would insist on wearing the same dirty clothes. In spite of all this, she would find it in her heart to thank me after she was clean, powered, dry, and in clean clothes. I was emotionally touched and gratified, and responded with a big hug and "I love you baby!" It was only by God's goodness and mercy that I was able to get through this unusual ordeal.

After insistent tips from her nurse, one day I bravely sneaked in to the bathroom, to see if her bowels were active. I was pleased that a little prayer, and a little laxative pill had done the job.

Ruby, your prayers and your constant encouraging words, "that honor your father and your mother," are being felt at 6415 Honey Hill. Keep it up my dear!

Love,
Dad

September 2, 2010

Ruby,

Charlene came while mom was still asleep. I had prepared mom's cereal on the table and left instructions. After a couple of hours, I came back, and everything was quiet and serene, with soft classical music on the radio. I was pleased that everything had gone well. Charlene, with her usual sweet spirit had really made friends with mom. They got along fine!

From time to time mom does not make it to the restroom in time, subsequently missing the target. On the toilet seat she sits "sidesaddle." Well, now she is losing interest in the commode all together! I have to point and persuade her that she needs to "SIT" to "do it." I even encourage her by saying that she is the queen and needs to sit on the throne.

Today, after a "peek inspection" (like you showed me), I came to the conclusion that she needed a change. After removing everything, we did a complete clean up job. Since she was already in her "birthday suit," I quickly grabbed some washcloths and gave her an impromptu sponge bath from top to bottom. I'm putting her clothes back on when suddenly she gets the urge again! We're in the bathroom so I quickly help her to the commode. I was envious, because I myself had constipation all that morning. My concern and meeting the needs for "my queen" is causing me to neglect my own health. Through my head rang the thoughts: "This is NOT real!" "This is bizarre!" "This is NOT happening to me!"

See Ruby, you're not the only one gifted to write deep profound e-mails. I don't mean to make fun of mom. You know I love her very much. But I found it amusing, and I knew I had to share it with someone.... and that someone had to be you.

(JUST ANOTHER DAY IN THE LIFE OF RICHARD AND LUPITA CORTEZ)

Love you,
Dad

September 16, 2010

Dear Ruby,

Yes, it is encouraging that you are thinking of me and mom. I've been thinking a lot about me too! I know, I need to think more upward, instead of inward. As we read in Isaiah 14:22, "Look unto ME, and be ye saved, all the ends of the earth. For I am God and there is none else." It just saddens me how totally dependent mom is on me. My time is not my own after I get home. I know you're always referring to mothers with young ones. And Mayra tells me this is not my role. Well, I sympathize with mothers, and I'm glad I am not one. But I'm blessed that I can do this for mom. This experience has molded our lives and sealed our love as we hold hands from room-to-room and in our going in and out. Then I think how the Lord might take her at any time, and you know what that does to my weary and aging heart. (Pause - excuse me, I have to blow my nose!)

Anyway, the Lord has been good to give me two thoughtful caring daughters, plus a host of loving saints from church. That is VERY encouraging! Of course Alex she is an angel in disguise! She has demonstrated an extraordinary Christlike love that has caused mom to respond quietly and cooperatively. At first I was a little concerned because she had never worked with elderly. But now she and mom get along beautifully! She knows how to respond to mom and tends to her quietly and gently. She is compassionate, considerate, and even reads her the bible. Praise the Lord for He is good and merciful!

I'll be happy to help you with the athletic finances for the kids. That is considered an educational activity, right? Hey, maybe you could teach Joy the flute, since she is still searching for her gift.

Say hi to Martha. Ask her to pray for mom and me.

And pray that mom and I can make it through the whole day at church on Sunday.

Love you,
Dad
P.S. I did not receive the note that Alex sent you.

ENDING THE GLORIOUS RACE: BY GOD'S GRACE

October 12, 2010 (letter To Grace Community Church)
Running The Race (up-hill), By God's Grace

Beloved Sister Connie - would you please relay this (Lupita's update), to the most wonderful people that I know. Thank you.

It is now October, 2010. Lupita sleeps comfortably. She is happy, content, and has no pain. However, Alzheimer's is taking its toll. It's a devastating disease that takes life away slowly, in degrees. Eventually it weakens the body and consumes the patient in stages. It appears to be the most frequent cause of irreversible dementia in adults. The intellectual impairment progresses gradually from forgetfulness to total disability. Another unexpected shocking crisis showed up. Lupita has been diagnosed with having an enlarged aortic aneurysm. The aneurysm is so close to her heart it cannot be operated on. It is only by the wonderful grace of a loving God that she still lives. Praise God, Hallelujah! Words are not adequate to describe my heart-felt gratitude toward my Lord God who gives and sustains life. Only He, who is sovereign, determines the extent of our lives. While I have her, I want to protect her, embrace her, love her, and share Christ with her, and pray with her, and for her. I want to please her and make her happy in every way while she is still responsive. I can't help but think of that beautiful lively vibrant person she used to be.

My love for her has not diminished - I can tolerate her child like behavior, eating with her fingers, poking her sticky fingers into everything, putting things away neatly – like my electric shaver in the clothes hamper, and the T.V. remote in the refrigerator. But I thank our loving Father that He keeps her calm, and peaceful, non-aggressive and nonviolent. Since I started bathing her, changing, and dressing her, brushing her hair, etc., she has gradually become less "combative." My daughters Mayra and Ruby have given me very helpful and practical ideas in all these areas.

As long as my beloved lifelong partner is holding my hand, she feels secure and is willing to follow me to the "ends of the world" - hopefully to my eternal home. The bond of love between us continues to grow. She depends entirely on me and I accept this tremendous responsibility which the Lord has brought to me. Who am I to question what my heavenly Father has predestined for me? I cannot ignore the commandment instilled in my heart from my youth, "that you love one another, just as I have loved you." And, after fifty-one years, I am constantly reminded of my sacred commitment - "Husbands love your wives, as Christ loved the church, and gave Himself up for her." (Ephesians 5:25).

The presence of God's love is reflected in my deeper love for my dearly beloved wife. He gives me an extraordinary calmness and the "peace that surpasses all understanding." Matt Haney spoke of a similar experience on October 10, 2010. I too have lived a very happy, healthy, and comfortable life. The Lord had not brought me any real challenges, or tested my faith. Now I am confronted with the most difficult trial of my entire life. At first I was devastated, feeling sorry, and having pity on myself. I felt helpless, and thought I would lose my sanity. Ruby and Mayra quickly pointed me heavenward to our heavenly Father, who hears the cry of the righteous, "and delivers them out of all their troubles."

The Apostle John tells us, "There is no fear in love, but perfect love casts out fear." Then I was reminded of Christ who suffered an excruciating death on that rugged cross, that I might die to sin and live to righteousness. My children, Rick, Mayra, and Ruby have been a bulwark of strength and encouragement for me. Alex Giuffre, a precious daughter of Zion, voluntarily comes three days a week to care for Lupita while I take much needed breaks outside the house. In her soft quiet manner she renders tender loving care while reading scripture and praying with her. Lupita listens and responds quietly. My heart swells with joy at how the Lord is providing! Plus, He is hearing the prayers of faithful saints who are dear to my heart. THANK YOU ALL! What comfort we find when we lean on God's Word - "Beloved do not be surprised at the fiery trial when it comes upon you to test you, as though something strange were happening to you. But rejoice insofar as you share Christ's sufferings, that you may also rejoice and be glad when His glory is revealed."(1 Peter 4:12 -13). Grace exposes our weakness, in order to give us greater strength. I can truly say - my greatest trial, has turned out to be my GREATEST BLESSING!....only by the outpouring of God's mercy and grace.

May God be glorified by the warm expressions of love, huge encouraging hugs, warm meals, visits, and fervent prayers by many beloved brethren. Sister Connie has brought us warm meals during a heavy rainstorm. One day she even climbed over the locked iron fence in front of our house to deliver a meal while we were exhausted and asleep. I have IMMEASURABLE love for all of you! I have witnessed the heart of Christ in His Body- (that motley group who congregate at Fattys on E. Commerce) - " So if there is any encouragement in Christ, any comfort from love, any participation in the Spirit, any affection and sympathy, complete my joy by being of the same mind, having the same love, being in full accord and of one mind." (Philippians 2:1-2). My prayer is that Jesus Christ be glorified throughout this whole challenging experience in our life.

"Only one life 'twill soon be past, only what's done for Christ will last."

"Papa"

Letter to Rick October 30, 2010

Hi Rick,

Hope you and your family are being blessed of the Lord.

The Lord has been faithful in sustaining me, in spite of my weakness, and inward despair. Yesterday (Friday) Mayra came, and we had a good day. Her labor of love for mom and me is overwhelming.

In the evening I took mom for dinner at Wendy's. She enjoyed the chicken sandwich and nuggets after playing around with it. But she ate most of it! At bedtime it's time for a change. We went through the usual routine - I reach and do a quick pull down of her slacks. If she grabs them before I do, it's a tug of war! By this time I'm on the floor pleading, and trying to remove her shoes (or slippers). Her feet are planted solid on the floor, like cement! If I'm smart I'll reach for the "Depends" (diapers), and rip them from the sides. They are designed with "rip off" seams on each side. Can you follow (or picture) what I'm saying?

Hey, those fancy diapers are a great invention! After doing all the necessary stuff, I quickly have to get back to mom to wipe, dry, and powder the area (front and back), like you do with any infant. (In fact I have a movie of mom doing this to you).

I have rubber gloves, but I'm not always fast enough to grab them. Through the whole procedure I'm telling her that I love her, and that she will be nice, dry, and clean. Then I have to rush the wet clothing to the washing machine. She is a grown woman and she still maintains her dignity, and resents all that I'm doing. I constantly reassure her with hugs and encouraging words. Sometimes she will say "I'm sorry," and afterward will thank me. I've become so attached to her, hand-in-hand, every day, everywhere. I cannot imagine losing her! The thought deeply saddens me! As exhausting as this challenge is, I accept it all as a trial sent from God. And He gives me much grace from day to day, and from moment to moment.

By the way Rick, what do you think about writing Alex an e-mail thanking her for the tremendous help and relief she has been for mom and me. Here is a young girl of 25, who left a successful career as a professional ballerina, performing as a "principle" with several ballet companies throughout the country. She came to the Lord, was converted, and left her career. In her conversations she always praises the Lord, and has a sweet, loving, caring spirit. I hope you get to meet her when you come. I've told her about you, and she looks forward to meeting the third member of my family.

Let me know the details of your trip to San Antonio, as soon as you know more.

Love,
Dad

Letter From Ruby October 31, 2010

Dearest Daddy,

I'm really glad that you gave Rick, Sister Alex's email address. I had thought to do the same thing. I'm glad you were able to give Rick a little "peek" in to the window of your life. I know if Rick lived here he would be doing his part in helping; he is a very caring person. But in God's perfect providence, he has Rick elsewhere...and email updates now and then of what is happening back "home" I'm sure are helpful and welcomed by him. I only hope that he doesn't feel guilty that he is not here because I know from talking to him through the years that if it were up to him he would have moved back long ago. Be thankful, Daddy, that the dominating desire of your son's heart is to follow Jesus as Lord. Fight any feelings of resentment (or whatever), grumbling or complaining that may try to creep into your heart.... and remember that God has not left you alone. The very God of heaven and earth promises to be with you always, never to leave nor forsake you... and makes this known experiential through His Spirit within as He supplies grace upon grace each day and the internal peace which passes all understanding.

In addition, He has shown you His love through His people; this, too, is a manifestation of His promise to you to never leave nor forsake you. So may God keep you encouraged as He brings His children your way to be His channel of His blessing for His glory and your joy now and forever. Alex, Mayra and all the others that God has purposely placed in your life are FOR HIS GLORY... that you would see His love and care for you and not look to the "gift" of the help they provide, but that you would look to the Giver of the gifts and worship Him... that your joy would be full!

I read a quote years ago that was very helpful that goes like this: "Live in the audience of One." This certainly applies to you as you perform all these selfless acts of love towards mom (just as you have described to Rick). God has privileged you in this season of your life to orchestrate details of each day in such a way that you would experience His power and grace like never before in your life - what a gift! As your pulling pants down, wiping "front and back," etc.... may all these good works of love and kindness be done as an act of worship to the God of your salvation. I appeal to you brother, by the mercies of God, present your body as a living sacrifice, holy and acceptable to God, which is your spiritual worship. May these very challenging days and nights with mom be a sweet act of worship for you, a sweet affair between you and our

Lord... may this "season" continue to grow you in your faith and in His grace... and may you "live in the audience of One" with the single purpose to joyfully serve this One as He is worthy to be served with all your heart, soul, mind and strength. Press on Daddy...the best is yet to come!!!

A happy slave of a most gracious Master,
Ruby

LETTERS BETWEEN RUBY AND ME

January 20, 2011

Dearest Ruby,

Mind you, I'm not complaining! But you've got to hear this, because it's hilarious! Coming back from the health club, I found mom and Ciara sitting quietly in the living room. I had not changed her because she was still asleep when I left. Plus, I thought the nurses' aide would be coming in the morning. Well, I gently walked her to the bedroom, lovingly and graciously. I did the usual thing of removing her slacks while whispering sweet things in her ear. She became resentful and starting hitting me.

I already had a towel on the bed for her to sit on, but she kept moving and turning while I was trying to clean her bottom. Then putting her feet through her pant legs is almost impossible when her toes are curled up. From there we headed to the bathroom to wash her hands. Well, that was another battle! For some reason, she refused to put her hands under the water. Again, I was not to reason, but to take necessary action. All clean and powdered up, I finally got her to bed after a big hug and a kiss. Just another "average" day. Exhausted, I went right to bed next to your mamacita for a much needed nap.

You were going to tell me something but you put it off. Don't forget what it was, I want to hear it.

Your prayers to a faithful God sustain me. Keep it up!

Love you,
Dad

January 20, 2011

Daddy - Praise God for His sustaining grace! Last Tuesday Tim did a wonderful bible study, as usual and it was on pride. At the end he talked about the "crosses" that our Lord calls us to bear... the very things that lead to our death. As I watch you as you daily pick up your "cross," I am thankful that you do not complain about the "instrument of death," if I can put it that way, that which is bringing about more and more of Christ out in you and less and less of Richard G. Cortez. Tim exhorted us all to embrace with thanksgiving to God those things that are actually answers to our own prayers (gifts from God perhaps wrapped unrecognizably, but precious nevertheless).

You know, we pray "Lord, give us patience... wisdom... greater faith... humility..." then the trial comes and we spend more time praying that God would deliver us than just remaining in it - the trial that our faith would be increased and that His grace would cause us to endure producing fruit now and for ever. I don't see that you are praying out of this trial, just mentioning that in context of Tim's msg. Every good and perfect gift comes from above... mom's illness would fall into that... and is working to accomplish God's infinite plan in your life and many others each and every day that unfolds. In everything give thanks, Pop. When you can thank God for "da kinde" that ends up in unspeakable places then you KNOW that you've reached a place that few will go... a place where our Lord lived every moment of His life.

When you think of Christ as God incarnate and how He so condescended to walk this world of wretched depravity daily without being hailed as sovereign King of the Universe by every person on the globe (that which He rightly deserved!) it can be seen, to me at least, as His daily dose of "da kinde" that He too had to deal with.

Sorry, that may be vulgar and crude but if we keep in mind what Christ our Lord did for us then ALL THINGS done in service to Him and out of love for Him will be understood simply as our "momentary light afflictions" that are only serving to prepare us for an eternal weight of glory beyond all comparison.

When you get like that, then you can say BRING IT ON!

Regarding that text in 2 Corinthians 4:17.. here are some thoughts (not original) that might encourage you:

The effect of these afflictions is to produce eternal glory. This they do:
1. By their tendency to wean us from the world;
2. To purify the heart, by enabling us to 'break off from the sins on account of which God afflicts us;
3. By disposing us to look to God for consolation and support in our trials;
4. By inducing us to contemplate the glories of the heavenly world, and thus winning us to seek heaven as our home; and,
5. Because God has graciously promised to reward his people in heaven as the result of their bearing trials in this life.

It is by affliction that he purifies them Isaiah 48:10; and by trial that he takes their affections from the objects of time and sense, and gives them a relish for the enjoyments which result from the prospect of perfect and eternal glory.

Well Dad, press on... and never forget... The best is yet to come!

Your daughter, your sister, your friend, your servant,
Ruby

MARCH 11, 2011 - THE SADDEST DAY OF MY LIFE

Friday, March 11, 2011 was the saddest and most heart-breaking day of my life. On this day at 5:22 a.m. my beloved wife and friend of 51 years took her last breath and was sent into eternity. I was devastated and gripped with emotion and sorrow as I wept over her uncontrollably. I felt as if part of me had been torn away. My daughter, Mayra and I had kept a vigil throughout the night when the crisis nurse, informed us that she would not last much longer. My son Rick, his wife Belle, and his daughters Tabitha, and Michelle arrived an hour and a half before she passed away.

We had talked to her and prayed loudly hoping she could hear us. Our loving wife, mother, and grandmother was gasping and her breathing was quickly getting weaker. The crisis nurse Adam Garcia had already graciously informed us that she was very near the end. He mentioned that she could probably still hear us even at this stage. She took her last breath just I said "Amen" to my last prayer. We embraced each other real tight and wept sorrowful tears. I had seen death before, but I personally had never experienced the sadness, emptiness, and loneliness that I felt that moment. It was sad, very sad; it was unreal! It was impossible to hold back the emotion and the relentless tears. Even days and weeks later, if anyone mentioned her name, or asked how I was doing, I would choke, and my eyes would swell with tears (as its happening right now!)

I could not talk about her, or think about her without getting flashbacks of the two of us walking hand-in-hand – walking in the park, going to church, or shopping at HEB. How can you forget a dearly beloved friend and partner whom you have lived with for 51 years.

I thank God for the outpouring of love and compassion from the brethren of Grace Community Church during my wife's illness. Ruby and Mayra did everything to relieve me of the pain I was going through. Without my knowing it, Mayra had removed all the clothes and other personal things from her room and closet. This was a huge thoughtful gesture!

The large funeral chapel at Sunset Northwest on Bandera Road was filled to capacity with people standing in the outside foyer. I was blessed beyond measure to see so many friends, old and new, as well as family and relatives. It was a glorious occasion, with my son Rick leading the singing and the grandchildren giving testimonies to the love of their grandma. Michael, in his Air Force uniform, gave a very touching farewell to his grandma. Tim preached a penetrating message on life and death. My tears of grief turned to tears of joy as God was glorified amidst the huge host of friends and family. I was thankful the Lord had sustained me through out the most difficult trial of my life. Looking back I could see the Lord's hand in everything that went on.

Sunset NW Funeral Chapel—Lupita's Memorial Service—March 14, 2011, 7:00 PM
Internment at Fort Sam Houston National Cemetery—March 22, 2011

Until Lupita's final days our beloved sister Alex had brought genuine love and comfort into our home. Her extraordinary labor of love was a testimony of her love for Christ. From the very beginning she refused to take pay and reminded me her purpose was to glorify Jesus Christ. She loved Lupita and was exceptionally patient with her, in spite of resistance and offensive language at times. After several weeks, Lupita appeared to appreciate and respond to the kindly affection she was receiving. Our whole family loves and has deep appreciation for this dear sister in the Lord.

Samuel, Joy, Lupita and I

"Blessed by the God and Father of our Lord Jesus Christ, the Father of mercies and God of all comfort, who comforts us in all our affliction, so that we may be able to comfort those who are in any affliction, with the comfort with which we ourselves are comforted by God."

2 Corinthians 1:3-4

CHAPTER 32
INVITED TO LIVE WITH THE CONWAYS

Shortly after Lupita's death, Ruby invited me to come stay at their home. "Indefinitely," she said. Several times she had asked me to move in with them and stay in the guest room. Grateful and still a little confused as a "loner", I packed my toothbrush and a few essentials and moved into the Conway house. Ruby and the rest of the family have always shown affection and been very hospitable to this old grandpa. The guest room that I would occupy had been a haven of rest for needy brethren, and weary visitors in the past. I felt privileged, plus it helped in the grieving process.

I was going through a rare and unusual season in my life. I was lonely not knowing what the future held for me. What I needed was to pull myself together and place my focus on Christ. Words are not sufficient to express my deep thanks to Ruby who has always been so gracious in listening to me, and taking me to the scripture for solace, comfort, and hope. Her words of wisdom would always put me back on track.

Cortez, Cerda and Conway Families—March 2011

(Row 1) Joshua, Grace, Joy, Samuel, Tabitha
(Row 2) Dorothy, Caleb, Benjamin, Grandpa, Michael, Charity

DENTON CONFERENCE – APRIL 21, 2011

The Conways invited me to a four-day Conference in Denton, Texas. This was a new and exciting experience for me. Camp Copass, which is just north of Dallas is a sprawling Christian retreat. It was sponsored by three churches, Grace Community Church, Lake Road Chapel, and Providence Church. Besides two convenient hotels, dormitories, and cabins, there were areas for camping. A huge assembly building came alive when people started pouring in.

There was fellowship with brethren and new friends from far and near. Some even came from outside the country. It's a blessing when brethren who have never met come together. Immediately there is a common brotherly kindred spirit. There are never strangers among brothers and sisters in the Lord. Then, our hearts were brought together in the singing of hymns. After that, we were fed with powerful biblical truths from special guest preachers. We were also privileged to hear testimonies from missionary friends that we had been praying for. The sweet fellowship extended to the immaculate dining room where we ate to our tummies' content. We enjoyed sumptuous cafeteria-style meals morning, noon, and evening.

Back home at the Conways, Tim would lead in daily bible studies, which I needed. At 7:30 a.m. promptly, the kids would scramble down the stairs to the dinner table. Some in bathrobes, hairs in disarray, and sleepy eyes half closed, they all sat quietly as their dad read from God's Word. This was a great comfort to me. The YMCA came next, that is, after rushing Charity to school. Ruby did the Zumba class while I engaged with The Silver Sneakers Senior Class. These activities served to keep my mind busy, and from thinking so much. I enjoyed all the attention Ruby and the family gave me to make my stay comfortable. But at night in my room, it was hard to hold back the tears when thoughts of my beloved Lupita kept popping up.

TRIP TO MICHIGAN - JUNE 20, 2011

Tim's mom invited the family to a week's vacation in Michigan on June 20th 2011. She rented a lake house that was nestled among giant shady trees. It was truly a refreshing and restful retreat. Together, with the kids, we enjoyed boating, swimming, and just leisurely lounging around. Of course, there was a generous amount of food and snacks for the hungry crowd. Tim drove us to Paw Paw, his birthplace, then to his old stomping grounds where he grew up. Then we visited Rich, Tim's brother, at his house, then went to eat at his restaurant. It was truly fun and a rare occasion for the Conway kids to play with their cousins, Austin and Hannah.

June 19, 2011

Dad,

This, I know, is not a traditional Father's Day type card... But I can't think of anything that I desire for you more than this, "Contentment in God," this card speaks of... especially in this new "season" of life the Lord has brought you to. I pray that you will grow in your love for the Lord as you seek to cling to Him more closely than any other relationship here on earth... For the love of God is the reality and substance while all else are mere shadows. I am exceedingly grateful to God for the beautiful "shadow" you have been to me (and Tim). Your unfailing, unconditional love has provided for me so clearly a picture of the love my Heavenly Father has for me/Tim – an unspeakable gift that not many share, I pray my life in some measure reflects my deep love and sincere gratitude I/we have for you because my words alone will never be enough.

Thank you Daddy – I/we l♥ve you very much. Happy Father's Day!
Love,
Ruby & Tim

VANGIE COMES TO LIVE WITH ME AUGUST 2011

God who is faithful, continued to guide and provide. My sister Vangie accepted my invitation to come live with me. She had been a widow and living with her daughter Debbie for fourteen years. Her move was a happy reality. She has been a tremendous blessing! Besides being my sister, she is my sister in Christ. Plus, she is a marvelous cook (just like mom used to cook). Is this a blessing or what? She keeps the house in order (including me!!). Our lifestyles are similar, and very peaceful. We are of like-faith and growing in grace and truth at Grace Community Church.

HAWAII TRIP WITH VANGIE OCTOBER 10, 2011

Vangie and I are both of "like mind" especially when the subject of Hawaii came up. We said "Why not!" We made plans, came up with ideas, and looked at maps. Kay Koike, a Hawaiian friend, had previously invited us to the Island of Kauai. However, we had to change plans because she would not be there at the same time we were going. That's when we made arrangements to visit a Bed and Breakfast on the Big Island and another one on the Island of Maui. After airplane reservations, we decided on rental cars. I knew we would have more liberty to drive around on our own. I deliberately wanted to avoid the big tour groups, expensive hotels, shops, and tourist traps.

On Monday, October 10, 2011, at 2 p.m. Vangie and I boarded a United Airlines flight headed to Hilo, Hawaii, with a lay over in Los Angeles. It was a special thrill flying across the spacious Pacific Ocean. We had requested seats with additional legroom, which made the flight over those fluffy clouds more tolerable. As we made the approach to Hawaii; I could see the mountains, the shoreline, and the palm trees swaying along the beaches and the avenues. Hilo Airport was larger than when I lived there forty years ago. But it was still small compared to other major airports. I thought back to the day when Continental Airlines made their initial flight to Hilo.

Me and Vangie in Hawaii

It was dark when we picked up our luggage. We could feel the cool clean air through the open air terminal. We were surprised as our names were called on the P.A. System. We responded to the reception booth to find a wahine (female) in a beautiful MuuMuu waiting to give us an aloha welcome with flower leis. After picking up our rental car it was easy to find our way to Kalanianaole Drive, which would take us to Maureen's Bed and Breakfast.

Maureen was a tall, stout Swedish woman who had turned her old rustic two-story house into a B&B. It did not compare with a modern hotel, but had simple historic elegance. Maureen hoisted our luggage up winding stairs to our rooms on the second floor. Being kind-hearted, she realized that these two "oldies" were not about to be running up and down those winding stairs. In the morning she moved us to two rooms on the first floor. When we first stepped into the backyard, it blew my mind! It was like a garden of Eden, with tall palm trees adorned with vines, surrounded by lush vegetation, including torch ginger, pandanas, hibiscus, plumerias, mangos, bananas, and a variety of other fresh exotic plants and flowers.

In spite of all that beauty, our first couple of nights were not very comfortable. We were kept awake by the high-pitched chirping of "birds," or so we thought! A lady at the airport had already described these exotic chirps as small Coqui frogs that you never see, but they multiply uncontrollably. Thousands of them are heard all night long! After a while you get used to these critters, or you just tolerate them.

Every morning Hilo had a fresh scrubbed down look. Why not, it rains just about every night! The relaxed lifestyle has not changed, neither has the natural beauty of the mountains, nor the rainforests with spectacular rainbows. The swaying palm trees along the ocean, Coconut Island, and the picturesque Queen Liliuokalani Park depicting ornate Japanese gardening, brought back wonderful memories.

Volcanoes National Park is still a major attraction for most visitors. The main vent, called Halemaumau, is perpetually smoldering, smoking, and threatening to erupt. It is the most active volcano in the world. After touring the park and taking pictures, Vangie and I had lunch at the Parks R and R (rest and recuperation) camp for military (active and retired). However, I was surprised and disappointed to find out that the policy had changed, and that ALL ex-military were permitted to stay there. I would have qualified for room accommodations there for a very nominal fee. Well, it was too late now!

The high points of the trip for me were visiting the schools where I had taught forty years ago. At Pahoa (middle and high schools) I had the pleasure of meeting with a few former students who were now teachers. They were surprised, especially since I had brought along a yearbook that had their pictures. Another school where we were received with much enthusiasm and aloha was Kalanianaole Middle School in Papaikou. A couple of the teachers and office staff were familiar with students who knew me from the past. One young teacher was the daughter of George Camarillo, a very good band director friend of mine, who has since passed away. Lina couldn't hug me tight enough when she knew that her father and I were very close friends. Later I would meet with her brother La Roma on the Island of Maui.

The cottage I used to live in had been torn down to build a new band room on that location. Now to my great disappointment, I discovered that the band program had been abolished, and the band room was used for other things.

The next day we visited James Sanbei, our former pastor from Kinoole Baptist Church. We saw him in the nursing home where he was recuperating from a stroke. His speech was limited, but we were still able to communicate with him. Mrs. Sanbei was so grateful that she invited us to dinner with her whole family the following Thursday. It was an interesting experience to get reacquainted with the young adult family that I knew only as small children. Sadau Tachibana, who is now a widower, is a good friend who was deacon at our church. He invited Vangie and me to dinner, where we had the opportunity to reminisce over the good old days.

On the way to visit Pastor Sanbei, we stopped off at Rainbow Falls, another refreshing attraction that is very near the nursing home. A touch of nostalgia came over me as we went past the Hilo Hospital. This is where our little Hawaiian girl Ruby Maile was born. The hospital is right across the street from the nursing home. I am hopeful that Ruby can visit her birthplace in Hawaii someday.

Another day we hit the Hamakua coast road headed toward the grandeur of Akaka Falls State Park. These majestic falls are in the center of a dense rainforest filled with wild orchids, bamboo groves, and draping ferns. The trails and paths which are always refreshingly cool, led to two falls. The main attraction is the stately Akaka Falls, cascading with a loud thunder, down 442 feet along a picturesque, green mountainside. Next, we continued along the scenic coast road with a view of the ocean on one side and lush green foliage covering the mountains on the opposite side.

On Monday, Oct. 17, we boarded a Hawaiian airlines jet headed to the Island of Maui. Hawaiians call this island "Maui No Ka Oi" (Maui, the best); also known as the Valley Island. It is indeed beautiful! We started out in our rental car from the Kahului Airport and drove to the Maui Guest House (Bed and Breakfast) in Lahaina, on the other side of the island. Not being familiar with this island, I drove very cautiously around one long, wind-swept mountain pass that would take us to the other side of the island. The warm Maui weather was quite a contrast from the Big Island.

The B&B was in a quiet neighborhood setting a short distance from the ocean, the beaches, and many shops, restaurants, and cafes. The guesthouse was small, practical and private, with a lot of aloha. We had immediate access to a colorful kitchen with a huge refrigerator filled with everything imaginable. The morning table was always adorned with flowers and big bowls of island fruits. Besides absorbing the breathtaking beauty of the ocean, the beaches with the swaying palms, the trips to the shops and cafes, we had the pleasure of a Luau. The scene was an oceanfront dining area in back of a hotel. It was completely surrounded by palm trees and all kinds of exotic plants, flowers, and torches. As the evening began to darken, Vangie and I were greeted with flower leis by a beautiful Polynesian girl in a colorful sarong, and a muscular kanaka (male) with a similar sarong. We were led to our table in this elegant lanai (a huge patio). It was a two-tiered deck with about fifty tables decorated with white tablecloths, orchids, and small candles.

The tropical scent in the air, the sun going down in the horizon, and the colorful servers prancing back and forth gave the promise of an exciting Hawaiian evening. It was a four-course dinner with dishes from four different islands, Hawaii, Samoa, New Zealand, and Tahiti. When each course was served, we would be entertained by dances of that particular island. The gyrating dances of Tahiti, the sword dances of Samoa, the fire dances, and the Hawaiian hulas were more exciting than the rare dishes that were served.

One day we took a guided tour to Haleakala National Park. Vangie and I were privileged to ride in a twelve-passenger van with no other passengers that day. We drove up a winding road that slices up volcanic Haleakala. It's a dramatic scurry to the clouds from sea level to 10,023 feet, over a distance of 35 miles. It was cold and windy, so the guide was kind enough to loan Vangie his jacket. It was awesome taking pictures from above the clouds at the observation center. You have the feeling of being on another planet. On the way down we had a couple of side tours, including lunch. Our tour driver surprised us by sitting us at a table in a quaint little gazebo right in the middle of a large exotic botanical garden. Out of the back of his van he brought out a complete lunch special for us, including an entree, sides, drinks, and dessert. It would be an understatement to describe this scene as delicious and delightful.

It was providential that we cancelled our "Road to Hana" tour. On that day we called and agreed to meet La Roma and Cora Camarillo. So we drove around a huge mountain pass to the City of Kihei to meet these new friends for the first time. They showed us much aloha with a dinner by the swimming pool at a hotel. We reminisced about his father and learned about his family who were all musicians and entertainers. In fact, halfway through the evening, they surprised us with a musical number. Cora who was a popular hula dancer at one time, danced the Hawaiian Wedding Song while her husband La Roma sang and played the Guitar. Amidst all the fun,

Vangie and I realized that it was now dark and we were a long ways from out guesthouse. Our return trip would take us up and around that treacherous mountain pass. La Roma convinced us to stay overnight at the hotel. It was very enjoyable! In the morning we had a leisurely breakfast, then visited Cora at her flower shop, and took time for pictures.

Back at the B&B in Lahaina, we had another surprise coming to us. Our checkout time had expired, and all our clothes and belongings had been removed from our room and placed in the lobby. The owner explained that there was another couple waiting to occupy the room. We were discreetly "kicked out." We were to blame and couldn't complain because they had treated us with extraordinary aloha hospitality. With our bags loaded in the car we had lunch at a near by cafe that overlooked the ocean. Afterwards, we drove around, lounging and taking more pictures along the beaches.

By evening we were headed toward the Kahului Airport taking an unfamiliar route that got us lost. By this time my little sister was getting a little nervous and anxious. I casually explained that at least we were getting to see new sights on this beautiful island. We arrived at the airport and checked in the rental car. Then we crossed the street to the terminal where we checked in our baggage. One of Vangie's suitcases was too heavy so the courteous agent suggested I put some of her clothes in my bag. No big deal, we did it! We were finally filing into the plane, one by one, inch by inch. It's strange how so many people can be so close and yet no words are spoken. The stewardesses usually break the ice with their big friendly smiles. Then comes the part where you need a shoehorn to squeeze into your cozy little seat. It's nighttime so you naturally think of being put to sleep by the humming of the engines.

You have to be a very heavy sleeper to sleep in that cramped little seat. With a swipe of your credit card you can watch a movie and hope it meets your taste. Or you can pray that the pilot stays awake and tries to avoid those huge air pockets that rock the plane. But praise the Lord, we were on our way home. We forgot one thing. We failed to throw a flower lei into the ocean. If the waves draw it back to shore it is believed that you will return!!

CHAPTER 33
MORE LETTERS

December 6th 2011

Sister Connie, Good morning. Would you be kind enough to send this to the brethren.

Beloved Brethren,

"Now concerning brotherly love, you have no need for anyone to write to you, for you yourselves have been taught by God to love one another..." (1 Thessalonians 4:9)

I was truly blessed with inexpressible and glorious joy at the Facebook messages, and the love and huge hugs from so many wonderful people who were reminding me that I was now 84 years old.

This aging and joyful heart is deeply grateful for the Lord's goodness and mercy! I pray Christ will keep me humble and faithful, that I may walk in a manner worthy of God.

May grace and peace be multiplied to all of you.

"Papa"

"A few more rolling suns at most, shall land me safe on Canaan's coast. There I shall sing the song of grace, to Jesus Christ, my hiding place." *"Hail, Sovereign Love"* Jehoida Brewer.

SHORT TRIP TO NORTH CAROLINA

DECEMBER 8TH 2011

A family that sticks together, travels together! Or is it the other way around? Anyway, Tim and Ruby were kind enough to invite me to travel with them into the Smokey Mountains region in North Carolina. We flew to Atlanta, then rented a car and drove to North Carolina. We visited Tim's mom in her breathtaking mountaintop home in Franklin, N.C. Franklin is an old-time town that reminds you of a fairytale. We drove up a narrow winding road surrounded by tall trees that hide the few homes that are visible. We finally reached the home of Mary Lou Gerke, which appeared to be at the very top of this mountain. The house was beautifully designed and left little to be desired in the way of comforts. On one of two outside decks facing the tall forests and the Smokey Mountains in the distance, I could stand in adoration and praise the Master of all creation. "I lift up my eyes to the hills, from where does my help come? My help comes from the Lord, who made heaven and earth." (Psalm 121:1-2) We were very comfortable and very relaxed. Mary Lou enjoyed having us and treated us to sumptuous meals. On Sunday, she took us to her church. It was a small, unique building nestled in the midst of tall trees. It was Episcopalian with a female pastor, so we sat very quietly. Franklin is a quaint little historical town. It's reminiscent of a movie set with mountains all around. We certainly appreciate the generous hospitality shown to us by Mary Lou.

December 31st 2011

Sister Connie - Happy New Year

Thank you so much for your labor of love, and for feeding us, as we seek to feast on the Word. Would you be kind enough to share this short message with the church?

Beloved brothers and sister,

I want to share with you my many blessings of 2011. It was an interesting and unique year. At the beginning of the year I faced the most difficult trial of my life. Lupita, my wife of fifty-one years, was diagnosed with Alzheimer Disease, which is a slow and devastating death. The Lord gave me the responsibility of caring for her, and the opportunity of demonstrating relentless love for her. God's love was manifested through the outpouring of kindness and support from the church, for which I am deeply thankful. I praise God for giving us two wonderful loving daughters, Mayra and Ruby. Their faith kept us united in spirit and in love.

Then, the Lord in His goodness and mercy, sent us a precious sister in Christ, who was filled with the love of God. Alex was truly a humble servant and turned out to be an enormous comfort and encouragement in our home. Her unselfish and inexhaustible labor of love was truly from Christ. And she kept reminding me of that! During Lupita's illness and after her death, God's amazing grace was sufficient and sustained me during the dark hours and saddest time of my life. Only Christ's wondrous love brought me peace and relief from my pain and inconsolable tears.

I turned 84 on December 5, by God's goodness and mercy. By His wonderful mercy I am happy, healthy, and growing in the grace and knowledge of our Lord and Savior, Jesus Christ. To Him be the glory both now and forever. "The days of our lives are seventy years; and if by reason of strength they are eighty years..." (Psalm 90:10)

I love our church, which is made up of many young people, and young couples. I know what lies ahead, cause I've been there! One reminder for those who are starting to build their nest - "Unless the Lord builds the house, they labor in vain who build it" (Psalm 127:1). My prayer, as we come to the end of this year, is that we seek to glorify God and be reminded of this glorious verse, "trust in the Lord with all your heart." And as the hymn writer says "Trust and Obey for there is no other way."

Happy New Year,
"Papa"

12-5-04

Dear Grandpa,

Thank you sooo much for all the gum, crackers, and other treats you give me!! You are soooooo SPECIAL !! to me, not just me but all of us!! I hope you have a great day. Happy Birthday!! "Te Amo Mucho."

with all my Love,
Charity

Happy Birthday. Have a great day.

Dad,

I HOPE YOU ENJOY OUR GIFT AS MUCH AS WE ENJOY GIVING IT TO YOU. HOW MANY TIMES CAN I THANK YOU (& GOD!) FOR THE OUTPOURING OF LOVE YOU HAVE DEMONSTRATED TO EVERY MEMBER OF MY FAMILY WITHOUT IT GETTING OLD OR LOOSING THE DEPTH OF MEANING EACH TIME I EXPRESS IT. I GUESS I'LL TAKE THE RISK — THANK YOU AGAIN! YOUR LIFE IS A GIFT AND EVERYDAY WE HAVE TO SHARE IS A TREASURE. MAY OUR LORD CONTINUE TO USE YOU AND PROTECT YOU ALL THE WAY TO THE END... AT WHICH TIME THE VERY BEST WILL JUST BEGIN. RUN HARD, DAD, THE PRIZE AWAITS!

This is the day which the LORD hath made; we will rejoice and be glad in it.
Psalm 118:24

May your special day be just the beginning of a year filled with God's blessings.

Happy Birthday

WITH OUR LOVES
TIM, RUBY and the CHILDREN

MORE LETTERS

I owe more than I can ever say to your wonderful influence and love.

DADDY,
  THIS CARD REALLY SPELLED OUT THE SENTIMENTS OF MY HEART. I COUNT IT NO SMALL BLESSING TO HAVE YOU IN MY LIFE. EVERY DAY IS A PRECIOUS GIFT, WHETHER IT'S SEEING YOU AT CHURCH OR HEARING YOUR VOICE ON THE OTHER END OF THE PHONE LINE OR EVEN AN EMAIL ABOUT DUCK! ☺ →

Happy Father's Day

THANK YOU, THANK YOU, FOR JUST BEING YOU AND FOR THE CHANNEL OF GOD'S LOVE THAT YOU ARE TO ME IN SUCH A REAL AND SPECIAL WAY.
  I LOVE YOU!
    RUBY (& TIM, too)

DADDY,
  AS ALWAYS, WORDS FALL SHORT... BUT SOMEHOW WITH MY ACTIONS AND WORDS I PRAY GOD WILL CONTINUE TO ALLOW ME THE HONOR OF LOVING AND SERVING YOU. OUR DAY TOGETHER YESTERDAY WAS A GIFT - I CHERISH EVERY TIME THE LORD GIVES US SPECIAL TIMES TO SHARE. THANK YOU FOR YOUR CONSTANT CHRIST-LIKE LOVE, THAT WHICH IS SHINING FORTH FROM YOU IN THIS SEASON OF YOUR LIFE LIKE NEVER BEFORE. WITH DEEPEST GRATITUDE TO THE LORD MY GOD FOR BLESSING ME (AND TIM!) WITH A DAD LIKE YOU... YOU, MY FATHER, MY FRIEND, MY BROTHER... I

...for being you.

THANK YOU!
THANK YOU!
THANK YOU!
  WE LOVE
   YOU VERY
    MUCH!
   RUBY & TIM

WISH YOU A GLORIOUSLY BLESSED DAY!

Daddy,
Just wanted to take a moment to tell you how much I love you and how deeply I appreciate all your love and help that flows to me from your sweet heart.
Thankful to God for you,
Ruby

Dear Grandpa,
thank you so much for being who you are. thank you for being such a wise giving and humble man and also for being a good influence to all your grandchildren. I hope you have a happy birthday and I hope that you will see many more.
with all the respect a grandson could give his grandpa

Love,
Benjamin

Dear Grandpa,

Thank you so much for all you have done! You are ALWAYS so giving. Thank you. I love you very much. Every second is a gift we have with you. ♡ You are very special! Your giving is behond words. You give and give and give. I wish I could give back a lot more. Feel free to ask our help in anything. Like if you need your yard raked or need help with your computer or camera or whatever. You will be missed so much when you go to heaven. We will miss not going to your house on Mons. While we have you, you are a great blessing. Ask anything you want from us. I can't wait to hear, or rather read, the story of your life. ~~All you have done~~ All the treats and blessings you give us means soo much.
I LOVE You sooo much. ♡

Merry Christmas! ♡

Love you tons, ♡
      Grace

P.S. Sorry my hand writting is so bad. I was writting in a moving car.

DEC. 2009

Dad,

This is truly our prayer for your life. May you continue, by God's grace, to strive for that perfection and for that reward of His smile now and forever more. Live each day as though it was your last till you stand before His Throne and hear those awaited words, "Well done, good & faithful servant."

We love and adore you and cherish each precious moment we have with you, our Dad, brother and friend. Happy Father's Day! Love, Tim & Ruby

Happy Birthday Gandpa!

I am truelly blessed to have such a good grandpa that is saved by the grace of God. I thank God for letting you be with us to this day, and I pray that we would be able to spend many more years together. Thank you so much for all the things you have given to us and all the times you have taken us out to eat. Even if I forget to say thank you I am so thankful. Even though this may sound childish I hope some day to be like you. In how caring you are, in how giving you are, and in all the little things. I love you so sooo much! I hope you have a wonderful day.

Love,
Joy Joy

Dear Grandpa,
this card is not just a birthday card but a thank you card for been a wonderful Grandpa. I love you so much.
Happy Birthday!
love,
Dorothy

DAD

He's a very special man
who cares deeply
about his family
and he shows it.
He's never too busy
for the little everyday things
that happy memories
are made of.
He is dedicated
to those who call him Dad
because he loves them
with all his heart.

WISHING YOU HAPPINESS

TODAY AND ALWAYS

Dad,
   You'll have to read this card again because it describes how we see you and how we feel about you.
   Our prayer is that God's grace and His Holy Spirit will be mighty upon you as you go through this season of growth in your race homeward. May God help us all.   Love, your Cerda family

CATARACT OPERATIONS - DR. LISA MARTEN

My eyesight was becoming weak and blurry at times. My ophthalmologist had already told me that I had small cataracts, but there was no need for operating until they increased in size. Finally, on January 16, 2012, it was decided that the cataracts had grown larger and needed to be removed. First the cataract on the right eye was removed and replaced with a new lens. The procedure was fast and the healing took about ten days, which was normal. On February 27, 2012, the left eye was operated on. This took longer, with a little "anxiety" and abnormal tension in the operating room. After a year, this eye was not completely healed. I suspect it was somehow damaged during the operation. The doctor did not admit it, nor did she deny it when I mentioned the problem. After getting a second opinion from Dr. Walton, I was diagnosed with astigmatism. He gave me two options, one, I could have a laser procedure which would improve my eyesight without glasses. Two, no operation but with prescription glasses. Being a little skeptical, I decided on the glasses.

During the period when my eyesight was weak and limited, I was thankful for brethren who offered to drive Vangie and me around, especially at night. Eddie Karisch and David Gonzales were two who were very helpful. David took it upon himself to be my chauffeur at every opportunity, even with his full-time job. This faithful friend and brother in Christ calls me every day, no matter where he is. Driving one of those large Star Shuttle buses, he travels all over Texas, and sometimes out of state. But he always avails himself to drive Vangie and me to church or wherever we need to go, any time of day or night, as long as he is off from work. We have a strong Christian bond and spend much time in fellowship and prayer at my house at every opportunity.

Richard & David Gonzales at the Fellowship Conference

DENTON CONFERENCE 2012

April 5th thru the 8th 2012

The much-awaited annual Fellowship Conference started on Thursday April 5. The Conference is organized by three churches: Providence Chapel of Denton, Texas; Lake Road Chapel of Kirksville, Missouri; and Grace Community Church of San Antonio, Texas. The location is Camp Copass, a Christian Retreat Center on the outskirts of Denton. As usual we congregated in sweet fellowship with brethren from all over the country, including some from the United Kingdom, Canada, Denmark, and Mexico. The singing of hymns was uplifting and the sermons were power-driven by the Holy Spirit. We met old friends, and made new ones. The room accommodations were comfortable and the food was excellent. We drove up from San Antonio to Denton on Thursday and returned Sunday after the last meeting. I was thankful that David Gonzales was willing to drive my car, especially since we drove through heavy rain most of the way home. Eddie Karisch, Bernard Dunn and I just munched on snacks and enjoyed good conversation all the way to San Antonio.

CHAPTER 34
MISSION TRIPS

BRAZIL — JUNE 6, 2012

Tim was invited to preach at a Fiel Conference in Sau Paulo, Brazil. The spacious campground had a tropical atmosphere with palm trees, exotic plants and flowers. Aric Diaz and I were his traveling companions who would share the gospel at every opportunity. This would be a challenge since the language in Brazil is Portuguese. Fiel knew of Tim because of our support to their Adopt-a-Pastor program in Brazil. We were surprised to see hundreds of youngsters coming in from different parts of Brazil. Tim would be preaching to about two-hundred young adults, mostly college students and some already in professional fields. He had good translators and the messages were well received. It was a joy meeting and sharing the gospel with so many Portuguese youth. I made several friends with whom I still communicate. It was an awesome experience! I was shocked looking at the map and seeing how far we had flown from San Antonio, Texas to Sao Paulo, Brazil.

GUADALAJARA, MEXICO – JUNE 18, 2012

Tim was scheduled to preach at a Conference in Guadalajara, Mexico, from June 18th to June 25th. The Conference was sponsored by Iglesia Del Centro. Josef Urban, a young man of 27, has been blessed as pastor of this church, located in a metropolitan center of Guadalajara. He is a missionary pastor that our church supports. Tim had brought David Gonzales, Selena Almorejo, and Cassandra Cortez and me. While there we would go with some of the brethren to the big plaza downtown, which is surrounded by statues, fountains, and huge gothic Catholic churches. While Josef or one of the other brethren preached, the rest of us would give out tracts and share the gospel with whoever would listen. Tim preached and Aaron Block translated during the evening services, which were held in a hotel assembly hall. Aaron is a young brother who assists Josef in preaching and accompanying with the guitar.

There were many that came from far and near, and were attentive and submissive to the Word of God. Many claimed they had never heard the truth preached with such clarity. As a whole, the fellowship was harmonious, the food was delicious, and we felt right at home with Josef and his wife Lina. Lina had the responsibility of caring and home schooling four precious little orphan boys while expecting her own baby in the near future. Sergio Valdovinos Santana was kind enough to take David and me on tours of the city and trying out some the favorite eating places. Selena and Cassie displayed their labor of love by helping Lina with the cooking during the Conference. After the Conference they were to remain there and continue helping Lina until she had her baby.

PUERTO RICO, "LA ISLA DEL ENCANTO"

NOV. 13, 2012

A Puerto Rican lady in our church invited my sister Vangie and me to go visit her mother and her family in Puerto Rico. She planned to take us to visit her mother and her family. After a few months, she got sick and said she would cancel the trip. But she gave us the option of going since she had already bought the tickets. Vangie and I were not going to pass this opportunity, especially since the tickets were very reasonable. And the Lord was faithful to provide, as He always does. I called Estela, a longtime friend from Free Grace Baptist Church, who lives in Puerto Rico. When she and her husband, Pastor Noble Vater, heard of our situation they immediately invited us to stay in their home in San Juan. This was the beginning of a beautiful reunion! They picked us up at the San Juan Airport and took us directly to dinner at the Sizzler, a diner on the Marina.

As they drove us to their house, we were enjoying every moment. Here was a beautiful tropical island that reminded us of Hawaii. It's no wonder they call it "La Isla del Encanto," which is displayed on all Puerto Rican licenses plates. Every morning we awoke to delightful breakfast treats. Estela is a fantastic cook. She is a dear sister in the Lord who sings in the kitchen, and loves to serve. Their big house allowed Vangie and me to sleep comfortably in two separate spacious rooms.

Every day after breakfast, Pastor Vater would take us on tours around the island. "El Yunque National Forest" is a dense rainforest with huge trees that extend over most of the road like umbrellas. The road has many sharp curves and winds up to higher and cooler temperatures. One of the many features of the park is a refreshing cascading waterfall which is ideal for picture taking.

One warm Puerto Rican night the Vaters took Vangie and me for dinner in Old San Juan. This town has government buildings, hotels, shops, cafes, statues, and other picturesque and historical landmarks that attract many tourists and visitors. It is surrounded by water, and adorned with palm trees, exotic flowers, huge trees and plants. We ended up at a Cafe called Tijuana, right off the boardwalk along the ocean front. After dinner we took a casual walk in the cool of the night. We were surprised as our eyes caught sight of three huge majestic white cruise ships docked in the harbor. From here these ships take cruises along the Caribbean and other tropical islands.

One day Rob Hendricks and his family took Vangie and me on a very unusual tour. By way of a ferry then a small open-air tram we reached El Morro. Castillo de San Felipe del Morro is a massive fortress built by the Spaniards depicting 400 years of military history. This huge bastion of defense encapsulates Puerto Rico's role as a guardian of the new world. It is perched on the northwestern-most point of Old San Juan and surrounded by water. The ocean views are breathtaking! We were thankful to Rob, Elizabeth, and their children who brought us on this thrilling tour. Plus, this gracious family, had us over for scrumptious dinners. They are Christian friends from years past. Rob, who is in the Air Force, was stationed in Puerto Rico.

On Thursday November 15, we visited two different women from the church, in two different hospitals. I was glad Pastor Vater was driving. I've seen bad driving, but San Juan is the worse! The laws are constantly compromised, and you feel like you're in a "Game of Chicken". I guess I was more critical, after having taught driver education for so many years. We celebrated Thanksgiving with all the trimmings at the church. The Wednesday night prayer meetings and the Sunday worship services at Iglesia Bautista Bereana were edifying.

One significant ministry of the church is the bookstore, which has an impressive number of sound biblical books. Pastor Vater, who has been in Puerto Rico for fifty years, preached sound solid truths from scripture. He preaches in impeccable Spanish, but there is still heavy Kentucky accent in his speech. After being a widower for several years, he met and was blessed with a godly and very domesticated widow. Estela was originally at Free Grace Baptist Church in San Antonio. She and Pastor Vader have had a happy and blissful marriage for twelve years.

Pastor Vater and other brethren from church were determined to show us as much of the island as possible. We drove from San Juan, south through well-developed highways, and then entered narrow roads with treacherous curves through the mountains. We came across quaint, rural mountain villages, went past Guaynabo all the way down to the southern coastal town of Ponce. We also visited a young Christian couple, Jeiren and Graciela, who live on the side of a breathtaking mountain surrounded by lush vegetation and numerous fruit trees on all sides. They are just a few minutes from the small fishing town in Guayama.

Another tour took us to Naguabo, a little town along the ocean that's famous for deep-sea fishing. At Los Makos Restaurant along the boardwalk, we were able to savor and taste the fish that is caught in that area. Another day, we visited one of the many famous beaches called Luquillo, on the far eastern part of the island. The water was warm, crystal clear, and irresistible, so I jumped in. Pastor Vater and Estela took off their shoes and decided to walk on a long stretch of clean white sandy beach. We saw much of the natural beauty of Puerto Rico, even though most of the names were difficult to pronounce.

"Brothers, I do not consider that I have made it my own. But one thing I do: forgetting what lies behind and straining forward to what lies ahead, I press on toward the goal for the prize of the upward call of God in Christ Jesus.

Philippians 3:13-14

CHAPTER 35
MY TESTIMONY

I was raised in a Christian home by God fearing parents. I have been attending church as far back as I can remember. As a very young child I remember sleeping on the floor in front of my parent's pew during Sunday night services. "El Templo Cristiano" was a large Assembly of God Church in San Antonio, where my parents were married. On Sunday nights this church came "alive" with continuous lively singing, praises, testimonies, prayers, and many speaking in "unusual tongues". We were too young to realize what was going on so we would just sleep through it all.

During my adolescent years, our family moved and we attended other churches. My dad made sure we attended church every Sunday no matter where we lived. He instilled in us the importance of a consistent church life. This "practice" became a vital part of my life. I realize now that from childhood to adulthood, the habit or tradition of attending church regularly was of upmost important to me. I responded and sought to adhere to my father's value system. My personal commitment and intimate relationship with Christ came much later in life.

We eventually joined La Trinidad Methodist Church. There, we got very involved and made a lot of friends. The pastor was a stern, pious, intellectual, who captured the attention of a full church during both morning and evening services.

I didn't steal, smoke, or drink, and I watched my manners as I had been taught at home. I always searched out protestant worship services on Sundays while I was in the Navy. I thank God for His constant protection in all my travels. Even though I was still void of solid gospel truths, the Lord in His mercy had sustained me in what is called "common grace".

As a maturing adult I naturally became more independent and readily accepted the pleasures and entertainment of the world around me. I had experienced life in the Navy, the university, life as a musician, a bandleader, and numerous other "important positions". So I felt secure and comfortable, especially since I had what I thought was a "clean record". I would drink a cold beer from time to time (on a hot day), only if it was cold enough and I was thirsty enough. I was content with myself, care free, and self righteous. I drove a beautiful 88 "hardtop" Oldsmobile, had money in the bank, and had many friends. Plus, I was attending church regularly, as per custom, so I felt guilt-free! I had a measure of pride, and had limited regard for the God that had created me, and provided for me in abundance.

I was a fickle 32 year old bachelor with a good education and a good job. My focus began to change as I became enamored by this beautiful young lady in church. At sixteen, she had moved to the U.S. from Sabinas Hidalgo, Mexico. Now, at twenty-five she was alluring and had a vibrant personality which caused me to forget all others. She knew that I had other "friendships" at that time, but she was being very patient. In time we got to know each other better and our relationship started to blossom.

It was a thrill just to hold her hand when we walked together. After we got better acquainted, I would drive her home after church. We had marvelous times just being together. Driving home one evening, we stopped at a little park with a quaint little gazebo on King Williams Drive. There is where I surprised her with an engagement ring and asked her to marry me. In her usual manner she let out a loud scream with excitement and almost choked me with her arms tight around my neck.

Our wedding was lively and well attended. We made a covenant before God and many friends and family. By God's grace, we had kept our vows. I say by God's grace, because it was ONLY by God's grace that our marriage survived. "Religion" was not helpful, and our lost depraved condition caused enmity, strife, and anger to creep in. We lacked the most important factor in a marriage – Christ.

Without Christ, a marriage is devoid of genuine love, joy, and peace. As I grew older, I could reflect on my weaknesses of the past. I started out with a college degree and thought I would have a better concept of marriage life. My wife had limited education, but was exceptionally wise. I made many decisions without consulting her. That was a mistake! "Husbands love your wives, as Christ loved the church and gave himself up for her". Ephesians 5:25

I wish I had read this sooner. As I look back, my jobs as band director were very demanding. Plus, during those years I had either part-time jobs, or was taking graduate courses. I had deep appreciation for my wife but was too busy to show it. She managed the homefront with sacrificial love and care for our children. For the most part, we had a "good" martial relationship. Our children brought great joy into our home and definitely resulted in unity and harmony between mommy and daddy. We continued our constant practice of attending church wherever we lived. But we still had not experienced the authentic grace and peace that results from an intimate relationship with Christ.

We enjoyed raising three children. However, during and beyond the high school years, our young offspring began to head in a worldly direction. They were surrounded by questionable influences and were exploring newfound freedoms of which I should have been aware. There were serious matters that caused me and my wife much worry and concern. There were countless nights that I spent on my knees in prayer and tears, feeling inadequate as a father. With this heavy burden that I carried, it appeared that God was not hearing my prayers. As I reflect back to those days, my conscience compels me to admit my neglect. I was too busy and letting my wife take more of the responsibility at home. I was devoting more time to my band kids, and driver's education students than to my own family.

My children were finally delivered from their corrupt minds and rescued from the clutches of Satan and the sinful worldly influences. This only happened by the mercy of a faithful and loving God. That is why today, and EVERY DAY, I thank Him for answering my fervent prayers and saving my children.

I cannot take credit, but I can say - "I have no greater joy than to hear that my children walk in truth" (3 John 4). Today my grown children and their spouses are faithfully serving the Lord. I praise God, and if He were to take me home today, I would go rejoicing. He has blessed me far beyond what I deserve,

I have lived a long, healthy, happy life. I had many friends and was pleased with the world around me. Later, I came to realize that my happiness before my salvation was self-righteous and world centered. In Romans 12:2 we read: "Do not be conformed to this world, but be transformed by the renewing of your mind, that you may prove what is that good and acceptable and perfect will of God."

I came under sound teaching at Free Grace Baptist Church. I started reading and studying the Bible seriously and prayerfully. I had heard

Pastor Billings preach both in Spanish and English. That was a double blessing for me. The Lord finally convicted me of a patronizing relationship with Christ, and the "secret" unrepentant sin in my life. In Romans 3:23, I read, "All have sinned and fall short of the glory of God.... and that there is none righteous, no not one." For the first time it occurred to me that I was included in that "all." My blindness and ignorance had never allowed me to comprehend what that really meant.

I justified myself because I was of good moral character and tried to obey the Ten Commandments. I honored my father and my mother and I didn't worship other gods. But something was telling me that I was not right with God. I had been living with "hidden" sin and was enjoying it.

I was considered a quiet, reserved, and moral person. I didn't hang around much with any particular group, but my friends had similar values. I was deceived by the reigning power of sin. I thought I was a good person, mainly because I didn't steal, didn't get drunk, didn't murder or use the Lord's name in vain. In comparison with many others, I looked okay.

But in reality, I lived in the "passions of the flesh, carrying out the desires of the body and the mind, and was by nature a "child of wrath". Ephesians 2 gives a good description of my comfortable and unassuming worldly life style.

I shared the joy of this exciting new life in Christ with my son Rick. He promptly assured me that the Lord had done a work in my heart, and I needed to share this with the church and be baptized.

The Lord had providentially saved my three children while I was still living with a false profession. They would admonish me and attempt to bring gospel truths that I was unfamiliar with. Rick, in his zeal would provoke my wife and me, claiming we were hell bound without the truth. I was a deacon in Baptist church and felt insulted. I would argue, "I am associated with the Southern Baptist Convention, a huge religious organization, known and respected worldwide. How could so many 'Christians' be wrong?" I suspected my young son of being involved in a cult that met out in the country, in Elmendorf.

My concern prompted me to contact Allan Martin, a long-time young preacher, whom I respected highly. His reply was "Rick is in good hands, you have nothing to worry about." He returned the message with a book titled "Elect in the Son", a Study of the Doctrine of Election, by Robert Shank. This was an eye opener for me. In reality, my son had the truth, and I was in error! Amazingly, God is able to save to the uttermost, even the hardest heart of a prideful 72 year old man.

Finally, after several years, the Lord through "His Word" revealed to me that I was guilty of sin that I should have been ashamed of. I thought I was wise in being able to hide my "secret" sins. I had been foolish and blind, not realizing that God is omniscient and omnipresent. He knows our lives, our hearts, and our minds better than we know them ourselves. He is holy and He hates sin. "And there is no creature hidden from His sight, but all things are naked and open to the eyes of Him to whom we must give account." (Hebrews 4:13).

I had not been accountable to anyone. I obviously did not have true love for Christ. I knew a historical Christ, and was more content in pleasing men. I was content in pleasing my pastor, and others around me. My relationships were more horizontal than vertical, (heavenward). We will all be accountable for our reckless and sinful lives on the Day of Judgment. "The wages of sin is death, but the gift of God is eternal life in Christ Jesus our Lord." (Romans 6:23).

In March 2000, the Lord truly and effectually saved me. I had been regenerated and had a changed heart. I had repented of my sins, and surrendered my life to Christ. He brought me out of darkness into light. I was brought out of deception and a "false profession," if you could call it that. I was saved by the blood of Christ who suffered an excruciating death on a cross. Worst of all, He endured the crushing wrath of His Father. He did all this for an unworthy worm. He washed me clean of all my sins: past, present, and future. And as the Word of God tells us in Romans 8:1, "There is therefore now no condemnation to those who are in Christ Jesus, who do not walk according to the flesh, but according to the Spirit." (New King James Version)

Christ said to Nicodemus, "unless a man is born again he cannot see the Kingdom of God." (John 3:5). I now had a new life, a spiritual birth from above. And it wasn't by anything I did. God, in His mercy granted me grace and faith. "For by GRACE you have been saved through faith, and that not of yourselves, it is a gift of God, not of works, lest anyone should boast" (Ephesians 2:8).

I confessed my sinful unrepentant condition to God, to my pastor, and to the congregation, and I asked to be baptized. "We were buried therefore with Him by baptism into death, in order that, just as Christ was raised from the dead by the glory of the Father, we too might walk in newness of life." (Romans 6:4). And the Apostle Paul reminds us when he says - "How can we who died to sin still live in it." (Romans 6:2). This does not mean we are perfect, but we are free from the lifestyle of sin. "For sin will have no dominion over you..." A radical change takes place in salvation, as described in 2 Corinthians 5:17. "If any man is in Christ, he is a new creation. Old things have passed away, behold all things have become new."

The greatest book ever written and the all-time bestseller, is the Bible, the inspired Word of God. It is "living and powerful, and sharper than any two-edged sword, piercing even to the division of soul and spirit, and of joints and marrow, and is a discerner of the thoughts and intents of the heart." "All Scripture is given by inspiration of God, and is profitable for doctrine, for reproof, for correction, for instruction in righteousness, that the man of God may be complete, thoroughly equipped for every good work."(2 Timothy 3:16-17) (New King James Version)

"God created me– and you– to live with a single, all-embracing, all-transforming passion– namely to glorify God by enjoying and displaying His supreme excellence in all spheres in life…" -John Piper

I am utterly astounded at the thought of being immediately thrust into eternity to my celestial home, and hear Christ say, "Well done, good and faithful servant."

www.ingramcontent.com/pod-product-compliance
Lightning Source LLC
Chambersburg PA
CBHW060452300426
44113CB00016B/2562